The Crucial Era

The St. Martin's Series in
20th-Century U.S. History

The Crucial Era

The Great Depression and World War II
1929–1945

SECOND EDITION

Gerald D. Nash
University of New Mexico

The St. Martin's Series in
20th-Century U.S. History

ST. MARTIN'S PRESS, New York

To Marie

Acquisitions editor: Louise H. Waller
Development editor: Douglas Bell
Development associate: Kristin A. Bowen
Production supervisor: Katherine Battiste
Text design: Gene Crofts
Cover design: Jeannette Jacobs Design
Cover photo: Courtesy of the U.S. Farm Security
Administration

Library of Congress Catalog Card Number: 90-63553

Manufactured in the United States of America.
65432
fedcba

For information, write:
St. Martin's Press, Inc.
175 Fifth Avenue
New York, NY 10010

ISBN: 0-312-03631-0

Acknowledgments: The Publisher gratefully acknowledges the
Franklin D. Roosevelt Library, Hyde Park, New York, for
providing the photographs used in this edition.

Preface

My chief purpose in this volume, as in the first edition, is to help students understand the lasting impact of the Great Depression and World War II on the American people, to recognize that these two events irrevocably altered the political, economic, social, and cultural life of the nation. The crises of depression and war stimulated the expansion of both government and corporate bureaucracy and paved the way for the dominance of great public and private institutions in American society.

In preparing a second edition, I have undertaken a number of changes to revise and update the volume and have profited greatly from comments by students and historians throughout the nation. Portions of the book have been rewritten and new materials have been added to reflect changed perspectives and greater timeliness.

The modifications are of various types. The analytical focus of the book has been sharpened and the materials presented have been unified. This edition contains a new introductory chapter that provides an overview of the period and presents the framework for the book. From the historical perspective of 1990s, the years from 1929 to 1945 constitute a crucial era in the history of the United States. These years set patterns and precedents that Americans were to follow decades thereafter. A new concluding chapter has been added to evaluate this theme in the context of history since 1945.

This edition also contains two new chapters focusing on the experiences of women during the Great Depression and in the Second World War. In addition, new sections and an individual chapter have been added to deal with the South and the West during the crucial era. Their rapid growth after 1945 was one of the most spectacular aspects of the national experience.

Finally, I have made numerous minor changes in the text for the sake of clarity and accuracy.

I am grateful to the reviewers who offered constructive advice, insights, and suggestions for the second edition of *The Crucial Era:* Patrick Allitt,

Emory University; Eileen Eagon, University of Southern Maine; Glen S. Jeansonne, University of Wisconsin at Milwaukee; Jordan A. Schwarz, Northern Illinois University; and Michael Sherry, Northwestern University.

Gerald D. Nash
University of New Mexico

Contents

CHAPTER 1

The Crucial Era

The Great Depression and World War II 1929–1945

 The years between 1929 and 1945 were some of the most fateful and decisive in the history of the United States. Americans set a host of precedents during this period, establishing patterns that were followed for four decades. Two major issues provided the main challenges of the era: domestic depression and foreign war. The responses to these problems were to serve as guidelines for the remainder of the century, resulting in a comprehensive restructuring of many aspects of American life, including the economy, the society, the environment, the culture, and the political system. In the process, Americans also transformed many of their values and beliefs. The restructuring amounted to nothing less than an organizational revolution.

In 1928, millions of voters endorsed Herbert Hoover for the presidency and implicitly approved his philosophy stressing the primacy of individualism in national life. The role of government, Hoover had argued in his book, *American Individualism,* should be limited. Government was to restrict itself to helping individuals and groups deal with the major problems of American society but not to intervene directly itself. It was to serve as a friendly counselor, not as a domineering chief executive. It was to be "on tap but not on top." The task of government was to advise and prompt. But it was the responsibility of individuals to provide for their economic well-being, to meet the hazards of life with their own resources, and to answer their own social welfare needs. Although the size of the federal civil service had grown steadily since the turn of the century, it was still the hope of Hoover and many of his supporters that the growth of bureaucracy could be contained. Certainly a distrust of big government was still deeply ingrained in many Americans—a heritage from the Jeffersonian age.

1

Big Government

By 1945 American theory and practice had undergone a remarkable transformation as big government had become a reality, overshadowing the previous emphasis on individualism. Under the impress of the Great Depression and World War II the nation had undergone a profound change. Government had a much more prominent role in American life than it had ever had before. Many Americans now believed that government, rather than individuals, had the prime responsibility for coping with the major problems that arose in an industrial society. Congress institutionalized this belief in the Employment Act of 1946, which declared that it was the prime duty of government to maintain economic stability in the nation and to ensure employment for individuals. Government was no longer to be a reticent adviser to private entrepreneurs. Rather, it was to be a prime presence in shaping the economic environment and in maintaining a measure of stability, through its tax powers, monetary and fiscal means, and a wide range of public regulations. Government had also begun to assume main responsibility for the social welfare of individuals. The Social Security Act of 1935 provided for old-age pensions, unemployment insurance, and limited federal aid to dependent children and the disabled. The Federal Housing Administration provided low-interest loans for millions of Americans seeking to acquire single-family homes, and the U.S. Housing Authority had begun extensive slum clearance programs in the cities.

Government now affected cultural life as well in the aftermath of the Second World War. Between 1933 and 1945, the federal government had become a patron of the arts. The New Deal had established programs to support unemployed writers, artists, musicians, actors, and archivists. During the war, new federal agencies, such as the Office of War Information, censored virtually all movie scripts in Hollywood and sponsored a wide range of motion pictures. Moreover, the Government Printing Office briefly became the nation's largest publisher, printing and distributing more than 200 million paperback books in Armed Services editions, designed to provide recreational reading for enlisted men and women. At the same time, the armed forces provided popular magazines such as *Yank* and newspapers like *Stars and Stripes* for millions of their personnel. Under the GI Bill of 1944, the federal government obligated itself to pay the tuition and living expenses of veterans who sought up to four years of special training or a college education. More than a million availed themselves of the opportunity. Clearly, unlike Hoover, his successor, Franklin D. Roosevelt, did not fear the positive use of federal powers. In the process of leading the nation through depression and war, Roosevelt persuaded a majority of Americans to modify their views toward government. In contrast to 1929, big government by 1945 had become an integral part of American society.

What conditions had led Americans to modify their values? Between the

Great Depression and the end of World War II, the American economy had gone on a violent roller coaster ride. The fluctuations were due to the culmination of various trends in the late 1920s. Farmers had been beset with declining prices and growing debts for a decade and saw their purchasing power steadily shrinking. Many banks and businesses had overextended themselves and become involved in speculative ventures that came crashing down with the stock market decline of October 1929. And organized labor had not been able to increase its purchasing power significantly in the pro-business atmosphere of the 1920s. These economic weaknesses at home were greatly sharpened by depressed economic conditions in Europe and Latin America after 1927, which earlier had served as important markets for the United States.

And so the roller coaster began its wild swings as Americans celebrated the new year in 1930. Just a little while before it had been riding high, reaching new peaks of production and frenzied highs in the stock market. But Black October, 1929, tilted things downhill. First came the precipitous drop of stock prices, followed in 1930 and 1931 by serious declines in industrial production and exports. By 1932 these consequences were reflected in massive unemployment. The roller coaster hit bottom in the winter of 1932–1933, when at least 15 million Americans (out of a total labor force of 45 million) were without jobs. Economic conditions improved slightly between 1933 and 1937, although at no time during this period did the number of jobless drop below 12 million. Temporary relief agencies like the Works Progress Administration (WPA) provided only temporary employment for a few million people. And when the Roosevelt administration decreased its deficit spending during the first half of 1937, hoping that the economy could sustain a recovery on its own steam, it provoked a rather serious recession, indicating that New Deal policies had not lifted the country out of the economic crisis. In fact, depressed conditions continued until the war mobilization program began to pick up steam two years later. As the federal government began to spend larger sums and induct men into the expanded armed forces, it fueled a speedup of the roller coaster. Starting fitfully in 1939, it gathered momentum during the next six years. By 1945 the economy had reached new peaks of production and employment, higher than the levels from which it had fallen in 1929. In the sixteen years after 1929, therefore, Americans witnessed extreme peaks and troughs in their economy, a breathtaking experience for those who lived through it.

The Welfare State

During the crucial era, Americans also fashioned the rudiments of the welfare state. What millions of people realized during the four years of Hoover's presidency was that private efforts to relieve unemployment and social distress such as hunger, homelessness, or medical crises were inadequate in dealing with a situation of such wide scope as the Great Depression. Only the federal government had the resources and the facilities to extend help on a national scale. That was also the view of many professional social workers during the 1930s, a consensus that was reflected in the Social Security Act of 1935. Although that measure was more modest than many contemporary reformers had hoped, it nevertheless established a foundation for the American welfare state. Three years later, Congress mandated minimum wage levels for many American workers, created standards for the maximum number of hours they could work, and prohibited child labor. The Second World War only further whetted the demand for social services provided by government. As wartime pressures fragmented families, and women entered the work force in larger numbers, the need for more child-care services arose, and government was expected to provide them in the interest of maximizing production. By 1945 the men and women who had served in the armed forces returned to civilian life and requested government aid to continue their educations, to secure decent housing, and to maintain full employment. In sixteen years, the expectations of Americans concerning social services to be provided by government had undergone a metamorphosis.

Government Management of the Economy

This was a crucial era in the restructuring of American economic life. First, in these years Americans made the decision to fashion a modified capitalist state, unlike those that were being adopted by Nazi, fascist, communist, or other totalitarian nations elsewhere. Such a state not only allowed the operation of free enterprise, subject to an increasing array of government regulations, but also maintained a wide measure of political and personal freedoms. In many ways, Franklin D. Roosevelt preserved an American form of capitalism. Second, the period was notable for the development of a government-managed economy. During the Great Depression, this was characterized by increased government regulation and restrictions on the power of big business. By the end of World War II, such regulation had evolved into active government management of the economy. That included government responsibility for full employment and the maintenance of economic stability. A third development of the era was government's assumption of the right to undertake a redistribution of wealth in the United States. Through its sweeping tax powers, Congress attempted to lessen economic inequalities among Americans and to seek a more equitable distribution of incomes in the nation. Finally, the Great Depression taught Americans a more intangible lesson. It left the psychological legacy of a pronounced fear of economic insecurity. This pervaded the outlook of the generation that lived through it and the succeeding generation as well. Their experience in the Second World War, however, persuaded them that perhaps such suffering could be avoided through positive government action.

Human and Civil Rights

This was a crucial era in building foundations for the human rights movement that was to gather momentum in the United States during the second half of the twentieth century. The Depression and the war uprooted millions of Americans and disrupted established social relations. Such conditions contributed to the growth of a more egalitarian society and consequently to the early stirrings of the feminist and civil rights crusades that became more prominent in the next generation. In these years, women's roles underwent various changes. In the Depression, more women left their homes to seek work in the labor market and to become breadwinners in their families. That altered social relations within family groups, broadened the range of opportunities for women, and in many cases altered their self-image. The presence of a greater number of women in the work force dramatized the issue of equal pay for equal work, since wages for women were almost uniformly lower than for men.

The severe labor shortage during World War II accelerated the trends of the Depression years. Women now entered many occupations previously restricted to men. For the first time, the armed forces recruited women as enlisted personnel and as officers. The responsibilities of many women were often greater than those of men, since they were still expected to maintain homes and to provide for the care of children. Help was slow in coming, but the establishment of day-care centers for children by private companies and by government agencies set precedents that were to be expanded in later years. Although a significant number of women left their wartime jobs to become homemakers in the decade after the war, the experiences of the crucial era left an indelible imprint and provided a foundation for the feminist movement that gathered strength in the 1960s and beyond.

In a subtle way, the conditions generated by depression and war laid the foundations for the civil rights movement after 1945 for ethnic and racial minorities. The economic crisis uprooted millions of black Americans in the South, where more than two-thirds lived. It destroyed their livelihood as sharecroppers and forced greater economic diversification and mechanization in the region. But in stimulating the movement of blacks to cities, it fostered greater political awareness and also more racial consciousness, which led to insistent demands for an end to job discrimination and segregation. During the Depression, the pleas of civil rights advocates received little

Women at work: riveting B-17 bombers at a Boeing plant in Seattle, Washington. (*U.S. Office of War Information*)

attention. But the severe labor shortage engendered by the Second World War transformed some of the demands into reality. Moreover, the ideological conflict between American democracy and German and Italian totalitarianism dramatized imperfections within the United States, such as racism. Since almost one million black men and women served in the armed forces and many others worked in war industries, it became clear that they would not be as submissive in the future as they had been in the past. Though many injustices remained to be rectified in the sphere of civil rights after 1945, the Depression and the war contributed considerably to the achievement of a greater measure of equality for blacks, Hispanics, Native Americans, and other ethnic and racial minorities.

Environmental Awareness

During this period, Americans also developed a heightened awareness of the environment, although this was to burgeon only much later. The Great Depression did much to reveal the social and economic costs of many decades of enormous waste of the nation's natural resources. Soil erosion, stream pollution, the denuding of vast stands of timber, the depletion of valuable minerals, and the destruction of fish and wildlife became prominent issues in the midst of economic crisis. New Deal programs attempted to address some of these issues, but many of these efforts were rudely disrupted by the war and the exigencies of maximum production. Although the United States emerged successful from the global conflict, thoughtful Americans were aware that military victories had been secured at high environmental costs. By 1945 the nation had lost much of its self-sufficiency in many raw materials. More deliberate and careful management of ecological balance was necessary, it was clear, if the United States was to seek affluence and growth in the future.

Political Heritage

The crucial era also left a political heritage. Between 1933 and 1945, Franklin D. Roosevelt set precedents for the growth of the "imperial presidency." That term was used by historian Arthur M. Schlesinger, Jr., to designate the vastly expanded functions and powers of the presidency as wielded by its occupants in domestic and foreign affairs in the four decades after the end of World War II. Roosevelt's successors often molded themselves in his image, consciously or not. Similarly, the actions that he took as leader of the Democratic party were to create patterns for national politics during the next generation. He fashioned the "Roosevelt coalition," an alliance of the less affluent segments in American society, including ethnic and racial minorities, organized labor and blue-collar workers, large segments of urban dwellers, and farmers, that served as the backbone of the Democratic party until the 1970s. Another part of the heritage was the increasing dominance of a growing bureaucracy. Both the Great Depression and wartime mobilization did much to stimulate the expansion of governmental functions and the growth of a bureaucratic apparatus. Despite much rhetoric about the alleged evils of bureaucracy and the need for its limitation, bureaucracy expanded steadily after 1945 on the basis of precedents set during the crucial era. Though many Americans were not quite ready to admit it, their attitudes toward bureaucracy and big government changed remarkably between 1929 and 1945. The Great Depression and the war had led them to transform their profound distrust to a reluctant acceptance of big government's role in many aspects of their lives.

Global Awareness

The crucial era had a profound influence on the conduct of American diplomacy. During the Great Depression, a majority of Americans strongly believed that the nation should follow a policy emphasizing isolation. Many in this generation still remembered extensive United States involvement in World War I, when Americans had hoped that they could make the world safe for democracy as President Woodrow Wilson had promised them. But that lofty goal was not achieved. By the 1920s, Americans looked back with considerable disillusionment on their efforts during the First World War. If that experience had any lesson for them, it was that they should not become embroiled in world politics again. From 1920 to 1939, therefore, a majority of Americans tended to be isolationists.

But beginning in 1931, Japan, Germany, and Italy embarked on aggressive policies of expansion, each determined to build a vast new empire of its own. With the United States and other democracies like England and France preoccupied with internal problems of depression and firmly committed to isolation, the expansionist nations found themselves virtually unopposed. Perhaps the most symbolic event that reflected totalitarian aggression and appeasement by the democracies was the Munich Conference of 1938. It was there that England and France allowed Adolf Hitler to expand into Czechoslovakia. The United States stood idly by. Within one year, however, Hitler made new territorial demands and precipitated the Second World War.

The Munich crisis cast a long shadow over American foreign policy in the twentieth century. Its immediate effect was to influence a growing number of Americans that isolationism as a policy did not strengthen national security. Appeasement had failed to avert war or to protect America's best interests. A strong military posture and close collaboration with other nations—collective security—was more likely to achieve the goals of the United States. After 1941 the nation increased its armed forces and became directly involved in World War II. By 1945 an overwhelming majority of Americans had rejected isolation as a principle of foreign policy and instead supported close collaboration with other nations around the globe. But the memories of foreign affairs during the crucial era did not fade; they continued to haunt American policymakers in succeeding years. During the Cold War years (1945–1989), defenders of United States diplomacy repeatedly referred to the Munich crisis to bolster their arguments against appeasement of the Soviet Union and for the need to maintain a strong military establishment. American diplomats justified intervention in Korea (1950–1953) and in Vietnam (1965–1972) in part on the nation's experiences during the crucial era. Military aggression by expansionist nations must be stopped early, they argued, lest it lead to even more widespread international conflagration later, as in the 1930s.

Even after the end of the Cold War, American leaders continued to use the analogy of Munich to defend their actions. When President George Bush sought to justify his decision to send American troops to Saudi Arabia to block Iraqi dictator Saddam Hussein, Bush likened him to Adolf Hitler and warned that appeasement of Hussein would only encourage further aggression as the Munich agreement had done in 1938. The impact of the crucial era on United States diplomacy was thus considerable. It created an outlook and bred assumptions that affected generations of American policymakers.

The years between 1929 and 1945 were therefore crucial in setting many precedents for Americans in the second half of the twentieth century. During this period they fashioned a government that functioned as manager of the economy; they created the American social welfare state; they brought government into the arena of human and civil rights, feminist causes, and the battle against racism; they expanded government's role in the management of natural resources; and they found a place for government as a patron of culture. In the process they did much to expand bureaucracy in American life. And they created patterns in American diplomacy that guided their successors in the next generation. In the context of the American experience in the twentieth century, these precedents, set during the Great Depression and World War II, made those years a significant and crucial era.

CHAPTER 2

American Society in Crisis

 In many ways the 1920s can be viewed as a decade in which Americans were seeking a sense of order in their rapidly changing society. The pace of technological change was increasing, and the consequent social and cultural disruptions were affecting millions of Americans. The problem for the American people was how to channel these shocks and to control them. Some Americans like Herbert Hoover believed that the task could be accomplished largely by private enterprise—by corporations, philanthropic foundations, private social welfare organizations, and private planners, with a modicum of help from government. Hoover distrusted a centralized state apparatus, however. Government should serve in an advisory capacity, he believed. But the Crash of 1929 and the Great Depression largely destroyed this vision of an associated state, one in which private groups played a major role in coping with prime social and economic problems while government served as a reticent adjunct. Between 1933 and 1945, Americans undertook to switch these priorities. The apparatus of the state came to occupy a dominant position, while private and voluntary groups played a supporting role in American society. But the competition between these private organizations and the federal bureaucracy created healthy checks and balances that placed both under public scrutiny and prevented either from accumulating excessive or abusive power.

Before 1929: A Search for Order and the Growth of an Organizational Society

The search for order and stability began in the late nineteenth century in the increasingly chaotic and insecure world ushered in by the age of industrialism. That search was to dominate Americans throughout the course of the twentieth century as they sought to achieve the elusive goal of economic and social stability. The generation of the 1920s contributed much to this effort by fashioning building blocks that would lay the foundations of the organizational society in twentieth-century America. Using the ideas and experiences of the Progressive Era (1900–1914) and World War I, they reorganized their economy, every level of government, many aspects of their social and cultural life, and their diplomacy. The process was often not deliberate but rather a pragmatic response to immediate problems. Nor was the extent of this reorganization always apparent to those who lived through it. If between 1933 and 1945 Americans responded positively to Franklin D. Roosevelt's call for help in coping with the problems of depression and global war, however, their acquiescence was not really due to a sudden conversion on their part. Their experiences from 1917 to 1932 had predisposed them to think and act within the framework of organizational imperatives in the pursuit of stability and order.

A distinctive characteristic of the technologically oriented mass production and distribution economy of the 1920s was the formation of organizations designed to minimize economic risks and to prevent destructive competition, competition based on unfair business methods. Trade associations, which mushroomed during the decade, reflected these efforts. Their functions ranged from attempts at price maintenance, sharing and disseminating useful information, and regulating competition to lobbying government at the local, state, or national level. Large American corporations such as Du Pont and General Motors joined international cartels to control the production and distribution of particular products on an industrywide basis. The proliferation of new federal agencies and increased regulatory activity on the part of the Federal Trade Commission, as well as the expanded activities of the Department of Commerce, were another reflection of the efforts to stabilize the highly competitive business world.

Similar trends characterized American agriculture. Caught in the throes of the Depression, most farmers abandoned some of their once-vaunted individualism to embrace organization as a key to greater prosperity and security. Like businessmen, they formed their own protective associations such as the American Farm Bureau Federation and the Farmers' Union, which lobbied for farm causes at various levels of government. Through the expansion of agricultural cooperatives and similar organizations, farmers tried unsuccessfully to achieve a more favorable balance between what they produced and what they could profitably market. They sought to stabilize farm prices and to increase their margin of profit. Low-cost credit, granted by the Federal Intermediate Credit Bank system created in 1923, and the purchasing of farm surpluses to maintain agricultural price levels, authorized under the Agricultural Marketing Act of 1929, were attempts to find support from the government.

To a lesser extent, workers also tried to organize themselves more effectively to secure stable wage levels and improved working conditions. Strong opposition from business and various decisions of the U.S. Supreme Court, however, kept labor union organizers from succeeding. Big corporations established company unions as a means of preempting workers from forming independent labor organizations. Such unions were organized and managed by particular firms. Some of the older and stronger unions, such as the railroad workers, turned to the federal government for help. The Railroad Labor Act of 1926, for example, imposed an organizational structure on railway labor-management relations by providing for federal mediation in disputes, arbitration, supervision of pension systems, and the maintenance of many of the benefits already secured by railroad workers.

While the 1920s saw the establishment of new organizations designed to minimize the insecurities of an industrial economy and new relationships among government, workers, and business, it also brought on the age of manager and the specialist. In large corporations, farm organizations, or unions, professionals and managers came to exercise a significant amount of power. Herbert Hoover noted this trend when he observed that the United States had entered a "new era" in which scientific and management experts would apply their particular skills to society's increasingly complex social issues. The special competence of the engineer, Hoover declared, could be used to solve the nation's problems. The term *social engineering* acquired great popularity during the 1920s. Americans who remembered the recent World War I experience, in which centralized management by experts provided the key to victory, enthusiastically embraced the concept. And those who had supported reform movements during the Progressive Era considered efficiency a prime goal, best achieved through organizations staffed by experts.

The organizational urges of Americans in the 1920s also affected racial and ethnic minorities. Sensing accurately that organization would enable them to exert greater influence on American life, millions of ethnic Americans banded together in civic and fraternal groups and formed political organizations. In the eastern and midwestern cities, they constituted large voting blocs, which by 1920 were beginning to wield sufficient power to influence the course of urban politics and to exercise a significant voice in state and national elections. In such states as Massachusetts, New York, Pennsylvania, and Illinois, ethnic minorities began to hold a crucial balance of power. Governor Alfred E. Smith of New York became a spokesman for urban minorities in the 1920s and through this voter base won enough support to be nominated as a presidential candidate in 1928.

Thousands of black Americans flocked to the banner of Marcus Garvey, a Jamaican who led a black nationalist movement. Garvey preached about the need for blacks to organize themselves more effectively to combat racial prejudice and discrimination. Native Americans strove more aggressively for their rights through newly formed groups such as the American Indian Rights Association. Hispanic Americans banded together in the League of United Latin American Citizens. The consciousness of women was higher in the 1920s than in pre–World War I America, spurred no doubt by their enfranchisement in 1920.

Such increasing awareness of ethnic and racial minorities and their effort to expand their economic and social status in American society was reflected in American politics during these years. Native-born, rural Americans saw their power wane as urban, immigrant Americans achieved positions of political influence. This trend was reflected in the growth of an urban coalition in the Democratic party. Until World War I the nucleus of the Democrats' power was in the South, but between 1920 and 1932 the prime base of their support moved to the large cities of the East and the Midwest. During this period the Democrats attracted the immigrant masses of the urban centers, an increasing number of blacks, and large numbers of blue-collar workers. As political analyst Samuel Lubell noted, this shift of political power in America was virtually completed by 1928. Somewhat more insecure than native-born Americans, who formed the core of Republican strength, the urban Democratic coalition looked to the federal government to maintain stability and order.

Cultural life in the 1920s was also affected by the emphasis on organization. A new age of mass culture emerged. This was the heyday of organized spectator sports, particularly major league baseball and prize fighting. Babe Ruth and Jack Dempsey were better known to many Americans than were leading businessmen or politicians. It was also the golden age of the silent film. Fifty million Americans went to the movies each week to follow the exploits of such stars as Rudolph Valentino or Clara Bow. Millions tuned in their radio sets to listen to programs beamed over the new national radio networks such as NBC. The circulation of mass-oriented magazines, of which *True Story* was an example, boomed in the 1920s. Improvements in recording techniques provided a new means for the mass distribution and popularization of all forms of music by record companies such as RCA Victor and scores of others. Entertainment—once largely provided by family and friends—was now packaged by large organizations.

Periods of rapid change in a society invariably lead to a questioning of traditional values. During the 1920s the Protestant ethic came under increasing attack as the writers of the so-called lost generation spearheaded an assault on the traditional values revered by many Americans before the First World War. Not only in literature but also in art, music, and philosophy, traditionalism was derided as being out of step with the new winds of change. American intellectuals were fragmented during the period as the conflict between traditionalists and nontraditionalists destroyed whatever consensus on cultural values Americans once held. The nineteenth-century system of values was beginning to disintegrate under twentieth-century pressures.

In foreign affairs as in domestic life, Americans sought stability and order. Although the United States did not assume the major responsibilities for world leadership that membership in the League of Nations entailed, neither did the nation retreat into extreme isolation. America's presence was felt around the globe. The United States worked informally with the League of Nations, played a major role in settling war debt and reparations problems via the Dawes (1924) and Young (1929) plans, and initiated the Kellogg-Briand Pact (1927) to outlaw war. The treaties arising out of the Washington Conference of 1921 were designed to impose an American-oriented balance of power in the Far East. United States policies regarding Latin America were designed to build a system of hemispheric solidarity that would no longer require direct military intervention. The State Department professionalized its staff during the decade and formed a corps of professional diplomats as specialized and competent as the managers of large corporations.

Between World War I and the eve of the Great Depression, then, Americans had opted for increased organization as a means of coping with the many problems of their rapidly changing society brought on by the industrial age. The pace of this organizational growth was to be greatly accelerated, however, by the Great Depression.

The Collapse of American Society

Within a few months of the Great Crash of 1929, Americans began to realize that they were not living through a mere monetary panic but were in fact trapped in one of the great crises of their generation. The economic collapse spared few individuals as business activity declined drastically. The gross national product of $87 billion in 1929 shrank to $41 billion four years later. Every day factories closed their doors, and scores of banks and businesses failed. Americans were gripped by a fear of worse things to come. The economic crisis crushed the human spirit, particularly of the growing number of individuals who lost their livelihood. In 1930 the jobless numbered 7 million; by 1931 their ranks had swelled to 12 million; and in 1932 perhaps only one of two Americans had a full-time job. Rural Americans often were no better off than their city neighbors. Hundreds of thousands of farmers lost their properties in foreclosures; those who stayed struggled with the depressed market and found it difficult to earn even subsistence incomes. In some agricultural areas of the Midwest, desperate, angry farmers revolted and formed the National Farm Holiday Association. Led by Milo Reno, they organized boycotts. To achieve higher farm prices, they blockaded roads to prevent farm products from reaching city markets.

What factors were responsible for the Crash and the consequent Depression? Contemporaries and later critics cited elements in both domestic and foreign conditions that created the basic problem: an imbalance between production and consumption. Several weaknesses in the domestic economy seemed to be operating: (1) maladjustments created by technological changes, (2) unequal distribution of the national income, (3) stock market abuses, (4) weaknesses in the structure of large corporations, and (5) questionable policies of the federal government.

In addition to these trends at home, the United States was affected by the international economic crisis. In a sense, the American Depression was but one aspect of a worldwide depression. Every major industrial nation except the Soviet Union was suffering widespread unemployment, declining production and trade, bank failures, and monetary instability. In a world connected by rapid transportation and communications as well as intricate financial arrangements, the United States could not escape this international crisis. It brought about a direct decline in U.S. trade and in foreign investments in the United States, and the disorganization of various national currencies seriously disrupted foreign debt and reparations payments to the United States and thus, willy-nilly, affected the soundness of the dollar. The consequences of the international economic crisis thus added materially to domestic weaknesses that were contributing to the development of a depression.

Technology's Adverse Effects

While the rapid pace of technological progress during the 1920s had laid the basis for the mass production industries, it also created some maladjustments in the economy. The new technology set apart a group of "sick" industries that were rendered increasingly obsolete, including some forms of agriculture, coal mining, and textiles. These declining industries were usually localized in certain areas such as New England, Appalachia, and portions of the South and the Midwest. The influence of their decline on regional economic activity was often pronounced and created pockets of unemployment. If the coal industry forced out more than 200,000 men in the 1920s, the textile manufacturers failed to hire proportionately larger numbers of employees after modernizing their manufacturing equipment. Indeed, unemployment was a consequence of technological change. Although the displacement of people by machines was most visible in farming, it was duplicated in many other industries that were affected by a succession of new technological inventions. In fact, between 1919 and 1929, manufacturing industries experienced a gain of 50 percent in output while employing the same number of workers. To be sure, technological displacement was usually only temporary, since in the long run machines tend to create new jobs. But during the Great Depression these temporary displacements were sufficiently disruptive to lead to chronic unemployment; one worker out of seven was unemployed, or about 5 million people yearly. As the purchasing power of these individuals shrank, so did their function as consumers. In short, as the number of potential customers diminished, the producers' stock of goods increased, creating a growing imbalance between supply and demand.

Unequal Distribution of Income

The gap between production and consumption was further widened by the persistence of poverty and underconsumption in the United States caused by a maldistribution of personal and corporate incomes. During the 1920s, production grew at a much faster rate than the relative number of potential new consumers. In 1929 fully 60 percent of American families had annual incomes below $2,000, which was then considered the minimum for self-sufficiency. This large group was increasingly unable to buy desired goods. In contrast, 1 percent of the population received 19 percent of the national income in 1929 (compared to 12 percent in 1919); 10 percent of the highest income earners garnered 40 percent of the national income. Unfortunately, these wealthy individuals provided an extremely limited market for consumer products. If income had been more equitably distributed among a larger number of people, the number of potential customers for consumer items would have been vastly increased.

Oligopoly

Another reason for the deepening Depression was found in the weaknesses and policies of the great corporations. The 1920s witnessed the emergence of oligopoly as a characteristic of American industry. A few giant firms—such as General Motors, Chrysler, and Ford in the auto business—tended to dominate production in an entire industry. By 1929 the 200 largest corporations in the United States (out of a total of about 400,000 corporations) controlled 49 percent of all corporate assets and received 43 percent of all corporate income. The 1,350 largest corporations secured 80 percent of all corporate profits. Corporations were being transformed from private into quasi-public institutions whose economic power no longer merely affected private individuals but was felt throughout the American economy.

How did oligopoly contribute to the Depression? First, it tended to lead to price rigidity. Secure in their control of a significant portion of their particular industry, oligopolies tended to set arbitrary "administered prices," ones not determined by supply and demand. In a period of declining economic activity and shrinking purchasing power, their rigidity in maintaining artificially high prices rather than making downward adjustments contributed to the imbalance between supply and demand. A second way in which corporate structure contributed to the Depression was through the abuse of holding companies, companies that held stock in hundreds of subsidiary corporations, following a practice known as pyramiding, especially in the field of public utilities. As in the case of Samuel Insull, the leading public utility magnate in Chicago, parent companies frequently followed policies that were detrimental to the firms they controlled. If one had financial troubles, it might affect all the others in the system. Consequently, the whole pyramid could collapse, as happened to Insull's utility empire after he encountered financial difficulties in 1929. Clearly, the unsound structure of some large corporations operating as holding companies introduced an element of instability into American industry. A crisis such as the Crash of 1929 could set off a chain reaction. The collapse of a great corporation easily created further unemployment, thus shrinking the purchasing power of the workers. The imbalance between consumption and production then only grew wider.

Speculation

An unsound corporate structure also contributed to the Depression by fostering a declining rate of investment in new enterprises. The concentration of capital in the hands of only a few hundred huge companies made their investment decisions crucial to the welfare of the entire economy. During the 1920s, large individual and corporate investors were not quick enough in plowing their surplus back into new productive enterprises in the United States. Many of these funds found their way into risky enterprises overseas or stock market speculation. Meanwhile, beset by a lagging rate of investment, the nation's economic growth rate became sluggish.

To some extent, excessive speculation on the stock market contributed to the outbreak of the Great Depression. After 1925 the speculative orgy gathered momentum. In that year, 300 million shares were traded on the New York Stock Exchange; in 1926, 451 million shares; in 1927, 577 million shares; and in 1929, more than 1 billion shares. During this period the market value of all stocks jumped from $27 billion to $67.5 billion. That some of this increase represented speculative expectation rather than real earning power was reflected in the ratio of corporate earnings to the market price of stocks. Although 10 to 1 was considered to be a safe ratio, by 1929 this average had climbed to 16 to 1. The speculative surge was also fired by many frauds and abuses. Speculators would often engage in "wash sales": by buying and selling to each other, they would drive up the price of a particular issue, then unload it before more gullible investors became wary. In other cases, insiders would act on confidential information concerning a particular stock and reap great profits.

Such conditions clearly contributed to the Depression. Investment capital was diverted from economic growth industries, which might have opened new sources of employment, into nonproductive speculation. Stock speculation helped to weaken the banking structure of the nation, since many banks were heavily involved in extending loans to speculators. When the Crash came, they were drawn directly into the whirl of failures. Speculation also created a tight money and credit situation. As interest rates for loans increased, less speculative enterprises found it increasingly difficult to secure loans themselves or to raise necessary capital. Although stock market speculation did not of itself initiate the Depression, it did aggravate existing weaknesses in the economy.

Passivity of the Federal Government

Another reason for the economic crisis was the attitude of the federal government in the 1920s. Neither President Calvin Coolidge nor Congress nor the Federal Reserve Board felt responsible for taking vigorous action to remedy some of the more obvious weaknesses in the American business and corporate structure, inequalities of income, or stock market abuses. Despite warnings from economists, President Coolidge refused to dampen the increasingly reckless spirit of speculation. Instead, in 1928 and again in February 1929, he publicly stated that in his estimation, stock market prices were not unusually high. Nor did the Federal Reserve Board take note of the danger signals. Although it had the authority to raise reserve requirements of member banks in the Federal Reserve System (and so to limit their capacity for making loans for speculative purposes), and although it could raise the rediscount rate for loans, it refused to do so. In fact, during 1927 it lowered its rediscount rate from 4 to 3.5 percent, making it even easier to secure credit for stock speculation. Very likely the board could have braked the stock market boom by raising margin requirements (the percentage of down payment required for stock purchases) or by official statements advising caution. Coolidge was not ignorant of the nation's need for sustained economic growth, of unemployment problems stemming from technological change, or of corporate abuses, but he took little direct action to deal with these issues or to alert Congress for necessary legislation. The federal government's passivity in the face of emerging economic problems contributed to the economic debacle of 1929.

International Crises

Whatever domestic conditions contributed to the outbreak of the Depression, these were worsened by the international dimensions of economic crisis. By 1929 the economies of Great Britain, France, Germany, and most European countries were beset with large-scale unemployment. Almost all of them sought to mitigate their problems by erecting trade barriers against their neighbors. The result was a further decline in world trade, which brought additional economic strains. Since the United States was tied to the international economy, it, too, was affected by these trends. One of the most direct effects was a great decrease in American trade between 1929 and 1932. U.S. exports declined from $5 billion in 1929 to a mere $1 billion in 1932. At the same time that American businessmen found their domestic markets shrinking, therefore, the number of their foreign customers was rapidly dwindling as well.

An unforeseen influence of the world economic depression on the United States was the withdrawal of foreign funds. As financial stringency affected the European economies, many European bankers and investors called back monies they had invested in American enterprises. As the New York Stock Exchange boom became more precarious in 1929, foreign stockholders in American corporations began to sell their shares in large numbers, thereby adding to the selling wave after Black Thursday, October 24, when stock prices crashed. The net result of this European liquidation of United States holdings was twofold. It placed a great strain on American banks by depriving them of an important source of credit. Also, the large volume of stock sales by Europeans added to the psychology of panic on Wall Street in 1929 and further demoralized stock prices on the exchange.

The international depression also destabilized foreign currencies, which unsettled the dollar. With heavy war debts and reparations payments, most European nations staggered under their burdens and suspended debts owed to the United States. The vicious cycle began in Germany, which between 1924 and 1932 underwent the most severe fluctuations in monetary cycles, from extreme inflation to deflation. Since the Germans were obligated to make large reparations payments to the Allies, their plight directly affected the others. By 1931 the currencies of most European countries were in disarray. A common remedy for many of them was devaluation, and one after another they abandoned the gold standard. In 1931 the Bank of England began the trend and was followed in rapid succession by France, Austria, Italy, and Belgium. Because of these international disturbances, American investors in overseas enterprises lost a substantial portion of their original investment as devaluations made previous monetary values worthless. Trade and commerce suffered because of the uncertain values of various national currencies. Finally, the world monetary crisis drained U.S. gold reserves and thus threatened the soundness of the gold-based dollar. Since the United States was also expecting European nations to make regular payments on their debts—payments they suspended after 1929—this added to the strains on America's supply of gold.

The Great Depression thus resulted from a combination of foreign and domestic factors. In the world of the twentieth century, economic problems were no longer confined to the boundaries of one particular country but also affected its neighbors and trading partners. The depression that broke out in Europe after 1927 could not fail to affect the United States. Within the American economy, the dislocations of technological development, inequalities of income, imperfections in corporate business policies, wild stock market speculation, and a lack of government economic leadership were all laying the groundwork for the most severe economic crisis in the experience of the United States.

Impact of the Great Depression

The Depression created a host of social problems. The loss of a job—and the status that went with it—caused suffering and brought much personal unhappiness into the lives of millions of Americans. Families were disrupted. Some took to the road in a vain search for better employment opportunities else-

Life during the Great Depression: the unemployed. (*U.S. Farm Security Administration/Dorothea Lange, photographer*)

where. Often the women in families sought to earn an income for the first time. Sometimes families moved in with friends or relatives. Other families disintegrated as individual members tried to make it on their own. Many young men and women—perhaps as many as 2 million—became "tramps," riding the rails to nowhere in particular, hoping to get a job or a meal at every stop. Numerous others were homeless, sleeping in parks, subways, or abandoned buildings. Thousands gathered on the outskirts of towns or along riverfronts, where they built primitive tar-and-paper shacks. These new communities were called Hoovervilles—monuments to the president who had promised Americans two cars in every garage and two chickens in every pot. In many communities, hungry people could be seen in back alleys, searching garbage cans for scraps of food.

The realities of the suffering could be grasped only through a firsthand look into the lives of millions of Americans. In July 1933, Harry Hopkins, in charge of New Deal welfare policies, sent Lorena Hickock, a reporter, on a journey through the country to report on actual conditions. Her impressions were quite vivid:

> There was the Negro woman in Philadelphia who used to walk eight miles every day over the scorching pavements just on the chance of getting, perhaps, a little cleaning to do, at 10 cents an hour. Then there was the little Mexican girl, aged 6, in Colorado, who said, sure, she'd worked "in the beets" two Summers already, and, yes, sometimes she did get pretty tired. There was the young musician who said: "For a few weeks it isn't so bad for a man and his wife and baby to get along on $4.80 a week, paying $3 out of it for rent. But when it runs into months, and you can't see anything ahead, you get damned discouraged." . . . There were the little boys who refused to go to school in Houston, Texas, wearing the trousers of terribly conspicuous black-and-white striped ticking that had been given them, because everybody would know they were on relief. . . . There was the small-town woman in Iowa who spent part of her husband's first CWA [Civil Works Administration] check for oranges, because she hadn't tasted any for three years. . . . There was the architect who said he didn't mind working on a road as a day laborer because "at least my children can tell the teacher their father is working. They don't have to say what he's doing." . . . There was the farm woman in South Dakota who had a recipe for Russian thistle soup and said, "It don't taste so bad, only it ain't very filling." There was the boy of 20 who limped wearily into his home in a Baltimore suburb one Autumn night . . . after having walked nearly 20 miles down into the center of the city and back, "just stopping at every place and asking if they didn't need somebody to work at anything."

Discontent was expressed through organized protests. Jobless men and women marched through the streets of New York and Chicago to draw attention to their plight. Groups of angry farmers with pitchforks and rifles prevented local banks from seizing the property of their neighbors. The Hoover administration appeared insensitive to the plight of the sufferers. When an organization of World War I veterans called the Bonus Expeditionary Force descended on Washington, D.C., in the summer of 1932 to express support for congressional legislation that would allow bonus payments for war veterans, President Hoover panicked at the presence of these peaceful protesters and called out the U.S. Army to disperse them.

The bewilderment of the American people filtered into the political ideology. With the deepening crisis all kinds of nostrums and remedies were proffered by critics of Hoover, who swore that they could set the country on its feet. To communists the Great Crash signaled the collapse of the capitalist system; to socialists, an opportunity to build a new utopian commonwealth; to neofascists, the dawn of a new totalitarian era; and to a host of less doctrinaire groups, an opportunity to place their special programs before the public. Although the faith of many Americans in the democratic system was shaken, these dissidents had surprisingly little impact on most voters.

The Great Depression disrupted American foreign policy. A growing atmosphere of fear, distrust, and insecurity throughout the world led to the failure of American efforts to secure disarmament. With high hopes, President Hoover in 1930 sent a delegation to the London Naval Conference to seek an agreement on force reductions among the world's leading naval powers. Bitter wrangling between England and Japan and a recalcitrant attitude on the part of the French led to failure. In the atmosphere of distrust, generated in part by the Depression, international disarmament had become an unpopular cause.

In 1931, Americans watched the outbreak of open warfare in the Far East when Japan launched a military invasion of Manchuria. A highly industrialized province of China, Manchuria was one of the most valuable regions in Asia. The Japanese invasion was a violation of the turn-of-the-century commercial Open Door policy of the United States, the Nine Power Treaty that Japan had signed at the Washington Conference of 1921, and the Kellogg-Briand Treaty of 1927, in which Japan had agreed not to resort to war. The Hoover administration vehemently protested Japanese aggression in Manchuria and the creation of the Japanese puppet state known as Manchukuo there, but a majority of the American people were unwilling to sanction any use of American military forces to chastise the Japanese or to support effective action by the League of Nations. American protests therefore remained largely rhetorical. Secretary of State Henry Stimson proclaimed the Stimson Doctrine, in which the United States declared itself unwilling to recognize any nation, such as Manchukuo, that was established as a result of military aggression. The Manchurian crisis contributed to undermining principles of American diplomacy such as the Open Door policy and self-determination.

The Great Engineer and the Great Depression

Great crises in the affairs of nations require great leaders. In 1929 many Americans felt fortunate to have as distinguished a chief executive as Herbert Hoover in the White House. Not only had Hoover served successfully in other important public positions, but he was regarded as a man of vision, a man who had a clear sense of America's future. Throughout the 1920s, Hoover's staff had carefully nurtured his public image as the Great Engineer, a man who was equal to even the greatest challenges.

Hoover was a prototype for the self-made man. Born on an Iowa farm in 1865, he was orphaned at the age of 10, whereupon he moved to Oregon to work on an uncle's homestead. After working to put himself through Stanford University, he became a mining engineer. Within a decade he achieved fame and fortune in his field. By World War I he was devoting most of his time to public service and had gained particular prominence as director of the U.S. Food Administration under President Woodrow Wilson. Between 1921 and 1928, while serving as secretary of commerce, he dominated the Harding and Coolidge cabinets. Considered the most prominent Republican of his generation, he won the first elective office of his distinguished career in 1928, the presidency of the United States.

Unlike most politicians, Hoover developed a comprehensive philosophy about national goals and the duties and limitations of government. His career strengthened his firm belief in individualism as a basic foundation of a democratic society. Individualism, he wrote, resulted in the highest fulfillment of each person's potential. Competition among individuals brought out the best in them and so benefited society as a whole. Hoover was by no means a follower of the nineteenth-century laissez-faire doctrines of Adam Smith, the eighteenth-century economist who opposed government interference in a market economy. Rather, he looked forward to an associational society, one in which individuals would form voluntary groups. Such associations would undertake rational, scientific planning to cope with the economic and social problems of a complex technological and industrial society. The role of governments at various levels was to stimulate and encourage these groups but not to intervene directly to resolve a society's problems. Such intervention, Hoover believed, would undermine individual initiative and the very vitals of democratic government.

The private Herbert Hoover differed considerably from the Hoover fashioned by public relations specialists. According to the public image, the Great Engineer was an original thinker, a superb organizer, a dynamic leader, a man who could solve the big problems that stymied others, be they in mining, engineering, business, social welfare, or government. Unfortunately, the image was embellished. Hoover may have been a good organizer, but only in situations where he controlled clear channels of command.

Where leadership was dependent on persuasion and compromise, as is so often the case in politics, he was not particularly effective. He tended to be intolerant of critics and unwilling to modify even ideas or programs that had proved to be unsuccessful. In addition, a certain shyness about showing emotion hampered his effectiveness as a leader during times of crisis.

Many Americans assumed that Hoover, known for his successful handling of major problems, would be adept at dealing with the economic crisis. However, in the eyes of numerous Americans in 1932, he proved singularly ineffective in coping with the greatest challenge of his long, outstanding career.

Certainly Hoover worked hard to alleviate the Depression. He summoned business and labor leaders to the White House and urged them to avoid panic; he persuaded Congress to create the Federal Farm Board to purchase farm surpluses as a means of maintaining stable agricultural prices; he created a national committee to solicit voluntary contributions for the unemployed and formed many other committees to deal with social problems; and by 1932 he had acquiesced to the establishment of a government bank, the Reconstruction Finance Corporation, whose purpose was to extend loans to ailing businesses and financial institutions. Yet the severity of the Great Depression made many of his efforts futile. Certainly his belief that Americans needed to organize more effectively as a means of confronting the problems of a technological society was inherently sound, but his profound conviction that such associational activity must be voluntary rather than subject to governmental action restricted the scope of his policies. Meanwhile, increasing numbers of Americans were coming to feel that only strong government policies could stem the growing chaos and restore order. Although Hoover was leaning toward greater use of governmental powers by 1932, he refused to abandon his cherished ideals concerning the sanctity of individualism and voluntary cooperation. In 1932 the tired and worn president was possibly the most ridiculed and hated man in the nation, a total reversal of his stature as America's most admired public figure a mere four years earlier.

The Politics of Despair

Optimistic forecasts by administration officials notwithstanding, the United States' fate in 1932 was perhaps more precarious than at any time since the Civil War. Many Americans wondered whether the democratic system would survive the shattering blows of the Depression. Too many had lost their homes, their livelihoods, and most important, their self-respect. Despite the dispirited mood, the Republicans renominated Herbert Hoover in June 1932.

Active competition for the Democratic presidential nomination ensued between former New York governor Alfred E. Smith, who had been the party's candidate in 1928, and his erstwhile protégé, Franklin D. Roosevelt, the incumbent governor of New York. After a bitter battle, Roosevelt was nominated on the fourth ballot. To their surprise, the conventioneers learned that their candidate would break precedent by appearing before them in person to accept the nomination. Roosevelt announced, "I pledge you, I pledge myself, to a new deal for the American people." Although he had few specific proposals for combating the Depression either then or throughout his campaign, he promised vigorous governmental action. Such pledges fell on sympathetic ears, and on election day 23 million Americans cast their votes for Roosevelt, 16 million for Hoover. Roosevelt won the urban minority vote in the large cities of the Northeast and the Midwest. He secured substantial segments of the farm vote in the Midwest and the West and carried the traditionally Democratic South. The electorate appeared to have given Roosevelt a mandate for change.

But four months lay between the election and the inauguration, and in the interval the Depression relentlessly worsened. The political vacuum that followed the election contributed to the crisis. During these months Hoover and Roosevelt met on various occasions to discuss pressing issues at the White House, yet found few areas of agreement. Roosevelt also listened to suggestions from all quarters but kept his silence and did not commit himself to any program or proposal during this period.

Roosevelt was elected to the presidency during one of the worst crises in the nation's history. Millions of Americans were uprooted from their homes, jobs, and families. Never before in America had 15 million people been unemployed. Never before had so many suffered hunger and want and lived under such wretched conditions as in the decade after 1929. America's future, which had seemed so bright during the 1920s, looked shattered beyond repair in the Hoover era. And the Depression unleashed a vicious cycle of poverty, social unrest, and political turmoil that each year became more intense. Many people feared that the Depression would destroy the foundations of American democracy. Certainly Herbert Hoover had shown himself to be incapable of dealing effectively with the disaster. Nor had he been able to retain the confidence of a vast majority of the American electorate. Whether another leader could revive the tottering system was an open question, for some argued that it was beyond repair. It was in this gloomy atmosphere that Franklin D. Roosevelt looked cautiously to the day when he would assume the heavy burdens of the presidency, and the country looked to him with hope.

CHAPTER 3

The New Deal Begins

The Hundred Days

 On March 4, 1933, millions of Americans sat by their radio sets listening to the ceremonies marking the inauguration of the new president. In the nation's capital the weather matched the nation's mood: somber, cold, and gray. A chilling drizzle fell steadily on the onlookers and dignitaries, further dampening their spirits as it dampened their coats. Yet in this gloomy atmosphere, Franklin D. Roosevelt stood out as a symbol of joviality and optimism. After taking the oath of office from Chief Justice Charles Evans Hughes, Roosevelt launched into a memorable and stirring inaugural address. "The only thing we have to fear," he said, "is fear itself, nameless, unreasoning fear."

Roosevelt did not promise easy solutions to the grave problems the nation faced, but he did exude an infectious optimism in his ability and in the ability of the American people to overcome the crisis. At a time when millions of people in the United States had lost faith in themselves and in their leaders, Roosevelt's call to action had an electrifying impact. Indeed, his ability to rejuvenate the American spirit was perhaps more important than any of his particular programs. Still, in the next three months he moved quickly to initiate laws and programs that he hoped would ease the Depression.

America's New President: Franklin D. Roosevelt

Many who had voted for Roosevelt in 1932 really knew little about the man; rather, the voters were registering their rejection of Herbert Hoover and expressing a desire for change. But large numbers of Americans were soon captivated by the new chief executive. His picture was hung on the walls of millions of homes. People who had never met him looked to him as a friend. The White House mail swelled to more than 80,000 letters a week, most reflecting the affection and esteem that millions of individuals felt for the president. Americans also developed an insatiable curiosity about Roosevelt, his past life, his family, and his friends.

Born into an upper-class family, Roosevelt was descended from Dutch settlers who came to New York in the seventeenth century. His forebears had made a prominent name for themselves as ship captains and merchants. Roosevelt's father, James, used his inherited wealth for prudent investments that enabled him to live in Victorian comfort on a sprawling estate in Hyde Park, New York, a few miles north of Poughkeepsie. James Roosevelt married Sara Delano, thirty years his junior, in 1880. Their only child, Franklin Delano, was born in Hyde Park on January 30, 1882. James Roosevelt was a reserved and retiring man of 50 when his son was born. Sara Delano was an aggressive and domineering mother who maintained a strong hold on her son throughout his life. The young Roosevelt grew up at Hyde Park, where he was educated by tutors. Summers he often spent sailing his own boat at the family's vacation home near Campobello, New Brunswick, or traveling in Europe.

But as Roosevelt neared adolescence, even his mother recognized the need for more formal schooling. In 1895 she sent him to Groton, an exclusive preparatory school for students from wealthy families. Roosevelt did well at Groton and entered Harvard College in 1900. Although his academic record at Harvard was average, he threw himself into many extracurricular activities and in his senior year was elected editor of the campus newspaper, the *Harvard Crimson.* Soon after graduation, in 1905, he married a distant relative, Eleanor Roosevelt, a favorite niece of President Theodore Roosevelt. Unsure of his career plans, Franklin Roosevelt enrolled in Columbia University Law School, where he was a desultory student for two years before he left without taking a degree. But he did pass the New York State Bar Examination and worked in various New York law offices until 1910. By then, somewhat bored, he had decided not to pursue a legal career.

He turned his attention instead to public life and politics. Inspired by Theodore Roosevelt, in 1910 he campaigned for and won a seat in the New York Senate as a Progressive Democrat. As an active supporter of Woodrow Wilson, Roosevelt was rewarded in 1913 with an assistant secretaryship in the Navy Department. For the next seven years he remained in this position while attracting many favorable comments. His popularity was one reason why in 1920 the Democratic convention nominated him to run as its vice-presidential candidate with James M. Cox. In the campaign he made innumerable speeches and made himself known throughout the nation. His budding political career was cruelly interrupted in 1921, however, when he was stricken with polio and paralyzed below the waist. For three years he was largely immobilized. But at the urging of his wife and close friends, he slowly sought to reenter public life, although he was never again able to walk unaided. In 1928 he was elected governor of New York, where he supervised an energetic state program designed to meet the problems generated by the Depression. As governor, he attracted a great deal of favorable nationwide attention, and thus in 1932 he became a prime contender for the presidency.

Roosevelt was not a dreamer, a profound thinker, or an idealist; rather, he had a sure sense of what seemed practical or possible. As president, he revealed himself to be a masterful politician. In part his political skill could be attributed to his personal charm, which he used as a potent instrument of manipulation. He also had a gift for self-expression that enabled him to communicate with persons in all walks of life. Roosevelt was as good a listener as he was a talker. Although his charming manner often led visitors to assume that he agreed with their views, he usually kept his own counsel and made his own decisions. Frequently, these decisions were a composite of the whole range of advice he had received from others, honed to what he felt was politically feasible. His sense of timing was superb and often strengthened his almost legendary ability to negotiate compromises. In combination these qualities made him one of the most skillful manipulators of power in the annals of American politics.

Although Roosevelt was a disabled person, paralyzed from the waist down, he was not perceived as such by the American public. People were aware of his polio, of course, but personally he exuded an image of vitality and strength. To many in the United States, he was an inspiring symbol of the ability of disabled persons to overcome their handicaps and to play a major role in public life or other endeavors they might choose. Newspapers and magazines rarely, if ever, mentioned his paralysis or showed photographs of him that revealed his disability. By dint of his personality, he even transformed his weakness into an asset. Millions of Americans suffering in the Great Depression felt a spiritual kinship with a man who himself had suffered but who had triumphantly overcome his paralysis. If FDR could do it, so perhaps could they.

Roosevelt's presidency cannot be fully understood without an appreciation of the very significant role of his wife, Eleanor. One of the great women of twentieth-century America, she made important contributions of her own. Their marriage had begun to founder during World War I when Franklin developed an affection for Lucy Mercer, his wife's social secretary. For the sake of expediency, however, Franklin and Eleanor decided against a divorce, which might hurt his political career. Nevertheless, in succeeding years Eleanor continued to be fiercely loyal to her husband. After he was struck down with polio, she sustained his spirits and urged him to return to public life—against the advice of his mother who wanted him to become a recluse. No less important was Eleanor Roosevelt's role in maintaining his political contacts between 1921 and 1928. She wrote voluminous letters on her husband's behalf, focusing especially on Democratic party leaders throughout the nation, and kept his name before the public. Without Eleanor's intensive political activities during this period, it is doubtful whether Franklin could have made the political comeback that he did.

Her importance grew steadily as the couple moved into the governor's mansion in Albany in 1929 and to the White House in 1933. As first lady, she played a crucial role. Contemporaries noted often that she was the president's "legs," as she traveled widely throughout the country to observe conditions firsthand and then reported to him. She was also a major adviser on appointments, especially in relations to women's, social welfare, and human rights causes. She was an unceasing advocate for civil rights for the poor and the underprivileged, answering (with her staff) tens of thousands of letters sent to the White House weekly. Through her writings and her travels, she developed an image as the social conscience of the New Deal and its most outstanding symbol for human rights. She was also significant in rallying women to support the New Deal. As she carved out a new life for herself in the White House, Eleanor Roosevelt emerged as the most effective and distinguished first lady in the nation's history. That accomplishment was a tribute not only to her own talents and character but also to the growing importance of women in the nation's political life.

Roosevelt's Advisers

A practical-minded politician rather than a theorist, Roosevelt adeptly surrounded himself with advisers who represented divergent views. Throughout much of his public life, Roosevelt's closest political friend and his mentor was Louis M. Howe, who had a background in journalism but who by World War I had decided to devote his whole life to furthering Roosevelt's career. His face scarred in a childhood bicycle accident, Howe preferred to exercise power behind the scenes. Eventually he moved in with the Roosevelts and became a combination of political confidant, adviser, manager, and secretary. Howe occupied a unique place in Roosevelt's life and also won the confidence of his wife and his mother. During the presidential campaign of 1932, Howe played an important role in persuading wavering delegates to come into the Roosevelt camp, using political contacts made in the course of two decades.

In a different category was the group of advisers known as the Brains Trust, whose views Roosevelt began to solicit while he served as governor of New York. Although membership in the Brains Trust between 1930 and 1934 varied with the particular problem under consideration, Roosevelt invited a few key individuals to advise him with some regularity. They included Raymond Moley, a Columbia University law professor, who was a firm believer in strong federal action in the business sphere. Roosevelt was often accompanied on his weekend trips to Albany and later to Washington by A. A. Berle,

On the way to the White House: Franklin D. Roosevelt and his Brains Trust. *(Left to right)* Cary Grayson, Norman H. Davis, Professor Raymond Moley, Professor Rexford Guy Tugwell, William H. Woodin, and Franklin D. Roosevelt. *(Wide World Photos)*

another Columbia law professor, who was an acknowledged authority on corporations. His book *The Modern Corporation and Private Property*, written in 1932, was a sensation. In it Berle focused attention on the growth of oligopoly in American business and on the separation of ownership and control that had developed in large corporate organizations. Berle often agreed with Moley about the need for greater federal control over business, but he had greater faith in the ability of the business community to police itself. Another regular in the Brains Trust was Rexford G. Tugwell, also a professor at Columbia University, whose specialty was agriculture. A firm believer in national planning, Tugwell was an unabashed advocate of federal action to deal with most Depression problems. Occasionally, M. L. Wilson, an expert in farm economics, joined discussions about proposed farm legislation.

Serving in still a different capacity was Sam Rosenman, Roosevelt's legal counsel in Albany. Rosenman was adept at transforming recommendations of experts into simple language that appealed to the press and the public. By the time Roosevelt entered the White House, Rosenman had become the president's chief speech writer. Still, the Brains Trusters often clashed over their differing philosophies. While Moley looked toward a Hamiltonian collaboration between government and big business, Tugwell espoused a vision of a Jeffersonian agrarian society. Roosevelt found these clashes stimulating. Although the Brains Trust was most important during the campaign of 1932, its influence continued until the summer of 1933.

Collectively, Roosevelt and his advisers drew on years of experience in the theory and practice of American politics and reform. Roosevelt himself had been greatly influenced by Theodore Roosevelt's doctrine of the New Nationalism, which emphasized the federal government's responsibility to right the wrongs of industrialism. He had also absorbed elements of Woodrow Wilson's New Freedom, which favored small rather than large business and government, and the desirability of restoring competition. Not only did Roosevelt accept the need to maintain competition, but he had also been profoundly impressed by World War I mobilization, which revealed how efficient federal centralization could be in time of crisis. At the same time, he and many of his advisers had been deeply influenced in their youth by the Progressive movement, especially the Progressives' concern for the underprivileged and for social justice in America. This common background shaped the outlook of the Brains Trust as it prepared to deal with the crisis.

The New Deal was not so much a consistent, carefully planned, comprehensive program as it was a series of practical responses to the various problems arising out of the Depression. Some observers even felt that there were two New Deals, one emphasizing recovery and relief and another focusing on reform. In recent years scholars have questioned such distinctions, noting that they imply greater order and design in administration policies than New Deal planners intended.

Some reform measures, including the Tennessee Valley Authority (TVA) and the Securities Act, were implemented in 1933; Congress also authorized relief programs such as the Works Progress Administration (WPA) in 1935. In short, it is difficult to compartmentalize New Deal measures. Nevertheless, it is true that Roosevelt proposed significant relief and recovery programs in 1933 and 1934 and clustered many of his reforms in the years from 1935 to 1937. Perhaps the distinction between two New Deals is artificial, yet political observers detected a decided shift of emphasis between 1934 and 1935.

Days of Gloom and Exhilaration

Roosevelt's inauguration on March 4, 1933, coincided with the lowest depths of the Depression. The night before he entered the White House, a majority of the nation's banks closed, some as a result of impending failure, others because they feared a run on their deposits. Business activity reached an unprecedented low—one-half of 1929 levels. Farmers found few profitable markets. Nearly 30 percent of the American work force was unemployed. Voluntary relief agencies had all but broken down. Despair characterized the mood of many Americans.

While communists talked of revolution, admirers of dictator Benito Mussolini of Italy spoke in favor of fascism. Nor was such talk of the need for strong rule unusual in the U.S. press and in private conversations. Americans desired order.

Roosevelt's immediate problem was to avert what many feared might be the impending collapse of the American economic and political system. Roosevelt himself shared this apprehension. His prime aim, he often said, was to save American democracy. He decided on three immediate steps. As a means of restoring the nation's confidence, he officially closed the nation's banks on March 5, 1933, by declaring a "bank holiday." To prevent a drain of specie from the United States, he limited gold exports, basing his authority to do so on a World War I statute, the Trading with the Enemy Act of 1917. Finally, he called a special session of Congress to convene on Thursday, March 9, 1933, to prepare further emergency measures. When Senators Robert M. La Follette, Jr., of Wisconsin and Edward P. Costigan of Colorado, two prominent Progressives, visited him the day before the special session to urge nationalization of the nation's banking system, he resolutely refused. Like Hoover, he favored maintenance of the existing structure through close cooperation between government and bankers. Unlike Hoover, however, the decisiveness of his actions and his political finesse won him widespread nationwide support.

Roosevelt presented his proposals for dealing with the immediate crisis to a frightened Congress. Few members were inclined to long debate: they listened to the president's message, and they wanted action. In essence, Roosevelt advocated government aid to banks so that they could safely reopen their doors. The Emergency Banking Act, which provided for federal loans to distressed banks and created guidelines for reorganization of shaky institutions, was passed. By the evening of March 9, both houses rushed the bill through, and by 9 P.M. Roosevelt had signed it.

During the first week of Roosevelt's presidency, the nation sighed with a sense of relief that at last it had a chief executive who did not shrink from the actions needed to restore a semblance of order.

Roosevelt had held his first news conference on March 8. He set the tone with an upbeat, friendly, informal approach that won over many members of the press. "It is very good to see you all," the president told the assembled journalists. "My hope is that these conferences are going to be merely enlarged editions of the kind of very delightful family conferences I have been holding in Albany for the last four years." He announced that he would not continue President Hoover's practice of receiving written questions only and instead would look forward to answering queries directly. More significant, on Sunday night, March 12, Roosevelt used the radio to address Americans directly in the first of his famous "fireside chats." In living rooms across the land, perhaps as many as 60 million Americans listened to the president, who said, "I want to talk for a few minutes with the people of the United States about banking. I know that when you understand what we in Washington have been about, I shall continue to have your cooperation, . . . sympathy, and help." Modulating his magnificent radio voice, he explained the nature of the banking crisis in simple, clear language and outlined the measures with which he proposed to meet it. Roosevelt seemed to be taking Americans into his confidence. They responded enthusiastically by lending him support—and affection. When banks were allowed to reopen seven days later, Americans deposited more than $1 billion, which they had previously hoarded out of fear of total economic chaos. During its first week, the Roosevelt administration managed to inject a feeling of elation into the nation that provided momentum for further action.

The Hundred Days

Roosevelt sought to capitalize on this momentum by keeping the special session of Congress at work until June. During what came to be called the Hundred Days, he proposed a wide range of emergency economic and social legislation that was designed to create order and stability in the nation. Although he did not always get his way as Congress sought to assert its own independence and bridled under the president's spur, this period was nevertheless a striking display of executive leadership that had few precedents in the American experience.

One of the president's prime concerns was over the nation's depressed agriculture. "Unless something is done for the American farmer," Edward O'Neal, president of the Farm Bureau Federation, told a U.S. Senate committee in January 1933, "we will have a revolution in the countryside within less than twelve months." Roosevelt instructed Secretary of Agriculture Henry A. Wallace to collaborate with Rexford G. Tugwell, his undersecretary, to formulate emergency farm legislation. Working closely with farm expert M. L. Wilson of Montana State College, and drawing on more than a decade of experience with farm problems and suggested remedies, they readied what was to become the Agricultural Adjustment Act. The fundamental assumption of this act was that farm production must be limited through balancing of supply and demand to achieve price stability. Since such stability had not been attained through private efforts, government must intervene to create order out of the chaotic price structure that had developed for farm products.

One means by which the federal government could persuade farmers to decrease their output was to pay them subsidies for their cooperation. Called the Domestic Allotment Plan, this program met with the approval of the nation's major farm organizations.

The Agricultural Adjustment Act also contained detailed provisions to carry out these objectives. It provided for restrictions on the amount of land to be planted, these to be administered by the new Agricultural Adjustment Administration (AAA), which was to pay the federal subsidies to cooperating farmers. The cost of the subsidies was to be borne by processors and canners, who became subject to a special processing tax.

A related measure, enacted hurriedly on the same day, was the Emergency Farm Mortgage Act, designed in part to head off a national farm strike threatened for May 13 by Milo Reno, a spokesman for farmers who was dissatisfied with the AAA. This act provided for federal refinancing of farm mortgages by the Farm Credit Administration in the Department of Agriculture. Before the year was out, it had lent $100 million to farmers who would otherwise have lost their farms. The Farm Credit Act also consolidated all federal agricultural lending operations in one agency, the Farm Credit Administration.

During the Hundred Days, the president and his advisers also tried to bring some order into the chaotic world of business. In his recommendations to Congress, Roosevelt urged the legislators to "provide for the machinery necessary for a great cooperative movement throughout all industry in order to obtain wide reemployment to shorten the working week, to pay a decent wage, . . . to prevent unfair competition and disastrous overproduction." Roosevelt was much impressed by the advice of Raymond Moley and General Hugh S. Johnson, the latter having had experience with mobilization of industry in World War I. Moley and Johnson felt that the Depression was a result of unrestricted and unregulated competition, which created serious imbalances between production and consumption. What was needed, they urged, was suspension of the antitrust laws; they proposed federal supervision of regulated industries, perhaps even including price controls. Stability in industry, they felt, could only be attained through the creation of a federal agency similar to the War Industries Board. Some business leaders such as Gerard Swope of General Electric had openly espoused such a remedy as early as 1931.

During April and May 1933, the Brains Trust and its staff worked feverishly to draft legislation designed to reflect Roosevelt's analysis of the crisis in industry. In May, Congress enacted the Truth in Securities Act, which required corporations issuing new securities to be truthful in their sales brochures or suffer penalties. Congress created the Securities and Exchange Commission (SEC) to administer the law. Such legislation had been common at the state level before 1930. Thereafter it had been advocated by President Hoover, particularly after a congressional investigation of the stock market in

1931 had revealed gross abuses by banks and brokers. In addition to the SEC, Congress accepted the president's proposal to establish a federal coordinator of transportation to recommend plans for stabilization and reorganization of the bankrupt railroads.

The major achievement of the New Deal was the rejuvenation of industry via the National Industrial Recovery Act of 1933. Largely the handiwork of Moley and Johnson, the act suspended the antitrust laws for a two-year period and created the National Recovery Administration (NRA), which bore a marked resemblance to the War Industries Board of 1918. Its primary purpose was to try to balance industrial production and consumption. To achieve this goal, the NRA called on more than 500 major industries or trade associations to draft codes of fair competition. These codes were to govern production quotas, business practices, standards of quality, and methods of competition. Once members of an industry had agreed to a particular code, the NRA and its enforcement agencies sought to secure the widest possible adherence to it. Roosevelt and his advisers had high hopes for this experiment in industrial self-government under federal supervision.

New Deal planners also increased federal supervision over labor. Section 7a of the National Industrial Recovery Act, designed to bolster labor's power and to boost its share of the national income, guaranteed workers the rights to bargain collectively and to organize unions. It also required NRA codes to provide for minimum wages and maximum hours. To mediate or settle management-labor disputes that might arise over the interpretation of these provisions, Congress created the National Labor Board.

The president and Congress agreed on several other measures to bolster economic recovery and feelings of security among Americans. The Emergency Banking Act of June 16, 1933, contained two important provisions: it required banks to separate commercial banking from investment banking as a means of preventing the stock market speculation that had undermined the banks' stability in the recent past, and it created the Federal Deposit Insurance Corporation to insure each bank deposit up to $5,000. Depositors no longer had to fear the loss of their hard-earned savings because of bank failures.

As an avid newspaper reader, Roosevelt was keenly conscious of the suffering and social unrest caused by widespread unemployment. He was aware that he must take immediate steps to ease the plight of the jobless. As governor of New York just a year earlier, he had recruited 10,000 unemployed men to work on forest conservation projects. Roosevelt now saw the possibility of enlarging the New York state experiment to a national scale. On the morning of March 14, he broached the idea of such a work program to Raymond Moley, and a week later, he asked Congress to enact a law to create the Civilian Conservation Corps (CCC). Despite opposition by the American Federation of Labor and some other unions, Congress agreed to the establishment of the CCC on the last day of March. The president announced that the corps would recruit 250,000 men between the ages of 18 and 25 from families on relief to begin work, he hoped, by early summer.

At the same time, Roosevelt listened to the urgings of Harry Hopkins, a social worker from Iowa who had directed relief operations in New York state while Roosevelt was governor. Hopkins advocated immediate direct relief payments by the federal government to unemployed persons to alleviate suffering. "We can eliminate to some extent at least," said the president, "the threat enforced idleness brings to spiritual and moral stability." Direct relief was "not a panacea" but "an essential step in this emergency." Acting in accordance with Roosevelt's recommendations, on May 12, 1933, Congress appropriated $500 million for relief. The lawmakers authorized the creation of the Federal Emergency Relief Administration to supervise disbursement of the money to state and local governments for distribution. Roosevelt appointed Hopkins federal emergency relief administrator. Hopkins, however, soon found himself at odds with state and local officials over the quickest and most desirable way of spending these funds. Hopkins was aware, too, that no matter how he distributed the monies, he could not aid more than 2 or 3 million of the 13 million unemployed at the time.

The president's recognition of the limited nature of relief legislation led him to recommend a more comprehensive public works program. When Congress authorized $3.3 billion for federal public works under the National Industrial Recovery Act, Roosevelt placed administration of the fund in the Public Works Administration under Secretary of the Interior Harold L. Ickes. Although Moley and other Roosevelt advisers saw public works projects as a means of helping business and industry by increasing purchasing power, the president tended to view such projects more as emergency measures than as real stabilizers of the economy.

Meanwhile, Roosevelt could not help but be aware that millions of Americans were in danger of losing their homes as a result of unemployment. Every day during the first half of 1933, foreclosure proceedings forced more than 1,000 Americans from their houses. Roosevelt was convinced that the federal government could do something to avert such a disaster. In April 1933, he asked Congress to establish the Home Owners Loan Corporation to buy or refinance mortgages of homeowners who could no longer maintain payments. Sometimes the agency advanced money for repairs. At least 20 percent of the nation's homeowners availed themselves of this federal assistance, which staved off a total collapse of the already depressed real estate market.

In June 1933, a weary Congress adjourned, thus ending the Hundred Days. The administration could look back on a spectacular performance, for never had a president and Congress worked so quickly to enact so extensive a range of programs. Even if the New Deal did not restore economic and social order to the nation—an elusive goal—the policies of these months provided the cement that maintained the fabric of American society.

Looking back just a few months, the New Deal seemed to many Americans to have swept the nation like a whirlwind. No one could yet predict whether Roosevelt and the New Deal would actually lead the country out of the Depression, but millions of Americans were encouraged by what they had observed during the Hundred Days. In contrast to Hoover, Roosevelt had humanized the White House. In a short time he had given millions of Americans the feeling that they had a friend in Washington. And immediate, if temporary, benefits from the administration's legislative programs flowed to business people, farmers, and workers. To be sure, the emergency measures did not generate a full-scale economic recovery, nor did they constitute the New Deal's greatest contributions. But Roosevelt had perhaps averted the collapse of the American system and had given his fellow Americans a renewed sense of hope.

A Period of Experimentation

1933–1935

 Roosevelt had responded to the crisis with vigorous action. What now remained to be seen was whether that action would be effective. Business people, farmers, and workers closely watched the new agencies, while the unemployed looked expectantly to the administration's relief programs. Whether the New Deal could succeed in lifting the country out of the Depression was a common concern of most Americans during the second half of 1933.

To a considerable extent, Roosevelt's approach to the Depression between 1933 and 1935 was characterized by experimentation. He had no clearly defined program in mind with which to cure the nation's ills. He preferred to experiment with a variety of alternatives, knowing that some might succeed—and others might fail. "I have no expectation of making a hit every time I come to bat," he noted. "What I seek is the highest possible batting average." When critics took him to task for this tendency to experiment, he responded with pride and disdain, saying, "The country needs, and unless I mistake its temper, the country demands, bold, persistent experimentation."

Experimentation in Business and Finance

Roosevelt and his advisers looked to the National Recovery Administration as the primary instrument to stimulate business recovery. To head this key agency the president had chosen General Hugh S. Johnson. This feisty army officer had worked with industrialist Bernard Baruch on the War Industries Board in 1918 and had gathered extensive business experience in the ensuing decade. Blustering, boisterous, and frenetic, Johnson liked to consider himself a man of action. Within four days after passage of the National

Industrial Recovery Act, he had the National Recovery Administration in operation. During the next two months, he traveled throughout the country to encourage industry representatives to meet with him and with one another to draft suggestions for acceptable NRA codes. His was an almost superhuman challenge, for by early September he had received almost 800 separate codes from industry groups and trade associations.

In part his success was due to a dazzling publicity campaign conducted during the summer of 1933. Using his World World I experience in promoting Liberty Bonds, Johnson employed bands, parades, and speakers to gather support for the NRA. In New York City in early September, more than 250,000 men and women marched down Fifth Avenue to demonstrate their support for the NRA, and similar but smaller parades were organized in towns and cities throughout the land. Meanwhile, General Johnson also conceived of a symbol to indicate compliance with the NRA. The agency's insignia was a blue eagle with spread wings. As President Roosevelt explained, "In war, in the gloom of night attack, soldiers wear a bright badge on their shoulders to be sure that comrades do not fire on comrades. On that principle, those who cooperate in this program must know each other at a glance." General Johnson was more pungent with his comments, saying,

Fighting the Depression: supporting the National Recovery Administration (NRA). *(National Industrial Recovery Administration)*

"May God have mercy on the man or group of men who attempt to trifle with this bird."

During the next eighteen months, however, the NRA largely failed to achieve its major objectives. The reasons for its shortcomings were complex. Enforcement of codes proved to be one major problem. Since a great many people, in government and out, had serious doubts concerning the constitutionality of the NRA, no one—not the NRA, not the Department of Justice, not the courts—was prepared to use sanctions to secure compliance. By fall 1933, violations were frequent. At the same time, NRA administrators throughout the country found the task of supervising the detailed regulations beyond their bureaucratic competence. Many small entrepreneurs and labor groups feared that suspension of the antitrust laws and collusion by big business would lead to a fully cartelized economy. By September 1934, opposition to the NRA was widespread and open, and this forced President Roosevelt to request General Johnson's resignation. In 1935, production indexes still lagged far behind the levels of 1929, and more than 12 million individuals remained jobless.

General Johnson often felt that much of his frustration with the NRA stemmed from his inability to control public works expenditures and to boost mass purchasing power. That authority the president had delegated to the Public Works Administration headed by Secretary of the Interior Harold Ickes. And Ickes, a miserly, if painfully honest, man, personally scrutinized every significant request that came to this agency to make sure that it would not result in fraud. During its first year, the PWA disbursed slightly over $100 million. Ickes spent PWA funds so slowly that his agency did not have the hoped-for impact in creating new jobs or in generating sufficient purchasing power to spur the national economy.

Meanwhile, the president decided to experiment with the manipulation of monetary policy to accelerate economic recovery. "The United States must take firmly in its own hands the control of the gold value of our dollar," Roosevelt declared, "in order to prevent dollar disturbances from swinging us away from our ultimate goal, namely, the continued recovery of our commodity prices." In particular, he toyed with the idea of stimulating inflation in order to raise price levels, thereby generating an increase in industrial activity. The instrument he used was the chief executive's authority to manipulate the price of gold, particularly to decrease the amount of gold backing the dollar. Roosevelt moved gradually. In March 1933, Roosevelt announced the abandonment of the gold standard; in October 1933, he informed the nation that the Reconstruction Finance Corporation would buy newly mined gold at fluctuating prices; and in January 1934, he fixed the value of the dollar at 59.06 percent of its last official gold value when the gold standard was in effect and set the price of gold at $35 an ounce. Unfortunately, the manipulation of the price of gold and the devaluation of the dollar did not unleash economic recovery, as Roosevelt hoped it would.

At the same time, inflationists in Congress were organizing their forces, hopeful that an increase in the nation's money supply would generate economic recovery. In April 1933, Senator Burton K. Wheeler of Montana introduced legislation to provide for the coinage of silver at a ratio of 16 to 1, as advocated by William Jennings Bryan in 1896. Senator Elmer Thomas of Utah advocated the issuance of greenbacks, or simply paper money. Though cautious in supporting these measures, Roosevelt found the political pressures exerted by westerners too strong to resist. In June 1934, Congress enacted the Silver Purchase Act, which instructed the secretary of the treasury to purchase silver until the supply reached one-fourth of the nation's monetary reserve—or more than $1 billion. Although this measure was undoubtedly of benefit to silver producers in the West, it contributed little to nationwide economic recovery.

Roosevelt's monetary experimentation between 1933 and 1935 did not effectively bring the country out of the Depression. As a practical individual, Roosevelt recognized this and began to search for more viable alternatives.

Experimentation in Agriculture

Experimentation also characterized Roosevelt's approach to farm problems between 1933 and 1935. The purpose of the New Deal farm program was clear. Roosevelt hoped to increase the farmers' share of the national income, which had been steadily declining ever since the end of World War I. Such a program required the reduction of output, which would bring an increase in farm prices. The means to accomplish these ends included a reduction of crop acreage, regulation of marketing, a lessening of farm debts, possible general currency inflation (which would benefit debtor farmers), and the expansion of farm export markets. The entire program was to be a cooperative venture between farmers and government. The federal government would act as initiator and guide for the millions of farmers who were to implement programs.

New Deal farm policies were characterized by duplication as well as uncertainty. "I tell you frankly," Roosevelt told Congress, "that it is a new and untrod path, but I tell you with equal frankness that an unprecedented condition calls for the trial of new means." Under Secretary of Agriculture Henry Wallace, Undersecretary Rexford Tugwell, and farm expert G. A. Peek, the Agricultural Adjustment Administration (AAA) moved quickly to reduce the vast agricultural surpluses. Some of its methods, however, invited serious criticism. Faced with increasing overproduction by cotton growers and hog producers in the spring and fall of 1933, Henry Wallace ordered farmers to slaughter 6 million pigs and to plow under 100 million acres of cotton, one-fourth of the 1933 crop. In return, the AAA paid producers $100 million. At a time when millions of Americans were hungry and had inadequate clothing, this decision was obviously controversial. In their defense, AAA administrators argued that such drastic measures were needed to prevent a total collapse of farm prices. And in October 1933, they organized the Federal Surplus Relief Corporation, which distributed more than 100 million pounds of pork to relief recipients.

Other programs of the AAA were not quite as desperate. Between 1933 and 1935, AAA benefit payments to farmers induced them to reduce their production significantly. The agency also imposed marketing quotas on producers of particular crops if two-thirds voted to impose such restrictions to maintain price levels. Meanwhile, the AAA also tried to expand overseas export markets, as when it boosted Pacific Northwest wheat exports to Japan. Price maintenance was another method the agency used. In fall 1933, at Roosevelt's suggestion, it established the Commodity Credit Corporation (CCC). Designed to stabilize production and prices, the CCC made loans to farmers to enable them to keep crops off the market until they could receive profitable prices. AAA efforts to reduce production were substantially aided by severe droughts and dust storms in 1934, which left portions of the Great Plains like deserts. Hundreds of thousands of small farmers and cattle growers were ruined by these catastrophes and were forced to leave their homes. A substantial number migrated westward in a desperate search for work. This was the worst drought in American history. One of its effects was drastically reduced farm output. The nation's wheat crop, more than 850 million bushels in 1932, shrank to 550 million bushels in 1935 and led to a rise in wheat prices. Other crop and livestock production declined proportionately.

The curtailment of agricultural output benefited many farmers. Their share of total national income increased from 11 to 15 percent in 1936; at the same time, their total debts decreased by more than $1 billion. Raymond Moley noted that the Agricultural Adjustment Administration was one of the most successful and most popular of New Deal programs, and a large number of farmers agreed with that assessment at that time. Without question, however, the AAA tended to benefit medium-sized and large farms more than it did small farmers or southern sharecroppers. Nevertheless, the New Deal restored a semblance of order to the Depression-wracked structure of agriculture. In retrospect, it is clear that the New Deal's farm program was based on the belief that farmers should cease to be individualists and instead seek to solve their problems through cooperative actions.

Experimentation in Labor

As in agriculture, the New Deal's early labor policies were also characterized by considerable trial and error. Since Section 7a of the National Industrial Recovery Act was broad and couched in general terms, its real meaning was to be determined by its administrators. Labor leaders such as John L. Lewis, president of the United Mine Workers of America, saw the legislation as a unique opportunity to organize large numbers of workers who were non-union. "The United States Government has said labor must organize," a labor handbill read during an intensive organizing campaign in the summer of 1933. Coal miners, clothing workers in New York, and steel laborers in Pennsylvania were solicited to join unions. The number of strikes doubled in 1934. Often strikers demanded the right to join a union rather than higher wages. Particularly bitter and bloody were a strike of truck drivers in Minneapolis; a longshoremen's strike in San Francisco led by Harry Bridges, at the time considered an avowed communist by many; a work stoppage by utility workers in Toledo; and a widespread strike by textile workers in New England and the South. Employers fought back, tensions increased, and by late August 1933, General Johnson had established the National Labor Board in the NRA to deal with labor-management disputes growing out of conflicting interpretations of Section 7a. Johnson appointed Senator Robert Wagner of New York as chairman, and three members representing industry and labor were chosen. In its first six months of operation, the board settled thousands of disputes and conducted open elections in which workers were allowed to vote on union membership. But by spring 1934, the board had become impotent because it lacked effective enforcement powers. Employers as well as employees openly flaunted its decisions. Senator Wagner became greatly distressed over the powerlessness of the National Labor Board, and in March 1934, he sponsored legislation to create a new federal labor commission with extensive authority. Since President Roosevelt was still cultivating the support of big business for the NRA, he refused to give his support to the Wagner bill.

New Deal labor policies from 1933 to 1935 generated much organizing activity on the part of unions, but they did not create order, nor did they help much in decreasing unemployment.

Experimentation with Relief

While Roosevelt was experimenting with programs designed to spur the nation's economic recovery, he was also acutely conscious of the social problems resulting from mass unemployment. In the summer of 1933, many millions of Americans were still hungry, ill-clothed, and homeless or poorly housed. Along with the undercurrents of bitterness, anger, and frustration were the rumblings of revolution, fanned by communist agitators and their sympathizers. Relief of social distress could not wait. Yet few of Roosevelt's advisers—neither business nor labor leaders—had constructive plans for dealing with these problems.

Nevertheless, Roosevelt was determined to try to do something. Most of the experts who testified early in 1933 before a congressional committee on relief felt that at this point only the federal government had adequate resources for the task.

The agency created to handle relief efforts, with Harry Hopkins at its head, was the Federal Emergency Relief Administration (FERA). It took Hopkins all of two days to assemble a skilled staff in Washington and set up all the state administrations. The $500 million allotted for distribution to the states was to be matched by the states, which were to administer it by making direct relief payments to the needy. Neither the president nor Hopkins favored direct relief payments, however, except as short-term emergency measures. Both believed that paying men and women to remain idle would undermine their morale and possibly destroy their sense of dignity and self-respect. Consequently, Hopkins quickly devised a broad range of makeshift work projects for relief recipients. These ranged from street repairs to classroom teaching in bankrupt school systems.

But as the fall of 1933 brought chilly weather, Hopkins brooded about establishing more extensive work-relief programs. Another winter was approaching, and the plight of the unemployed was no better than it had been at the beginning of the year. With the president's approval, Hopkins created the Civil Works Administration (CWA) in November 1933, with the avowed goal of employing 4 million people before the year was out. More than one-third of those hired worked to repair roads and highways. Others helped out in building playgrounds, parks, sewers, and airports. Hopkins never conceived of the CWA as more than a temporary expedient, and Congress abolished it in 1934 after it had dispensed more than $1 billion. Despite charges of political corruption and favoritism, the CWA had helped more than 4 million unemployed persons to survive the winter of 1934.

The Civilian Conservation Corps (CCC) was providing work-relief for a limited number of young Americans. By June 1933, the War Department had made 1,300 camps available. Some 300,000 men, from every section of the United States, including significant numbers of black Americans and Native Americans, were enrolled. The CCC engaged in a great variety of conservation projects such as tree planting, forest firefighting, and forest disease control. The corps did much to improve national and state parks and beaches and worked on erosion control projects in thousands of local areas. Over the course of two years, the CCC enrolled more than 2.5 million youths who, in addition to receiving a monthly work allowance of $30, learned new skills or a trade. The CCC was too small-scale to ease the nation's unemployment problem, but it was a popular means of sustaining the morale of a significant portion of America's young unemployed.

To provide financial aid for students and to keep them out of the job market, Congress in 1935 authorized the creation of the National Youth

Administration. This agency provided direct monetary stipends for more than half a million college students. Often they performed part-time clerical work for their home institutions, in libraries or as research aides. One and a half million high school students received similar aid, usually enough to enable them to remain in school. And more than 2 million youths who were not in school also received stipends, often in exchange for work on construction projects. Between 1933 and 1939, the federal government became involved in a wide range of educational activities, prompted largely by the nation's economic crisis.

The New Deal's relief programs in fact affected only a segment of the nation's needy. By 1935, approximately 7 million Americans had received some form of federal relief, but 12 to 15 million were still not employed regularly. Although the New Deal's experiments with social welfare seemed radical to contemporaries, in retrospect they appear to have been too limited to generate economic recovery and full employment. They ameliorated the nation's unemployment problem, but they failed to solve it.

The administration's tentative experimentation in 1933–1935 produced mixed results. The NRA did not prove to be the mighty engine of economic recovery that Roosevelt had hoped it would be. The PWA was disappointing. And monetary manipulation failed to achieve the much desired economic recovery. The administration's attitude toward labor was so ambivalent that little was accomplished in this sphere. The AAA did succeed in attaining a limited recovery for agriculture.

Despite some successes and some failures, however, the various measures comprising the New Deal during the years of experimentation did not bring economic prosperity and full employment. At best, Roosevelt had sustained the hopes of millions of Americans, who sympathized with his efforts to lift the nation out of the Depression—even when they did not succeed. And without doubt the New Deal's economic and social programs during these years cushioned the suffering that the Depression inflicted on millions of people.

CHAPTER 5

The New Deal
under Attack

Leaders and Nostrums
1933–1935

Although the New Deal won a large following in 1933 and 1934, at the same time it aroused vociferous opposition. Convinced Marxists, of course, had never looked upon Roosevelt with much favor, and as he struggled with the Depression, some mounted more vehement attacks. They loathed the experimental nature of the New Deal and yearned for a tightly structured, government-controlled society. At the same time, various neopopulist critics decried the seeming lack of social conscience on the part of Roosevelt and proffered alternative programs of their own. They were latter-day descendants of Populist reformers of the 1890s, who believed that government should right economic wrongs. Some intellectuals viewed the New Deal skeptically because of its tentative, experimental nature. Economic depression, they believed, required a more thorough reorganization of American society than Roosevelt was prepared to undertake. A very different attitude was expressed by the extreme right in the American political spectrum. Staunch adherents of the status quo, they charged Roosevelt with undermining the very vitals of free enterprise and the American democratic system.

Growing Opposition to the New Deal

The reasons for growing opposition to Roosevelt and the New Deal were varied. Perhaps the most obvious was the dogged persistence of the Depression. No matter what virtues its defenders might claim, the New Deal failed to bring economic recovery to the nation, nor did Roosevelt succeed in significantly reducing unemployment. At the same time, he made many personal enemies. His political decisions often aroused envy and hate. And glaring gaps in the president's legislative programs frustrated many groups. Roosevelt's initial reluctance to undertake extensive social welfare programs, for example, incurred the suspicions of many progressive reformers. Moreover, the passing of the crisis of 1933—when the country had seemed near collapse—vitiated the sense of national unity and purpose from which Roosevelt had benefited during the first Hundred Days. Increasingly, therefore, the anti-Roosevelt forces subjected the New Deal to searching criticism.

Thunder from the Left

The Communist Party of America aimed some of its severest barbs at the New Deal. Expressing a hope that the collapse of the American system was at hand, the Communist party offered voters its particular programs. In a book published in 1932, *Towards Soviet America*, William Z. Foster, the Communist party's presidential candidate in 1932, proposed a Marxist program for the reorganization of American society. The experimental nature of Roosevelt's actions to end the Depression was anathema to Foster and other Communists, who felt that they already held the key to economic stabilization. They urged the nationalization of all private enterprise in the United States, for government ownership and operation of business would create economic order. The abolition of all political parties except the Communist party would end political strife and establish political order. By embracing communism, Americans would enjoy social benefits denied them by a capitalist system—a living wage, job security, health care, and old-age pensions. The Communist program was reiterated during the first two years of the New Deal by Foster and by Earl Browder, a Kansas bookkeeper who came to be the party's leader during the Roosevelt era. Browder said, "The suffering masses have been told to look to Washington for their salvation. . . . But the bitter truth is rapidly being learned that Roosevelt and his New Deal represent the Wall Street bankers and the corporations—finance capital just as Hoover before him." No piecemeal reforms could ameliorate the Depression, the Communists argued. Rather, a comprehensive reorganization of society was needed to bring the nation out of economic crisis. Although the Communist party had no more than 15,000 members in 1932, its positive program appealed to many thousands more. While most politicians seemed to flounder, the Communists had a clear sense of purpose—and a comprehensive program with which to fight the Depression.

Some Americans were not party members but expressed their sympathy with Communist aims by participating in organizations that were affiliated with the Communist party. College students were drawn into such groups as the American Youth Congress, a federation of the Young People's Communist League, and the Young People's Socialist League. On most domestic or foreign issues, their spokespersons were sharply critical of the New Deal and at times espoused the usual Communist positions.

The most distinguished of the Communist fronts during the New Deal was the American Writers Congress, held in 1935. In an ambitious attempt to rally America's leading intellectuals under a Communist banner, the party secured participation of such well-known writers as John Dos Passos, Theodore Dreiser, James T. Farrell, Lewis Mumford, Richard Wright, Erskine Caldwell, and Ernest Hemingway. "The capitalist system crumbles so rapidly before our eyes," the congress declared, that "today hundreds of poets, novelists . . . and . . . writers recognize the necessity of personally helping to accelerate the destruction of capitalism and the establishment of a workers' government. . . . Communism must come and must be fought for." The purpose of the congress was to parade some of America's leading thinkers in a public condemnation of the New Deal. The effort backfired, however, because most of those who participated soon became utterly disillusioned with Communists, particularly as they learned of the extensive Stalinist purges and mass executions occurring in the Soviet Union.

The Socialist Party of America was also attracting a growing following. Led by Norman Thomas, who ran for president five times, the Socialist party drew nearly a million votes in 1932 and made a respectable showing in national, state, and local elections during the 1930s. Thomas was an indefatigable speaker. Through the hundreds of speeches he made yearly in the course of his extensive travels, he kept the Socialist position before the American public. He enjoyed cordial personal relations with many leading political figures, including the president and Mrs. Roosevelt. American Socialists drew much inspiration from the Marxist vision of society, but they were more flexible and pragmatic. The Socialists devoted much of their energy to criticism of New Deal measures. In particular, they bemoaned Roosevelt's seeming lack of concern for the nation's poor, not only the urban poor but also the sharecroppers and tenant farmers of the South. Thomas focused attention on blacks as well as on whites. Alone among political leaders, he stood out as a fervent and articulate advocate of civil rights for black Americans. His stand won him much praise but little political support. "You know, Norman," Roosevelt is reputed to have said to him once, "I'm a damned sight better politician than you are."

Neopopulist Critics

Most critics of the New Deal were not as doctrinaire as the Marxist left in the United States. American voters have traditionally spurned ideologues or even reformers who advocate major changes in the structure of the American system. Rather, they tend to support leaders who promise to devote themselves to the solution of specific problems by working within the organizational framework of American society. This the neopopulists did with a vengeance.

The most brilliant of Roosevelt's challengers was Huey Long, the affable U.S. Senator from Louisiana. Born in the Louisiana backcountry on August 30, 1893, Long received little formal education after he left home as a youth. A fast talker, he rose steadily in state politics. In 1918 he was elected as a state railroad commissioner after basing his campaign on an appeal to poor backcountry "rednecks." Within a decade he was Louisiana's leading politician. Campaigning on a promise to "make every man a king," Long was elected governor in 1928. During the next four years, he made himself an absolute ruler of the state. He personally directed a vast public works campaign to construct colleges, schools, roads, and bridges; this provided much needed employment. By increasing corporation taxes, he also secured funds to expand and improve public education. Meanwhile, he used the state police to back up his power, occasionally permitting them to manhandle state legislators or coerce political opponents. In 1932, Louisianans readily sent Long to the Senate, which gave him a national platform from which he could—and would—challenge Roosevelt.

Long was unlike any other American politician. Roosevelt feared him as his most powerful political rival and took great pains to cater to him. The senator from Louisiana was a brilliant stump speaker, a vitriolic demagogue who knew how to arouse or to charm his listeners. Although he loved to play his role as the poor man's advocate, Long was equally at home in the boardrooms of corporations. Moreover, the senator was not all bluster. With considerable insight he grasped the need for more comprehensive social welfare policies. Positioning himself as a neopopulist, he advocated a redistribution of wealth in the United States. Long felt that the wealthy should underwrite the cost of social programs for the poor.

By 1934, Long was ready to challenge the New Deal and to place his own "Share the Wealth" program before the American public. Although an early supporter of the New Deal, Long was angered by restrictions that Washington officials placed over his right to appoint WPA employees in Louisiana. Moreover, his own personal ambitions to become president were evident. In 1934 he wrote a book titled *My First Days in the White House,* in which he sketched out in graphic detail what he would do if elected president. Many observers believed that Long planned to run for president as an independent in 1936 and would draw perhaps as many as 4 million votes from the Democrats. Even if he could not prevent a Roosevelt victory in 1936, Long hoped he would attract a significant enough vote to make him a prime contender for the Democratic presidential nomination in 1940.

Long consciously developed his role as a neopopulist. With his acute political acumen, he pointed out glaring weaknesses in the New Deal's social welfare policies. Long carefully shaped his own program to fill the vacuum.

After unveiling his Share the Wealth plan in 1934, Long organized thousands of Share the Wealth clubs in every part of the nation to provide him with a grass-roots organization. He proposed a far-reaching redistribution of wealth in the United States that would provide each American family with a home, a car, and a free college education for its children. Affluence for the common people was to be secured via high taxes on corporations and confiscation of private fortunes. Long's plan to end poverty and unemployment in the United States included provisions for free public health programs, a vast expansion of public education, extensive public works projects for the unemployed, and pensions for the elderly. His Share the Wealth program—fueled mostly by his fiery and brilliant oratory—obviously held wide appeal. Its popularity during 1934 forced Roosevelt to give higher priority to social welfare legislation, if only to forestall Long and his followers. Long's campaign was cut short by his assassination on September 8, 1935; his proposals for social reform, however, did not die with him.

If Long was the most skillful critic of the New Deal, Father Charles E. Coughlin was one of its most consistent detractors. A Catholic priest of Canadian-Irish background, Coughlin had a mellow and melodious speaking voice. As a student at the University of Toronto, he became deeply impressed by the moral wrongs of usury and the need for economic justice in the world. In 1926, while a priest in the Detroit suburb of Royal Oak, Michigan, he began broadcasts of his sermons over radio station WJR; soon his "Golden Hour of the Little Flower" attracted thousands of listeners. Every Sunday his soothing voice could be heard attacking bankers, financiers, and Wall Street moguls, pouring venom on men such as Herbert Hoover, J. P. Morgan, and the Rothschilds. Gradually, his sermons took on an increasingly anti-Semitic tone. By 1933, Coughlin was estimated to have a Sunday audience of 10 million Americans and had become an imposing national figure. During Roosevelt's first year as president, Coughlin supported the New Deal, but when the president abandoned monetary experimentation, he incurred Coughlin's wrath.

In 1934, Coughlin organized the National Union for Social Justice, an organization designed to provide support for his program. That program was not as comprehensive as Huey Long's, but it concentrated on reform of the nation's banking and monetary system. Like other neopopulists, Coughlin believed that the surest way to end the Depression was through inflation. He was confident that the unlimited coinage of silver and the abandonment of the gold standard were the keys to national prosperity. With increasing rigidity, he viewed these two changes as the only effective means to bring justice to the farmers and workers of America. Coughlin also urged the nationalization of all banks and public utilities in the United States as a means of eliminating what he considered to be the pernicious influence of Wall Street on national affairs. After 1935, when Roosevelt further deemphasized monetary reforms as a cure for the Depression, Coughlin's attacks on the president became more hateful. Coughlin once said, "Is it democracy for the president of this nation to assume power over Congress, to browbeat the Congress, and to insist that his 'must' legislation be passed? Is that democracy? I urge you to purge . . . Franklin Double-Crossing Roosevelt."

As Coughlin became more extreme in his anti-Semitism and in his attacks on the Roosevelt administration, prominent leaders of the Catholic church tried to restrain him. After an abortive attempt to enter national politics in 1936, Coughlin's influence waned as church leaders forced his retirement from public life. His significance in the early years of the New Deal was to carry on the neopopulist tradition of cheap money and to encourage Roosevelt's experimentation with monetary policies.

To most Americans during the Great Depression, the name of Francis Townsend was as familiar as that of Charles E. Coughlin or that of Huey Long. Townsend had an unusual and varied career in his long lifetime. Born in 1867 on an Illinois farm, he spent much of his youth as a farm laborer, miner, teacher, and homesteader. In 1900 he received a medical degree and for the next twenty years practiced medicine in South Dakota. Soon after World War I, he migrated to Long Beach, California, where he sold real estate before he secured a job as a county health officer. In this position he witnessed poverty firsthand, particularly among the elderly. At the time Long Beach had one of the highest concentrations of persons over 65 years of age of any urban area in the nation, about 20 percent (only around 10 percent of the U.S. population was over 65 in 1933). And here in the depths of the Depression, Francis Townsend, at the age of 66, himself lost his livelihood. As he pondered his own fate and that of his contemporaries, Townsend became bitter. And as he grew angrier, he resolved to bring the plight of the aged before the entire nation.

Out of these experiences Townsend developed, over a period of years, the Townsend Old Age Revolving Pension Plan. He explained:

> In 1933 when it began to look as if calamity to business would eventually engulf all of us, and we would have to repudiate all obligations of a financial nature and start all over again, the epidemic of despair . . . had reached an all-time high. I had given a great deal of thought to this problem . . . when at the age of 66, I lost my job with the Long Beach health department.
>
> An idea came to me which might alleviate the hopelessness of aged people.
>
> It is estimated that the population of the age of 60 and above in the United States is somewhere between nine and twelve millions. I suggest that the federal government retire all who reach that age on a monthly pension of $200 or more on condition that they spend the money as they get it. This will insure an even distribution throughout the nation . . . thereby assuring a healthy and brisk state of business. Where is the money to come

from? . . . A sales tax sufficiently high to insure the pensions at a figure adequate to maintain the business of the country in a healthy condition would be the easiest tax in the world to collect.

Townsend was hardly unique in putting forward a scheme for old-age pensions. Such programs had been widely discussed by social workers, reformers, and politicians for more than two decades, but Townsend crystallized much of this debate and captured the imaginations of millions of Americans, young and old. Townsend's plan had several advantages. By requiring compulsory retirement at 60, Townsend hoped to exclude such persons from the labor market and thus to alleviate some unemployment. At the same time, if the pensioners spent their monthly allowances, they would do much to increase the flow of money in circulation. And, of course, the hardships and sufferings of millions of destitute aged Americans would be relieved through the pension. The cost of such a plan would be high, Townsend admitted, perhaps $2 to $3 billion annually, but it could be met by the imposition of a national sales tax. In this way relief for the elderly would generate economic recovery for the whole nation.

Townsend proved adept in mobilizing widespread support for his proposals. In 1934 he organized the Old Age Revolving Pension Plan, which eventually grew to more than 5,000 local Townsend Clubs. Unemployed teachers or ministers often took the initiative in establishing such community groups. Through speeches, magazines, and lobbying activities in Washington, D.C., and in state capitals, the Townsendites impressed on the conscience of America the plight of the aged poor. Although Roosevelt and his advisers feared the cost of the Townsend plan if Congress were to adopt it, they could not ignore him and his followers. In a real sense the provisions for modest, federal old-age pensions in the Social Security Act of 1935 were an attempt to still the demands of the Townsendites, although the Social Security Act fell far short of the proposals made by Townsend. Townsend himself considered social security unfair and inadequate. Yet it dampened the ardor of many of his followers, and after its passage, the Townsend movement rapidly declined.

Townsend had hoped to broaden the base of his support through collaboration with a group of midwestern neopopulist agrarians led by Congressman William H. Lemke of North Dakota. Lemke was born on a North Dakota farm and early in life came to know the hardships of small farmers on the Great Plains. After graduating from the University of North Dakota, he attended Yale Law School. Soon he was back in his native state, however, where he became a prominent politician in the Non-Partisan League, the neosocialist party that dominated North Dakota politics between the two world wars. In 1932, Lemke was elected to the House of Representatives. There he emerged as one of the champions of the distressed farmers on the

Social Security for Americans: Franklin D. Roosevelt signs the act into law, August 14, 1935. *(Wide World Photos)*

Great Plains. Almost two-thirds of the farmers in his own state lost their properties due to foreclosure. Between 1933 and 1936, Lemke sponsored a series of bills to lighten the debt loads of farmers, to postpone foreclosures, to allow refinancing, and to issue greenbacks. Lemke saw himself squarely in the populist tradition and took pride in his agrarian radicalism. Since the Roosevelt administration opposed most of his proposals, Lemke, once a nominal Republican, openly opposed the administration.

Lemke led a new party composed of New Deal opponents. In July 1936, Coughlin, Townsend, and Gerald L. K. Smith, a self-proclaimed successor to Huey Long, united in their support of Lemke as the presidential candidate of the newly formed Union-Labor party. Although the party claimed to represent 20 to 30 million voters, it consisted of a rather unlikely combination. Except for their hatred of Roosevelt, the party chiefs had little in common. In fact, within a month, rivalries among the leaders largely disrupted whatever influence the Union party might have had. In the elections of November 1936, the party drew fewer than 1 million votes.

Intellectuals

To many intellectuals, academicians, writers, and thinkers who eschewed Marxism, the neopopulist programs of Long, Coughlin, Townsend, and Lemke seemed unsophisticated. In their view, only far-reaching changes in the organization of American society could lift the nation out of the Depression. And whereas neopopulist critics of the New Deal had the support of millions, the intellectuals could only count on a following in the tens of thousands. Nevertheless, their views were sometimes important in shaping the attitudes of New Deal administrators responsible for policy formation.

The American Commonwealth Federation was one of the significant critics of the New Deal and its programs. Founded in 1932 by Selden Rodman and Alfred Bingham, two young college graduates with upper-class backgrounds, the federation sought nothing less than the reconstruction of American society. In his book *Insurgent America: The Revolt of the Middle Classes*, Rodman explained his reorganization plan. Meanwhile, Bingham edited the federation's journal, *Common Sense*, which attracted leading intellectuals to its pages. Philosopher John Dewey wrote extensively for it, offering criticisms of New Deal programs and suggesting alternative measures for coping with the Depression.

Less influential than the American Commonwealth Federation were the Technocrats. Founded by Howard Scott, an engineer, and Harold Loeb, a journalist, the Technocrats attempted to analyze the Depression scientifically. A modern industrial society, they believed, could function effectively only with large-scale, comprehensive planning. The absence of such planning had led the nation into the morass of economic crisis. What was needed, therefore, was a drastic change in American values and institutions. Technical efficiency must replace economic profit as a main goal of society; economic planning by specialists and experts must replace democratic processes and institutions. Planning was necessary not only for the economy but for society as well. The Technocrats envisaged planned communities—in cities, rural areas, and suburbs—to create an orderly, scientifically organized society. Since they couched many of these proposals in obscure language, however, the movement lacked mass appeal. Yet its emphasis on social and economic planning struck a responsive chord among both supporters and critics of the New Deal.

Fascists

The Depression policies of the New Deal and the alternatives suggested by its critics in the 1930s developed at the very same time that totalitarian movements were sweeping through Europe. In the Soviet Union, Communist dictator Joseph Stalin was becoming increasingly repressive; in Germany, Adolf Hitler unveiled the Nazi system; in Italy, Benito Mussolini instituted a fascist dictatorship; and in Spain, Francisco Franco aped his Italian neighbors. Inevitably, the followers of these totalitarian movements in the United States sought to further their respective causes. The Communist Party of America faithfully followed the policies determined by its counterpart in the Soviet Union; and a German-American Bund—composed of American Nazis led by Fritz Kuhn—agitated to institute Nazi policies in the United States. At the same time, American proponents of fascism advocated their brand of totalitarianism as an alternative to the New Deal. Fascism's leading exponent in the United States was Lawrence Dennis, a Georgian of upper-class background who, after graduation from Harvard, spent a decade in the Foreign Service. After some experience as an investment banker in New York during the first year of the Depression, Dennis became convinced that capitalism was doomed and that the efforts of the New Deal to save it were futile. He explained his reasoning in several cogently written books. One, *The Coming American Fascism* (1936), provided a blueprint for a fascist government in the United States. In urging the abolition of the existing American system, Dennis proposed the creation of a centralized dictatorship. A fascist state would have absolute control of the economy and could eliminate unemployment, especially by increasing military expenditures. In a fascist America, the suppression of all political parties except that of the fascists would result in political stability. And strident nationalism and aggressive foreign policy would bring national unity to a divided America. With economic conditions improving slightly after 1933, the fascist movement did not attract a significant following, but it aroused concern and alarm. Novelist Sinclair Lewis became so disturbed about the specter of fascism that he wrote the book *It Can Happen Here* to warn his fellow Americans of the potential danger.

Echoes from the Right

Among Roosevelt's most vitriolic detractors was the extreme right. Some of the richest individuals in the nation became increasingly disturbed by the New Deal, opposing most governmental social and economic programs. In 1934, members of the Du Pont family—which controlled the nation's largest chemical corporation—organized the American Liberty League specifically to oppose Roosevelt and his programs. The Du Ponts provided most of the money used to further the league's lobbying and publicity ventures. Other rich individuals who contributed included bankers such as Winthrop Aldrich and Felix Warburg and corporation lawyers such as Dean Acheson. A few of Roosevelt's personal enemies also joined the league, most notably the embittered Al Smith. The league made little pretense of offering a positive program to combat the Depression; instead, its leaders vented their hatred on the president and castigated the whole range of New Deal legislation. One of their oft-repeated charges was that Roosevelt sought to establish a socialist dictatorship in America.

Some of the criticism Roosevelt got was inevitable for any administration in power—which, as a seasoned politician, the president realized. But Roosevelt was acutely sensitive to the most telling charge of his critics, namely, that the New Deal had failed to put the nation back on the road to economic recovery. That much-sought-after goal still seemed distant in 1935. With the presidential election of 1936 looming on the horizon, one of Roosevelt's chief goals was to steal the thunder of his most important critics and to soften their strident demands. Even if he could adopt only a portion of their suggested programs, Roosevelt reasoned, he would still be able to attract large numbers of their followers to his own banner. So he paid some attention to the suggestions of the socialists for greater government aid to the nation's poorest farmers, to Long's loud cries for social welfare legislation, to Coughlin's urgings for greater monetary inflation, and to Lemke's complaints about the need for additional farm credit legislation. Roosevelt also appeared to be impressed by the call of intellectuals for more emphasis on national planning. In fact, the only groups he ignored were totalitarian ideologues and the advocates of rigid laissez-faire—a reflection of his distaste for extremism. By adopting portions of the proposals made by the various critics of the New Deal, Roosevelt was able to win the support of many of their followers while at the same time deflating the importance of their leaders. Thus in 1935 the president was fashioning a program that was an amalgam drawn from a varied range of proposals made by his opponents. This program was to constitute the nucleus of the New Deal during the next four years.

CHAPTER 6

The New Deal and Reform

1935–1939

 By 1935 various pressures on Roosevelt were leading him to shift his approach to Depression problems. In 1933 he had largely been concerned with economic instability and the possible collapse of the American system; in 1934 he tried experimental legislation to lift the country out of the Depression; but the persistence of the Depression in 1935 seemed to dictate another approach—an emphasis on reform. This was also a wise strategy for a politician who had to run for reelection in the coming year. Moreover, in the first half of 1935, the Supreme Court had handed down a series of decisions that all but invalidated the New Deal. Most far-reaching was *Schechter v. United States*, in which the court unanimously declared the NRA unconstitutional. Other decisions negated New Deal farm and labor legislation. The Supreme Court's actions were a clear indication to the president's opponents that they could prepare for another round of combat.

The Reform Persuasion

The president's own convictions also played some part in persuading him that the time was ripe for a greater emphasis on reform. Throughout his political career, Roosevelt had shown sympathy for reform causes. In 1910 as a freshman state senator in the New York Senate, he had aligned himself with reform Democrats against Tammany Hall, the New York political machine; as a member of the Wilson administration, he had attracted reform Democrats who supported his vice-presidential nomination in 1920; and between 1928 and 1932, as governor of New York, he developed one of the most reform-minded state administrations to be found anywhere. Thus it seemed unlikely

57

that Roosevelt would put aside his predilections for reform after he reached the White House. Rather, he suspended them temporarily while he dealt with the immediate pressing problems of the Depression, but once these had been stabilized, his reform instinct could be expected to emerge again.

As Roosevelt viewed the nation's problems in 1935, he came to realize that long-range reform might be more effective in dealing with the Depression than the short-range solutions already tried. The crisis seemed too deep-seated, too deeply rooted in structural weaknesses in the American system to be remedied by palliatives. Substantial modifications in the economic and social structure of the nation were required to make the system function more effectively. The president was not seeking to transform American capitalism but rather to preserve and strengthen it by protecting it against its own worst excesses. This could be accomplished by increased federal supervision to ensure the more efficient operation of American institutions. In 1933, Roosevelt had hoped that big business could assume prime responsibility for leading the nation back to prosperity. But by 1935 he had come to the conclusion that his faith had been misplaced and that the federal government must assume the role of arbiter among the contending interest groups in American society. He felt it necessary to implement on a national scale many reforms already being administered by local and state governments between 1900 and 1933.

By 1935 former Progressives were urging Roosevelt to take a more pronounced reformist stance. As a sense of crisis abated, business executives had become increasingly disenchanted with the New Deal, and they now openly attacked it. At the annual meeting of the U.S. Chamber of Commerce in May 1935, speaker after speaker arose to condemn Roosevelt and his policies. Meanwhile, at a White House meeting during this same period, Progressive Senator Robert M. La Follette, Jr., urged him to take the lead in the reform movement. Similar advice came from Professor Felix Frankfurter of the Harvard Law School. Frankfurter shared many views of Supreme Court Justice Louis Brandeis, who had once been a close adviser of President Woodrow Wilson in formulating the doctrines of the New Freedom. Brandeis advocated smallness in a decentralized society. He abhorred big business, which he considered to be inefficient economically and dangerous to political democracy. Hoping to restore a more competitive society, Brandeis believed that the federal government could function best as the supervisor of orderly and regulated competition. Roosevelt was well acquainted with his views, which were also espoused by Frankfurter and scores of dedicated New Dealers.

Thus began one of the most far-reaching reform movements in the history of American politics. Between 1935 and 1937, Congress, at Roosevelt's prodding, undertook the reorganization of the economic system, the environment, and social policies. Although the pace of reform ebbed after 1937, the reforms also extended to the government itself.

Reorganizing the Economic System

As the Depression continued, Roosevelt launched a comprehensive program in 1935 to strengthen the structure of the American economy. With the NRA invalidated, Roosevelt now threw his support behind legislation designed to bring greater order into the nation's banking system by expanding federal supervision of it. The Banking Act of 1935 increased the authority of the Federal Reserve Board in various ways. It permitted the board to regulate discount rates to determine reserve requirements of member banks and to buy and sell in open markets. The act also authorized the board to issue new types of federal bank notes, thus providing the federal government with more direct control over the nation's monetary system.

The strengthening of federal regulatory authority was also evident in the Holding Company Act of 1935, designed to affect the nation's utility companies. In an effort to create orderly and regulated competition, this act required the integration of utility companies and their subsidiaries, largely in the hope of increasing their efficiency. At the same time, Section 11a of the act required dissolution of most utility holding companies. Such holding companies had been common in the utility industry since 1920 and, in the opinion of many experts, were responsible for much waste, inefficiency, and instability. The act also required all new securities issues to be approved by the Securities and Exchange Commission, a provision designed to discourage fraud and inefficiency.

Other legislation was also designed to bring greater stability to the power industry by increased federal control. The Federal Power Act of 1935 created the Federal Power Commission, which was given extensive authority to regulate the rates charged by companies engaged in interstate business. In a supplementary act in 1938, Congress granted the Federal Power Commission the right to regulate the price of natural gas flowing between states. This legislation supplemented one of the New Deal's proudest accomplishments, the Tennessee Valley Authority (TVA), established in 1933 after more than a decade of efforts by Senator George W. Norris of Nebraska. The TVA was a government corporation that operated a multipurpose development in seven states of the Tennessee River valley and engaged in the production of public power, flood control, soil conservation, improvement of river navigation, forest conservation, and development of recreational areas. The program was widely praised. In addition, by competing with private public utilities, the TVA put pressure on them to provide efficient service at low rates and set a "yardstick." Under the leadership of Arthur Morgan and David Lilienthal, the TVA was a vivid demonstration of the New Deal's determination to create regulated competition via federal controls.

Drawing on the advice of Brandeis, Frankfurter, and progressives hostile to big business, early in 1937 Roosevelt revitalized the Department of Jus-

The Tennessee Valley Authority (TVA) in action: Appalachia Dam, 1942. *(TVA Annual Report)*

tice's antitrust division. He appointed Yale Law School Professor Thurman Arnold as assistant attorney general and provided him with a large staff to undertake extensive investigations and prosecutions. Within two years, Arnold had initiated ninety-two major antitrust actions. Meanwhile, Roosevelt appointed the Temporary National Economic Committee to investigate monopoly power in the nation's major industries. After exhaustive inquiries, the committee advocated the dissolution of companies characterized by monopolistic power; however, the advent of World War II prevented the implementation of its recommendations. In fact, the antitrust phase of the New Deal did no more to lift the economy out of Depression than did the NRA, but it represented an effort to increase competition within industry with the hope that such competition would contribute to the revival of prosperity.

Federal supervision of competitive practices in business was also a major goal of the Miller-Tydings Act of 1937. Sometimes known as the Fair Trade Act, it required retailers to sell nationally advertised products at price levels stipulated by manufacturers. This effort to avoid cutthroat competition and price instability was but another attempt to establish a stable price structure that would lessen the economic chaos seemingly created by the absence of federal planning and regulation prior to the New Deal.

Since the Depression had also torn apart the nation's transportation system, the New Deal planners hoped to bring order and stability to the industry by placing it under federal supervision. Roosevelt recoiled from the suggestion that the federal government nationalize the rail carriers, and between 1933 and 1935, Federal Coordinator of Transportation Joseph B. Eastman never did more than advise carriers on more efficient modes of operation. But by 1935, Roosevelt and his advisers had concluded that government supervision of competition would result in a more efficient and balanced transportation system for the nation. The railroads were already operating under the regulatory power of the Interstate Commerce Commission, but other forms of transport were still free from federal controls. Acting in part on Eastman's recommendations, the administration persuaded Congress to approve three measures: (1) the Motor Carrier Act of 1935, which placed the nation's trucking industry and inland waterways under the authority of the Interstate Commerce Commission, which was granted powers to regulate rates, services, and routes; (2) the Merchant Marine Act, which provided the maritime industry with government subsidies and loans, to be administered by the U.S. Maritime Commission; and (3) the Civil Aeronautics Act of 1938, which established the Civil Aeronautics Board to regulate rates, routes, and services. These three acts effectively reorganized the nation's transportation system.

During its reform phase, the New Deal sponsored additional legislation to promote stability in agriculture. One of its most successful measures was the Rural Electrification Act of 1935, which provided low-cost federal loans to farmers who sought access to electric power. In a few short years, this act resulted in the electrification of more than 90 percent of the nation's farms.

Meanwhile, bitter disputes broke out between various factions in the Department of Agriculture over extension of more federal aid to the nation's poorest farmers. Many New Deal agricultural programs benefited middle-class or rich farmers but not poverty-ridden sharecroppers, tenant farmers, and farm laborers, even though this group constituted one-third of America's farmers. In response to their pleas, and with a hope of conciliating the various factions in American agriculture, Roosevelt threw his support behind the Bankhead-Jones Farm Tenancy Act of 1937. This measure authorized federal loans to tenants to enable them to become self-sufficient landowners and provided for limited resettlement of farmers currently living on exhausted or nonproductive land. It also sought to provide aid to the increasing number of farm migratory workers.

One of the New Deal's last significant farm reform measures was the Agricultural Adjustment Act of 1938. It reiterated many provisions of its predecessor in 1933 but also attempted to meet constitutional objections voiced earlier by the Supreme Court. The Agricultural Adjustment Administration (AAA) controlled farm production by making soil conservation payments to those who cooperated and by allowing the imposition of marketing quotas if two-thirds of the farmers producing a single crop desired them.

Roosevelt was not particularly eager to extend federal regulations to the sphere of labor relations, but pressures from organized labor narrowed his options on this issue. Preoccupied with the problems of economic recovery that seemed so elusive, the president was loath to enter upon experiments in social planning unless they would directly contribute to ending the Depression. The National Labor Board, created under the NRA, became increasingly frustrated by its lack of authority, and by 1935 it was virtually impotent. The invalidation of the NRA by the Supreme Court in the *Schechter* decision was the final blow.

During this phase, United Mine Workers president John L. Lewis was seeking to spur his reluctant colleagues in the American Federation of Labor to organize workers into industrial rather than craft unions, for the vast numbers of unorganized workers in manufacturing industries were unskilled. Lewis and the advocates of industrial unionism were convinced that without federal support, their organizing drive would have scant success in view of strong opposition from big business. In Congress, labor's leading spokesman, Senator Robert F. Wagner of New York, was sponsoring a bill to extend benefits labor had enjoyed under the NRA, namely, federal guarantees of the rights to organize and to bargain collectively. Roosevelt did not actively support the Wagner bill, although he could scarcely oppose it. Despite the president's reluctance, he had few options but to approve the bill after Congress passed it by a large majority.

The Wagner Act of 1935 was organized labor's Magna Carta. It prohibited a broad range of unfair labor practices by employers—among them the organization of company unions. The act also guaranteed labor the rights to organize and to bargain collectively. To ensure the effective administration of these provisions, the act established the National Labor Relations Board (successor to the National Labor Board created in 1933), appointed by the president. Its functions included hearing complaints by workers or employers and conducting elections where workers sought to organize into unions. The immediate impact of the Wagner Act was to spur unionization and to stimulate the organization of the Congress of Industrial Organizations (CIO), the nation's largest industrial union. In a broader sense the Wagner Act did much to systematize employer-employee relations in the United States. It was an essential building block in the construction of the organizational society.

The Fair Labor Standards Act of 1938 further extended federal guidelines concerning labor management relations. It stipulated minimum wage levels throughout the United States (25 cents an hour) as well as a maximum 44-hour workweek. At the same time, it embodied the hopes of reformers for more than a half century by prohibiting child labor.

The main thrust of the various measures in the New Deal's economic program was to reorganize the American economic system and set it on a firm foundation. Believing that unrestrained competition and laissez-faire had contributed heavily to the Great Depression, New Deal planners hoped to repair the American system. This could be done, they believed, by letting the federal government play an increasingly important role in maintaining economic stability, in supervising contending economic interests, and in regulating competition.

Reorganizing the Environment

The crisis of the Great Depression also spurred New Deal efforts to organize the nation's environmental resources more effectively. From early childhood, Roosevelt had felt a deep love for nature. As president, this passion did not wane. Soon after he entered the White House, Roosevelt instructed his advisers to work on various phases of conservation programs. "Unlike most of the leading nations of the world," he noted in 1934, "we have so far failed to create a national policy for the development of our land and water resources." The development of such a policy was one of his fervent hopes.

Roosevelt did much to invigorate existing conservation agencies. The activities of the Forest Service were considerably expanded. Roosevelt prevailed over skeptical experts to promote the planting of 200 million trees in a 100-mile zone along the 100th meridian on the Great Plains. Stretching from Canada to Texas, the shelterbelt was designed to break up winds and to avoid the disastrous dust storms that had swept away surface soils. With the enactment of the Soil Conservation Act (1935), the Soil Conservation Service in the Department of Agriculture took on the task of preventing soil erosion on a national scale. Similarly, the Taylor Grazing Act of 1934 protected the vast cattle ranges of the West by stipulating federal regulations for users of federally owned range lands. To coordinate the increasingly numerous federal programs concerned with the environment, the president on June 20, 1934, created the National Resources Planning Board (after 1935 called the National Resources Committee). The board did much to stimulate local resource planning and encouraged development of regional plans, acting only in an advisory capacity, however, since existing organizations such as the Departments of the Interior and Agriculture and the Corps of Engineers became increasingly jealous of possible encroachments on their powers. Although the New Deal fostered a variety of specific conservation programs, Roosevelt's desire to formulate a comprehensive national policy concerning the environment was not fully realized. Yet the New Deal focused the attention of Americans on the need to develop more systematic resource policies.

Reorganizing American Society

More than any other single event, the Depression highlighted the unequal distribution of wealth in the United States. Although Roosevelt did not propose profound changes in American society, he did seek a more equitable distribution of economic and political power in the United States by shifting more from the upper to the middle and lower classes.

Roosevelt was keenly aware of the sharp impact of federal taxing powers in separating classes of Americans. In a real sense, the Revenue Act of 1936 was a social as well as an economic measure. Throughout the first half of 1935, the president was clearly on the defensive against the growing popularity of Huey Long and his Share the Wealth platform. Hoping to steal Long's thunder, in 1935, Roosevelt sent a tax message to Congress, influenced in part by Louis Brandeis and Felix Frankfurter, who were urging an attack on concentrated wealth. The president asked Congress to redistribute wealth by new taxes on inheritances, gifts, and high incomes and by corporate taxes that increased in relation to the size of the corporation. This program aroused bitter reaction from business groups and occasioned a lively debate among the lawmakers. Congress revised the president's proposals and enacted the Wealth Tax Act of 1935, a much more moderate program than Roosevelt's original plan. It increased gift, estate, and capital stock taxes and contained an excess profits levy. Although far less sweeping than Huey Long's proposals, it clearly indicated Roosevelt's determination to use tax powers for limited social planning.

The struggle for a national social security system was just as heated. Demands for social welfare legislation came not only from some of Roosevelt's sharpest critics—Huey Long, Francis Townsend, and Father Charles E. Coughlin—but also from social reformers such as Abraham Epstein, Paul H. Douglas, Harry Hopkins, and others who had been advocating some form of federal welfare programs since the turn of the century. Social security represented the culmination of decades of agitation and planning. Beset on all sides by conflicting demands for various forms of social welfare, Roosevelt reacted with characteristic caution. He appointed the Special Committee on Social Security, chaired by Secretary of Labor Frances Perkins, which represented some but by no means all of the divergent viewpoints. Out of the deliberations of this committee came recommendations that ultimately found their way into the Social Security Act of 1935. Considering the many proposals for federal social programs made at the time, it was really a very moderate and tentative approach by the federal government. Nevertheless, it was a milestone in federal social policies.

The Social Security Act of 1935 reflected the president's effort to reorganize American society by removing fears and insecurities induced by unemployment, illness, or old age and so to stabilize social tensions. It provided for unemployment insurance, aid to the needy, and old-age pensions. To provide some economic security against joblessness, the act established a fund, administered largely by the states, from contributions by employers and employees. The law also provided for direct federal aid for dependent children, the blind, deaf, or disabled, achieved with matching federal and state funds. In addition an omnibus measure created a pension fund for certain categories of workers over 65 years of age, drawn from tax contributions by employers and employees.

The act had some drawbacks in a depressed economy. By requiring employer and employee contributions, the measure had a deflationary effect because it took money out of circulation. Moreover, its coverage of individuals was limited, and no provision was made for joblessness due to extended illness. Still, it was a beginning.

Housing and health each also had a place in the social reform proposals. "I see one-third of the nation ill-housed, ill-fed, and ill-clad," Roosevelt noted during his second inaugural address in 1937, and he was determined to take effective action to improve conditions for those in greatest need. Congress responded with the Wagner-Steagall Act of 1937, which established the U.S. Housing Authority. This agency was authorized to grant $1 billion in loans and subsidies to public housing authorities for slum clearance and public housing projects. Roosevelt also sponsored legislation for national health care, but the strong opposition of the American Medical Association helped to defeat the bill in Congress.

Some of the New Deal planners also had visions of a more orderly and content society, to be achieved through governmental planning. Rexford G. Tugwell, in particular, saw a new America, "a land in order, wisely used with the hills green and the streams blue." To achieve this happy society, community planning was essential. Roosevelt, too, felt that new land settlements could provide subsistence homesteads for at least a portion of the unemployed and that a better balance between city and country life in the United States could be established. This was first attempted in the National Industrial Recovery Act in 1933, under which Secretary of the Interior Ickes created the Subsistence Homestead Division, designed to attract rural as well as urban slum dwellers to newly planned, self-sufficient demonstration communities. The first project was built in Arthurdale, West Virginia, at considerable cost to the federal government. During the next two years, the New Deal sponsored sixty more model communities. Although many of the settlers who came improved their lives, no more than 7,000 individuals were involved in these community experiments. And most of the unemployed were not prepared for life in a cooperative anyway.

In 1935, Roosevelt consolidated the various rural planning efforts by creating the Resettlement Administration. In addition to resettling farmers from exhausted lands in well-managed, federally sponsored cooperative farm communities, the Resettlement Administration created Greenbelt towns, model suburban communities that took their name from Greenbelt, near Berwyn, Maryland, a showplace for the program. None of the experiments in community planning attracted widespread support, and by 1937 Roosevelt ordered the liquidation of the programs.

Reorganizing American Government

Roosevelt's vision also embraced the reorganization of American governmental institutions, particularly the judicial and executive branches. Soon after his smashing electoral victory at the polls in 1936, he sent Congress proposals to reorganize the Supreme Court. Throughout 1935 and 1936 the president had been increasingly irritated by the majority of conservative justices on the Court, who had invalidated many of the New Deal's major programs. In 1935 the Court had invalidated the NRA in *Schechter* v. *United States,* the Railroad Retirement Act in *Railroad Board* v. *Alton Railroad,* and the Farm Mortgage Act in *Louisville Land Bank* v. *Radford.* In 1936 the justices declared the Agricultural Adjustment Act unconstitutional in *United States* v. *Butler* and the Guffey Coal Conservation Act in *Carter* v. *Carter Coal Co.* In 1937, Roosevelt feared that the Wagner Act and the Social Security Act might meet a similar fate. Thus he advocated the Judicial Reorganization Bill of 1937, which proposed to grant the president authority to appoint a maximum of six new justices to the Supreme Court and to allow him to replace any justice who did not retire after reaching the age of 70. Much to Roosevelt's surprise, his Court reorganization plan aroused a storm of fury. He was accused of trying to pack the Court. Many prominent leaders in his own party, such as Senators Carter Glass, Joseph Robinson, and Walter George, openly denounced him as a would-be dictator and usurper of judicial power who would eventually undermine the democratic process. The Republicans were even more vehement. So powerful was the combined opposition to the Judicial Reorganization Bill that in July 1937, Roosevelt withdrew it. The battle deeply divided the Democratic party and eroded some of the president's support. Within two years, ironically, four justices died or retired, and Roosevelt was able to place on the Court men whose thinking was more compatible with his own.

Roosevelt was more successful in reorganizing the executive branch of the federal government. In 1937 he appointed a group of experts in public administration headed by Louis Brownlow to the President's Committee on Administrative Management. Their task was to recommend improvement of the government's vast bureaucracy. Congress adopted some of their recommendations by approving establishment of the Executive Office of the President, which authorized a staff of six administrative assistants to aid the president in his conduct of public business. In addition, a number of overlapping federal agencies were consolidated in the interest of administrative efficiency.

The New Deal and Organizational Society

Administrative reorganization was the last segment of the New Deal's reform program. After 1939 the waging of World War II in Europe created issues that dominated Roosevelt's attention. Then, too, the passions of reformers seemed to have spent themselves in the extraordinary burst of legislative and executive energy that characterized the years between 1935 and 1939.

What the New Deal accomplished during this period was a comprehensive reorganization of American society. Economic reforms modified the structure of the American economy as the federal government, through regulatory and direct action, assumed major responsibility for modulating booms and recessions. New Deal social welfare legislation attempted to stabilize the effects of economic insecurity by having the federal government assume increasing responsibility for problems of old age, unemployment, and housing. And since these expanded public functions greatly increased the size and scope of the federal government—in Washington and throughout the nation—the New Deal's administrative reforms were designed to render the workings of bureaucracy more efficient.

The total effect of much of the New Deal reform program was to accelerate the growth of an organizational society. Such a society depended on the action of groups rather than of individuals. New Deal policies accelerated the organization of interest groups in formal organizations such as business, agriculture, and labor, and these groups, which represented large numbers of individuals, became important influences in shaping federal policies, policies that expanded the role of government in most phases of American life. Roosevelt was one of the founders of the welfare state in the United States and also one of the progenitors of the organizational society in America.

The New Deal and the South

The South was hit particularly hard by the Great Depression. Heavily dependent on agriculture, especially cotton and tobacco, the disastrous drop in farm prices directly affected millions of its poorest farmers. Many of them were sharecroppers, or tenants, who eked out a precarious marginal subsistence even in the best of times. The seemingly endless decade of depression after 1929 brought them unprecedented misery and poverty. Industrial production as well as the timber and coal industries felt the shock waves of the economic crisis. As President Roosevelt noted in 1938, "It is my conviction that the South presents right now the nation's number one economic problem."

Roosevelt had a special relationship with the South. Blacks and whites in the region admired him. He was not a Virginia planter but a Dutch country squire with a large landed estate in the Hudson valley. Southerners admired his pastoral gentility. His speech bespoke the old American upper class, prized in a region where family and traditions were held in high esteem. Best of all, he was a part-time resident of Georgia. He had first come to Warm Springs, Georgia, after developing polio; he later established the Warm Springs Foundation in 1926 to provide therapy for sufferers of the disease. Six years later he built a simple cottage there that became his second home. Meanwhile, he also acquired some timber lands in the area and enjoyed showing his neighbors his prize cattle. This southern connection served Roosevelt well. At the same time, his election to the White House gave southerners political power such as they had not enjoyed for many years. In 1933, southerners chaired nine of fourteen important committees in the Senate and twelve of seventeen in the House. The South had come into its own again with Roosevelt, and for the next five years it played a major role in shaping New Deal legislation.

No wonder, therefore, that the impact of the New Deal on the South was far-reaching. The New Deal did much to alter the economic structure of the region. It hastened the decline of the sharecropping system and the mechanization of agriculture. It relieved poverty in rural areas and cities and raised wage levels. And it gave the South greater influence in national as well as international affairs.

Various New Deal measures were designed to help farmers in the South. Among these, the Agricultural Adjustment Administration of 1933 was prominent. That agency had three tasks. It was to maintain farm prices at parity (1914 levels), to regulate production, and to dispose of surpluses. Under the Cotton and Tobacco Control Acts of 1934, the AAA allotted production quotas to each southern state. When the U.S. Supreme Court declared the AAA unconstitutional in 1936, Congress met its objections by enacting a similar measure two years later. New Dealers also extended additional farm credit in 1933. In a special effort to help southern tenant farmers, the lawmakers passed the Bankhead-Jones Act of 1937, which granted low-cost loans to sharecroppers. The program was less successful than its sponsors hoped, which was also true of 164 experimental cooperative farms created by the Farm Security Administration. Yet these programs helped more people in the South than in any other section of the nation. The net result of all of these laws was to undermine the sharecropping system of the South, to stabilize prices, and to encourage expansion of larger mechanized farm units.

Also significant for the South was the Rural Electrification Administration (REA). Established in 1935, it provided low-cost loans to local farm

cooperatives that built electric lines in rural areas. It was particularly important because in 1933 only 10 percent of southern farms had electricity. By
1943, the REA had succeeded in bringing power to 80 percent of the farms in
the South. Such statistics do not adequately describe the human impact of
this agency, which raised living standards immeasurably. Many farm families
could now use refrigerators, radios, hot water heaters, and other appliances
that improved the quality of their lives. In a similar vein, the Tennessee
Valley Authority (TVA), created in 1933, improved the lives of millions living
in the seven-state area it served.

By 1939 the New Deal had helped the South to stage a moderate economic recovery. Industrial production that year equaled that of 1929. Per
capita incomes in the South had increased somewhat from 55 percent of the
national average to 59 percent in 1940. The region was still poor, but it had
shed some of its gloom and despair. On the eve of World War II, southern
business operators had embraced a growth orientation that led them to
anticipate a brighter economic future, a future that World War II soon made
a reality.

The social programs of the New Deal left their mark on the South. In
1933 and 1934 the Federal Emergency Relief Administration made grants to
the states for direct relief payments. In the South these reached more than 4
million people and about one-fifth of all families. These funds kept 35,000
schools open in the South that would otherwise have had to close because the
states were mired in bankruptcy. The agency paid teachers' salaries, made
library services available, and provided special classes and programs. Hardly
less important was the Civilian Conservation Corps because of its emphasis
on soil conservation projects. It operated 106 camps in the South. When the
Works Progress Administration (WPA) was established in 1935, it took over
most relief programs. From 1933 to 1939 these various New Deal agencies
spent more than $2 billion in the South in direct relief and work-relief
programs.

Additional federal funds poured into the South to improve its housing.
The Public Works Administration built twenty-one new housing projects in
the region, out of a total of fifty-seven that it sponsored nationally. When
Congress created the U.S. Housing Authority in 1937, that agency allocated
a substantial portion of its funds for slum clearance in the South.

Although the social needs of the region were great, ironically, southerners did not benefit as much from the Social Security Act as Americans in
other sections. Initially, farm workers and domestic servants were not covered in the measure, and the South counted a significant portion of its labor
force in these categories. Moreover, the South had a larger percentage of
people over 65 than other regions had, and thus the funds it received had to
be allocated to a larger number of individuals, resulting in smaller grants.

The New Deal stimulated labor organization in the South. Section 7a of the National Industrial Recovery Act of 1933 and the consequent Wagner Act of 1935 did much to restrain employers from interfering with the formation of unions. The immediate result was the organization of the Congress of Industrial Organizations (CIO) in 1937, which recruited 11 percent of the southern labor force in its first three years. It experienced special success in the southern coal and steel industries, including whites and blacks. Although the union also began to recruit textile mill workers in Kentucky, Alabama, and Tennessee, it faced greater opposition there. Progress was slow, but by 1940 the New Deal had left a legacy of union organization, increased wages, and work standards.

If the New Deal did not bring an immediate change for blacks in the South, its total impact was to loosen the restraints of segregation. The so-called black cabinet—a group of black professionals who were advisers to the president—also performed a symbolic function for many blacks, who felt that they had some representation in Washington. At least half of all PWA housing projects in the South were for the benefit of blacks, and construction contracts for these projects stipulated nondiscriminatory hiring. Blacks constituted a larger percentage on relief rolls than their proportion in the population. Blacks still lived in a strictly segregated world in the South, but as a contemporary observer, the Swedish sociologist Gunnar Myrdal, noted, "Segregation was only a temporary balancing of forces which was just on the verge of being broken." New Deal policies contributed toward that goal.

The New Deal affected southern life in various ways. It stimulated the decline of sharecropping and diversification of the southern economy. It increased the political influence of the South in national politics. It alleviated poverty and economic distress and improved housing, health, and educational facilities. It fostered unionism, and it undermined some pillars of racial segregation in the region.

The New Deal and the West

The influence of the New Deal on the West was unique because this was the youngest and least developed region in the United States. A major aspect of federal programs in the West was extensive construction of dams and irrigation projects and shoring up the rural economies of many western states suffering the repercussions of extensive farm foreclosures. Social programs did much to relieve tensions and distress but did not succeed in nursing the economy back to recovery. In part this explained the political ambivalence of the West toward the New Deal. On the one hand, westerners welcomed federal aid. On the other, they resented federal interference and often provided only reluctant support for New Deal programs.

Economic problems of the West differed from those in other regions.

The West had little heavy industry, contributing only 10 percent to the national manufacturing output. But it was not, like the South, primarily an agricultural section. Instead, it was a land of wide open spaces, semiarid areas, and deserts. Its major sources of income came from mining, petroleum, cattle and livestock, lumbering, and some agriculture. Its economy was unique.

New Deal programs in the West thus differed somewhat from those in other areas. Farm policies such as those of the AAA were of greatest benefit to large farms, especially on the Pacific coast. The policies were not as successful in raising farm income for small farms like those on the Great Plains. The New Deal saved tens of thousands of cattle ranchers from bankruptcy in 1933 when the federal government bought up large quantities of beef for which there were no markets. And the Farm Credit Administration extended low-interest loans to the hard-pressed cattle raisers when private bankers balked. In addition, the Taylor Grazing Act systematized national grazing policies on public lands to make them more accessible. Western miners also secured relief. Under the Silver Purchase Act of 1934, the U.S. Treasury obligated itself to buy $1 billion of silver, much of it mined in Idaho, Colorado, Utah, and other western states. Industry codes of the National Recovery Administration for lumber and oil staved off the complete collapse of those industries in 1933 and became part of more permanent legislation in later years.

Some of the most significant New Deal measures in the West were the large-scale dam-building and reclamation programs. Their purpose was to irrigate arid lands to make them more productive and to allow for the creation of thousands of new family-sized farms. At the same time, New Deal planners hoped that these programs would also generate vast amounts of electricity that would not only improve the quality of rural life but also attract new industries and lead to economic diversification of the West. With those goals in mind, President Roosevelt in 1935 watched over the completion of the Hoover Dam and inaugurated massive new projects in seventeen western states, including Bonneville and Grand Coulee dams in the Pacific Northwest, the Big Thompson in Colorado, and the Central Valley system in California.

The economic impact of these various economic policies on the West was considerable. On a per capita basis, federal expenditures were higher in the West than in the East. Western states received three times as much in federal funds as they sent back to Washington in the form of tax revenues. That disparity was due to some extent to the relative poverty of this underdeveloped region compared to the industrialized East and also to the vast scale of the reclamation projects. But this uneven balance of payments underscored the significant reliance of the West on the federal government.

Social programs of the New Deal also left their mark on the West. Of the various new agencies formed in 1933, the CCC was particularly important because its mission of soil conservation and reforestation was especially well suited to conditions in the West. Although some western leaders, in Colorado and Wyoming, for example, resented the increasing intrusion of federal relief programs such as the FERA and the WPA, most westerners welcomed such relief. In the Dakotas, the WPA provided the only source of outside cash income for drought-ridden farmers and for most Native Americans on reservations. In New Mexico, old-age pensions under the Social Security Act provided the main income for more than one-half of the Hispanic farmers in the northern part of the state. Indeed, for the Sioux Indians in the Dakotas, the Navajos in Arizona, and Pueblo tribes in New Mexico, payments from the CCC, the WPA, and social security often provided their only major cash income.

New Deal social policies in the West held special significance for Native American tribes in other ways as well, particularly in allowing them greater self-determination. Before 1933, federal policy had attempted integration of Native Americans into the mainstream of American society by deemphasizing their languages, religions, and cultural traditions. That policy had not met with great success, and by 1933, Roosevelt was prepared to offer a new deal to Native Americans. He appointed John C. Collier to direct Native American affairs and to follow a policy of self-determination. During Collier's tenure (1933–1945), he encouraged a revival of native cultures, languages, religions, ceremonial traditions, arts and crafts, and greater political participation through the establishment of tribal councils. These various programs did not solve many of the problems of Native Americans—such as poverty or acculturation—but they did a great deal to restore ethnic and racial pride and an awareness of the unique cultural heritage of Native Americans.

The New Deal also affected western politics. In stimulating political party realignments, it increased the power of Democrats, as state and local leaders used economic and social benefit payments to increase patronage. Also, inevitably, the disbursement of large sums by the federal government brought a shift in the federal system: the states lost influence while that of Washington increased.

In the West the cultural programs of the New Deal did much to foster regional pride. The WPA guidebooks produced by the writers' program were particularly successful in the West since much of its recent history—in contrast to that of the long-settled regions—remained unrecorded. In fact, the guide for Idaho was the first to appear in the series. The federal theater program had a notable role in the West because Hollywood, as the nation's film capital, had very large numbers of unemployed theater people, such as actors, directors, and set designers. In fact, more than one-third of the 13,000 individuals in the program resided in Los Angeles. A similar situation affected musicians.

The federal cultural programs did much to aid Hispanics and Native Americans in developing their traditions. The arts program encouraged Hispanic and Native American painters and Hispanic woodcarvers. The music program for the first time recorded Hispanic and Native American musical expressions. And the history programs did much to emphasize the region's distinctive ethnic and cultural heritage. It restored many of the old Spanish missions in California. Altogether, the New Deal cultural programs did much to heighten regional as well as national awareness of the West's distinctiveness.

The New Deal thus had a far-ranging impact on the West. It bolstered the economy; it lessened the independence of westerners as they increasingly looked to Washington for social services, whether in relation to problems of employment, relief, health, or old age; and it led to significant political realignments as the federal government assumed a dominant role in its relations with the states. Furthermore, government patronage of cultural affairs did much to sharpen the region's identity.

CHAPTER 7

Social Consequences of
the Great Depression

Women in Crisis
1929–1939

 The Great Depression bore heavily on both men and women, yet each had distinctive perspectives. In many ways, those of women were unique to their sex in view of the structure of American society. For one thing, the majority of women viewed the crisis from the home rather than from the workplace. Thus women felt the economic impact of the Depression differently from their male counterparts. Such changes altered the social roles of many women and to some extent increased their prominence in national politics. Like other disadvantaged Americans, they rallied behind Roosevelt. Women also made some gains in the cultural sphere. As Susan Ware, a leading women's historian, has noted:

> The Depression propelled many women into new patterns of behavior that might not have occurred otherwise. Women's activities outside the home— especially their participation in the work force, in the professions, in politics and social reform, and in fine arts and popular culture—add further dimensions to the experience of women in the Depression decade of the 1930s.[1]

The Depression clearly dampened the mood of most women, in contrast to the ebullient self-confidence of the 1920s. This was a period of somber apprehension, and women felt it both inside and outside of their homes. Eleanor Roosevelt in 1933 reflected the contemporary mood when she noted that "practically every woman, whether she is rich or poor, is facing today a

---

[1]Susan Ware, *Holding Their Own: American Women in the 1930s* (Boston: Twayne Publishers, 1982), p. 17.

reduction in income." That meant a multitude of constraints in everyday life that were peculiarly the province of women. In a thousand different ways they had to "make do." They bought day-old bread, darned worn-out socks, altered adult clothing to fit children, put patches on skirts and pants, and made meatless meals. Leftovers were carefully stored where in a more prosperous age they would have been thrown away. Recreational trips—to the movies, amusement parks, or the mountains—became less frequent. As Mrs. Roosevelt commented: "It means endless little economies and constant anxiety for fear of some catastrophe such as accident or illness which may completely swamp the family budget." Many times making do was not enough, and families were forced to do without. But whatever allocation of weekly salaries was made—the average for those fortunate enough to have a working income was $20 a week—it was most often the responsibility of women to do the budgeting.

In many instances, the tribulations of the Depression tightened the bonds of family. The majority of women centered their lives on their homes and families and devoted more than sixty hours weekly to them. When money was scarce, women often increased giving of their own time and labor. So instead of purchasing canned fruits and vegetables, an increasing number of homemakers reverted to canning, and instead of buying ready-made clothes for themselves and the family, they relied on their own sewing skills. Most Americans accepted the notion that a woman's place was in the home. "Women, the wives and mothers," wrote Mrs. Roosevelt, "are the inspiration of the homes, the persons for whom the men really work." Women's spheres embraced husband, family, and domesticity. Consequently, even though the Depression created many new strains, the world of women was not as totally disrupted as the workaday world of men. As Robert and Helen Lynd, two eminent sociologists, noted in 1937:

> The men, cut adrift from their usual routine, lost much of their sense of time and dawdled helplessly and dully about the streets; while in the homes the women's world remained largely intact and the round of cooking, housecleaning, and mending became if anything more absorbing.[2]

Economic Impact

Not all women stayed at home, however, and the percentage of women who worked outside increased even during the Depression. Many were young, single females. But a significant trend was the entry of married and middle-aged women into the labor force. Some of them, no doubt, were seeking to

[2]Robert S. Lynd and Helen M. Lynd, *Middletown in Transition* (New York: Harcourt, Brace and Co., 1937), pp. 178–179.

maintain family incomes when their husbands became unemployed. When women became the major breadwinners in a family, it sometimes brought fresh strains, considering most contemporary views of women's role as home-maker. Fully 25 percent of American women labored for wages during the 1930s. The majority were in domestic service; others worked in factories, in clerical positions, and in the professions. In whatever category, however, women earned less than men. The average yearly pay for women, the Social Security Administration reported in 1937, was $525, compared to $1,027 for men. Household workers earned only $312. A large number of these were black women whose wage rates were usually lower than that of whites.

Most Americans did not approve of women in the work force. A 1936 *Fortune* poll of a sample of Americans, including many business executives, inquired: "Do you believe that married women should have a full-time job outside the home?" Only 15 percent of the respondents approved, and 48 percent said no, but 37 percent gave conditional assent. Those who were critical feared that women would take jobs away from men; they believed that a woman's place was in the home and that it was more beneficial for children to have a mother in the house. One contemporary skeptic com-mented that "few of the people who oppose married women's employment seem to realize that a coal miner or steel worker cannot very well fill the jobs of nursemaids, cleaning women, or the factory and clerical occupations now filled by women."[3]

Two million black women, one of every six women who worked, were among the most poorly paid during the Depression. While about two of every ten white women worked outside the home, twice as many black females were in the labor force. Most of them could find only menial labor during the Depression. Nine-tenths were in domestic service as maids and house cleaners or worked in agriculture, usually as cotton pickers in the South. In one Louisiana parish, black women cotton pickers averaged only $41.67 a year, since they worked seasonally for about ninety days annually. Men earned about three times as much. Black women often experienced discrimination when they applied for work in factories by being refused outright, even when qualified. Only 100,000 black women worked in manu-facturing during the 1930s, in tobacco, food, and textile operations.

Various New Deal measures designed to improve working conditions benefited women less than men. In part this was due to the fact that occupa-tions in which women were numerous, such as domestic service or certain spheres of agriculture, were exempt from federal regulations. Though the National Industrial Recovery Act of 1933 stipulated minimum wage stan-dards, one-fourth of the industry codes approved by administrator General

[3]Ruth Shallcross, *Should Married Women Work?* (New York: National Federation of Business and Professional Women's Clubs, 1940), p. 17.

Hugh S. Johnson required salary differentials, with a lower scale for women. Women also found it more difficult to secure work with the Federal Emergency Relief Administration. Only 12 percent of its workers were female. Male administrators of such programs often did not perceive women to be competent for particular jobs. As one regional WPA director wrote to Eleanor Roosevelt: "One can put practically all of the men eligible for work in a community to work on a couple of major work projects. Not so with women." Stereotyping led to the assignment of women to research and clerical work, library programs, recreational activities, health and nutrition programs, and above all, sewing projects. Sewing was the largest WPA activity for women, involving 56 percent of the women employed. They repaired old garments or made new ones from donated surplus; the clothing was then distributed by the WPA to relief clients. As one woman summarized it: "For unskilled men we have the shovel. For unskilled women we have only the needle." Just one member in each family was eligible to be on WPA relief rolls, so usually only women who were heads of families could qualify. The Civilian Conservation Corps was restricted primarily to males, having a token force of 8,000 young women (out of 2.5 million enrollees). Most beneficial for women was the Social Security Act, which included maternal and pediatric programs and aid to mothers with dependent children.

Social Conditions

The grim psychological and economic conditions of the Depression were clearly reflected in the social trends of the decade of the 1930s. A more somber mood could be detected in the public image of American women during this period. In the 1920s the ideal American female was the flapper, a frivolous young irresponsible fun-loving party animal with short hair, slim boyish figure, and narrow hips. That role model did not at all suit Americans a decade later when they were desperately seeking to survive. Instead, an insecure age found it far more comforting to visualize motherly figures. These were expected to display curves and fuller bosoms, indented waistlines, long tapering hips, and a molded bust. The mood of the Depression did not favor the risqué styles so popular in the Jazz Age. Women who could afford them wore formally tailored suits. Others chose skirts that were longer than in the 1920s, about 12 inches above the ground. The fall of the stock market was accompanied by a fall of hemlines.

But if women of the 1930s shed the fashions of the previous decade, they did not as readily dispose of its sexual mores. Women continued to have greater sexual freedom than in the early years of the century. Courtship by the 1930s had left the family home for the automobile. While one-half of male college students reported having premarital sex, now one-fourth of the females confessed to similar practices. Condoms became more widely available in the decade than in earlier years. Many gasoline stations had automatic dispensers, and drugstores provided them discreetly. Abortions were illegal in most states but could be obtained surreptitiously, usually under frightful conditions. Each year about 10,000 women died from botched abortions, often performed by unskilled practitioners in unsanitary places. Social pressures of the time strongly favored marriage as an institution and frowned on single mothers. Psychologists of the era considered motherhood as the ultimate fulfillment of female sexuality, and that conclusion well suited a nation with high anxieties.

Nevertheless, economic realities contributed to a decline in the marriage rate and the number of new births during the Depression. A significant number of young people—perhaps as many as a million and a half—were forced to postpone marriage. Some women remained single for life. Whereas the marriage rate in 1929 had been 10 per 1,000 persons, it had dropped to 7.8 per 1,000 by 1934. Many couples also delayed childbearing. In 1930 the Census Bureau reported 21 births per 1,000 people, but 3 years later this had declined to 18 per 1,000. A few observers at the time speculated that the decrease might have been due in part to a decline in the frequency of sexual activity. Some contemporaries reported that fear of pregnancy was very common. Men who were unemployed often felt somewhat inadequate, and sometimes women lost respect for men who were no longer wage-earners or major breadwinners for their families. Moreover, some women were so tired from their manifold duties and chores that they limited their sexual activity.

Political Status

Women made considerable strides in the political arena during the Depression era, more in informal situations than in formal ones. Not many women served in Congress during the decade; the only woman elected to the U.S. Senate was Hattie Caraway of Arkansas. In the House the voters usually chose four or five women in each session. But in the states 132 women served in legislatures. The percentage of women on town councils and county governments was considerably higher. Eleanor Roosevelt believed that these women had exerted a considerable influence on public policies. Evaluating the preceding twenty years in 1940, she wrote:

> Government has been taking increasing cognizance of humanitarian questions, things that deal with the happiness of human beings, such as health, education, security. There is nothing, of course, to prove that this is entirely because of the women's interest, and yet I think it is significant that this change has come about during the period when women have been exercising their franchise.

Civil rights advocates of the Roosevelt Era: union leader A. Philip Randolph, Eleanor Roosevelt, and former New York City mayor Fiorello LaGuardia, 1946. *(UPI/Acme)*

And Molly Dewson, a leading feminist and major figure in the Democratic party during the New Deal, noted aptly: "The change from women's status in government before Roosevelt is unbelievable."[4]

Women made great strides in securing administrative positions in the bureaucracy that the New Deal did so much to expand. In this endeavor Eleanor Roosevelt played a major role. For the first time in the century, women found a champion for women's rights in the White House. Mrs. Roosevelt gave impetus to the appointment of women as social welfare services expanded, and she lobbied unceasingly for women. The changes represented a striking example of feminism in public life. The president appointed Frances Perkins to the post of secretary of labor, making her the first woman to hold a cabinet position. Ellen Sullivan Woodward became head of Women's and Professional Projects at the Works Progress Administration. Josephine Roche served as assistant secretary of the treasury, Marion Glass Banister as assistant treasurer of the United States, and Nellie Taylor Ross as director of the U.S. Mint. The president nominated Florence Allen to the

[4]Quoted in Ware, *Holding Their Own*, p. 90.

U.S. Court of Appeals. In the Department of Labor, Perkins chose Clara
Beyer to direct the Division of Labor Standards, Katherine Lenroot to head
the Children's Bureau, and Mary Anderson to supervise the Women's Bureau. Since the percentage of women in social work was high, many were
especially qualified for the new positions created by New Deal programs. As
historian William Chafe noted: "Washington seemed like a perpetual convention of social workers as women from the Consumers' League, the Women's
Trade Union League, and other reform groups came to Washington to take
on government assignments."[5] Presiding over this growing New Deal political sisterhood was Eleanor Roosevelt, who equaled her husband in providing
political skills and leadership. She also helped to create a Women's Division
within the Democratic party and devised special activities to provide women
with greater political power. The division's director, Molly Dewson, was a
close personal friend of Mrs. Roosevelt's and a former women's suffragist.
She proved to be a key figure in dispensing patronage among women and,
next to the first lady, the central figure in finding qualified women to fill
government positions.

The best-known black woman in the New Deal administration was Mary
McLeod Bethune, president of Bethune College in Florida. An advocate of
equal rights for blacks and an experienced administrator, Bethune was one of
the few black females to hold high office. She served as director of the Office
of Negro Affairs of the National Youth Administration and as assistant director
of that agency. In that position she was able to obtain for black youths an
equitable share of grants made to students in high school and college. In
addition, she was instrumental in organizing the National Council of Negro
Women in 1935 and served as its first president. This organization coordinated more than 100 black groups, representing about 800,000 black
women. Once they were organized, these women were able to exert some
measure of political pressure.

When women did not occupy political or administrative offices, they at
times exercised political influence through scores of women's organizations.
These included the Women's Joint Congressional Committee, an important
lobby group; the American Association of University Women; the General
Federation of Women's Clubs; the National Consumers' League; and the
Women's Christian Temperance Union. Some groups, like the International
League for Peace and Freedom, focused mainly on foreign policies, while
those dealing with domestic matters emphasized issues touching on women
and children. The League of Women Voters not only trained women for
citizenship but also advocated old-age insurance and disarmament. For
women who spent most of their waking hours in the home, such organiza-

---

[5]William Chafe, *The American Woman, 1920–1970* (New York: Oxford University Press, 1972),
p. 42.

tions provided one of the few windows on the world and brought stimulation and diversity into their lives. Moreover, members in such groups also received training for public service that they could call on when they went into government service. In an indirect fashion, then, women helped to shape New Deal social policies. They aided in the drafting of New Deal legislation such as the Social Security Act of 1935, the Wagner Act of 1935, the Fair Labor Standards Act of 1938, and the Hatch Act of 1939. They provided important testimony at congressional hearings and did much to spread favorable publicity for New Deal measures that they approved.

More specialized women's associations paralleled such efforts. Among these, the National Council of Negro Women and the National Council of Jewish Women were representative. In 1930, Jessie D. Ames, a Texas businesswoman, organized the Association of Southern Women, a biracial organization whose primary goal was to prevent lynchings. Also controversial was the National Women's Party, which advocated an equal rights amendment to the U.S. Constitution. Led by the articulate Alicia Paul, the party never had more than 20,000 active members, but its influence was much greater because many upper-class, wealthy women were engaged in its activities. On the issue of the equal rights amendment women were split, however, and during this period no consensus emerged on the issue. In the debates about it, supporters argued that with such an amendment, special protective labor legislation for women concerning wages, hours, and working conditions would no longer be necessary if equal treatment of men and women was assured. Opponents argued that women had special needs that had to be reflected in protective laws. Although the Republicans in their platform for 1940 supported an amendment and the Democrats followed in 1944, the various groups could not find common ground when they appealed to Congress to vote on a specific measure.

Cultural Influence

In rather unexpected ways, white women were able to increase their influence in the nation's cultural life during the crucial era. To a considerable extent this was because the Depression spawned cultural nationalism, which led to greater government patronage of the arts. Such patronage was more gender-neutral than that of private benefactors and involved women on a much larger scale since it was supported by public funds. In art, literature, music, theater, and popular culture such as moving pictures, women found more work outlets than had been available to them in previous years. And women served as cultural administrators in various New Deal programs. As mentioned earlier, Ellen Sullivan Woodward supervised WPA cultural programs in 1935; she was succeeded later in the New Deal by Florence Kerr.

One of the most influential individuals in the WPA was Hallie Flanagan, who served as director of the Theater Project. A drama professor at Vassar College, she had a major impact on the theater during the Depression.

Women received considerable encouragement in the WPA art program because projects they submitted were judged anonymously. Ruth Reeves, a reputable mural painter, was appointed national coordinator of the Index of American Design, an inventory of distinctive American buildings and arts and crafts. Audrey McMahon, a New York City artist, was offered directorship of the Arts Project but declined in order to direct the program in New York, at the time the most important center of the arts. She made it a point to award a sizable number of commissions to talented women artists and photographers, including Olive Gavert, Constance Rourke (Juliana Force), Berenice Abbott, and Gwendolyn Bennett. About 40 percent of artists on relief were women. Not all were distinguished, but a few, like Louise Nevelson, became famous in later years. Much of the work of these individuals adorned public buildings in Washington and around the nation. Women were especially pleased with the Arts Projects because it provided them with an opportunity to have their work judged on the basis of equality with men. In selecting work for display, government officials often judged entries without knowing the artists' gender. Unexpectedly, therefore, the Depression created conditions that encouraged greater equality among artists.

Women also had a hand in the design, writing, and editorial functions of the Federal Writers Project. The plan for many of the WPA guidebooks was developed by Katherine Kellock, an extremely able editor. She undertook the laborious task of editing and processing most of the series of more than fifty volumes. Women served as directors of the Writers Project at the state level. Corita Corse supervised the program in Florida, and Eudora Richardson did so in Virginia. Relief aid helped some women writers to complete their works, among them novelists Anzia Yezierska, Meridel Le Sueur, and Tillie Olsen. Depression conditions encouraged a new literary genre, the photoessay or documentary. These books combined striking photographs of aspects of American life with accompanying text. Women figured prominently in the development of this art form as the Farm Security Administration hired a group of brilliant photographers to record the travails of common people, particularly the poor, in the Depression. Among the best of these photographers were Margaret Bourke-White and Dorothea Lange; their work has rarely been surpassed.

Understandably, the best-known women writers of the decade were not directly involved with federal programs. These included authors with worldwide reputations such as Pearl Buck, Margaret Mitchell, Edna Ferber, Katherine Ann Porter, and Lillian Hellman. Despite the Depression, their books sold in the millions.

But the most widely admired heroines of the 1930s were in the world of popular culture—in sports, aviation, and the movies. During the 1920s most American sports idols were men, but in the 1930s women also received their due. Among the stars were Sonya Henie, the Norwegian figure skater; Alice Marble, the national tennis champion; and golf pro Patti Jane. Gertrude Ederle, the first woman to swim the English Channel (on August 6, 1926), became one of the nation's leading professional swimmers. These women reinforced popular conceptions of femininity, including physical attractiveness, with their sports prowess. Sports like skating, tennis, and golf, many Americans at the time believed, were especially well suited for women, unlike boxing, football, or baseball. The outstanding all-around female athlete was Babe Didrickson Zacharias, who excelled at basketball, hurdles, the high jump, the shot put, and the javelin and won gold medals at the 1932 Olympics. Eventually, she became the nation's leading woman golfer.

Women also left their mark on the newly developing field of aviation. The most famous pilot of this decade was Amelia Earhart, who became the first woman to fly across the Atlantic and was determined to prove that women could equal men's achievements. She set many new records, including one as the first person to fly alone from Hawaii to the Pacific coast. Her tragic disappearance on a flight across the Pacific added to the heroic image that most Americans had of her. Her example inspired other women to pioneer in flight, including Jacqueline Cochran, Louise Thaden, and Anne Morrow Lindbergh.

Women had a pervasive impact on American life—on dress, manners, behavior, sexual mores, and appearance—through the medium of motion pictures. During the Great Depression, movies played an especially important role because, along with radio, they provided a most accessible form of entertainment and escape from the grim realities of the decade. Each week 60 to 90 million people (out of a total population of 140 million) attended local cinemas. Women who were movie stars earned more money than women in any other field. Before the Film Production Code of 1934, which imposed certain moral restrictions on films, actresses like Mae West, Marlene Dietrich, Miriam Hopkins, and Greta Garbo portrayed passionate, assertive females who flaunted their independence. Jean Harlow, Bette Davis, and Joan Crawford sought to perpetuate such role models after 1934, when film makers also began portraying model homemakers and women in the domestic sphere. Reflecting changing conceptions of women's roles in American society, by 1938 Hollywood directors were casting single working women as well. Rosalind Russell played a star reporter in *His Girl Friday*, as Jean Arthur did in *Mr. Deeds Goes to Town*. Ginger Rogers, in *Kitty Foyle*, struggled with the choice between marriage and a career. Lucille Ball portrayed an independent struggling actress in *Stage Door*. Katharine Hepburn engaged in a battle of the sexes with Cary Grant in which she more than held her own in *Bringing Up Baby*. The spate of films featuring smart single women mainly oriented toward careers reflected the aspirations of much of the younger generation of women who were contemplating lifestyles other than homemaking.

The experiences of women during the Great Depression thus differed somewhat from those of men. In some respects, women fared better than their male counterparts. Unemployment was more serious in the industrial sector than in the service and clerical occupations in which women were more numerous. Women were often more likely to be hired than men since they were usually paid less. And New Deal programs, especially in social welfare and in cultural activities, opened up opportunities for women that had not existed previously. In somewhat paradoxical and unexpected ways, the Great Depression furthered feminist goals, greater independence for women, access to a wider range of occupations, a greater degree of sexual freedom, and for some, a changed self-image.

CHAPTER 8

Minorities during the Great Depression

Among the unheralded reforms of the New Deal was greater recognition of the role of minorities in American life. Until 1933 ethnic and racial groups had achieved only limited visibility in politics and public life. This was true of many ethnic Americans who were first- or second-generation descendants of immigrants, particularly the Irish, Italians, Germans, Poles, and Jews. Black Americans, Native Americans, and Hispanic Americans, eager to play a greater role, were submerged in American society. Constituting almost one-third of the American people, these minority groups looked to the New Deal to help them achieve a more prominent place in American society. If Roosevelt was not exactly the avowed champion of minorities, he still displayed a sympathetic attitude toward their aspirations, thereby earning their overwhelming support.

Minorities and the New Deal

Since New Deal programs were broad in their appeal, they also embraced some of the desires of minorities. By emphasizing equal rights for all Americans, to be achieved through governmental action, the New Deal attracted millions of minority Americans who came to feel—rightly or wrongly—that they had a sympathetic friend in the White House, for this administration did not ignore these groups as previous ones had done. Roosevelt and many of his advisers believed that most forms of ethnic, racial, and religious discrimination emanated from poverty or economic exploitation. Improvement of economic conditions for minorities, they felt, would strike at the roots of prejudice. The sons and daughters of the millions of immigrants who had poured into the United States at the turn of the century, in turn, were particularly fearful that the scant economic and social gains they had made in earlier decades would become casualties of the Great Depression.

Also unlike his Republican predecessors, Roosevelt appointed members of minority groups to public office. From 1920 to 1932 only one out of every twenty-five judicial appointees was a Roman Catholic, for example, but from 1932 to 1940 at least one out of four was.

Roosevelt's policies toward minority groups paid off. Clustered in the great cities of the Northeast and the Midwest, minority group members voted Democratic in overwhelming numbers in 1936 and 1940. Of 106 cities with more than 100,000 population, Roosevelt captured 104 in 1936. Minority groups gained enough power to be instrumental in 1936 in abolishing the Democratic party rule requiring a two-thirds majority for the presidential nomination, a requirement often used by southern Democrats to exert strong influence.

Many American Roman Catholics gravitated toward the New Deal and the Democratic party. In the large cities of the nation, Irish-Americans and Italian-Americans flocked to the Roosevelt banner in large numbers. In the Midwest equally large numbers of Slavic-Americans and other ethnic groups with roots in central, eastern, and southern Europe voted for New Deal issues and candidates whom they perceived would best represent their special interests. Most of these ethnic groups still had a vision of America as a land of opportunity. If the Depression had destroyed that vision, Roosevelt at least promised to restore it.

A majority of American Jews also enthusiastically supported Roosevelt and the New Deal. Since many Jews were first-generation Americans, their parents having immigrated to the United States early in the twentieth century, they, too, feared the loss of gains they had made in recent years. They saw Roosevelt not only as a protector of their existing status but also as a leader in the struggle to extend the social and economic opportunities of the middle classes, with which most Jews tended to identify. At the same time, the Roosevelt administration was for the most part sympathetic to the plight of persecuted Jews in Nazi Germany. Over 100,000 entered the United States under existing quota laws between 1933 and 1939. Conscious of the large number of unemployed in the nation, however, Roosevelt, as well as Congress, was reluctant to provide a haven for larger numbers.

Black Americans

The New Deal took greater cognizance of the aspirations of black Americans than any previous administration in the twentieth century. True, Roosevelt did not support all of the demands of the black community, for he was unwilling to antagonize southern Democrats who occupied key positions on congressional committees and could jeopardize his entire reform program. As Roosevelt explained, he had to get "legislation for the entire country passed by Congress. If I antagonize the southerners who dominate congressional committees through seniority, I'd never be able to get bills passed."

Although historians have argued over the degree of the New Deal's dedication to the cause of racial equality, the fact remains that the overwhelming majority of black Americans, in a major shift in their voting patterns, enthusiastically supported Roosevelt. From Reconstruction until 1928, blacks had traditionally cast more than 80 percent of their ballots for Republicans. But various conditions were undermining that loyalty. The failure of Republicans to respond to the demands of the black community was especially evident during the Hoover administration. Moreover, blacks increased their political consciousness when they moved from the rural South to the big cities of the East and the Midwest. And since blacks were the most marginal group in American society, they were hit particularly hard by the Depression. In short, they were ready to shift their political loyalties. In the election of 1932, therefore, 90 percent of the black voters supported Roosevelt and the Democrats. In 1936, fully 95 percent of those voting preferred Roosevelt, and in 1940, a record 97 percent of black voters closed ranks behind him. In the South as well as in the North, thousands of poor blacks affixed a picture of Roosevelt on the walls of their dwellings, for he was considered a friend of the black community. Black Americans were a significant force in the urban coalition that provided Roosevelt with much of his support.

To some extent Roosevelt earned the support of the black community because of his sensitivity to their desires. Early in his administration, he established the "black cabinet" to maintain channels of communication with black leaders. The idea was first suggested to him in 1933 by Charles G. Johnson of Fisk University in Nashville, who urged Roosevelt to be aware of the special needs of blacks during the Depression. Roosevelt asked Harold Ickes to find black civil servants to fill key federal posts and to relay advice back to the White House.

Ickes asked Clark Foreman, a white Atlanta civil rights advocate, to assemble a representative group of advisers culled from the black community. Foreman invited black representatives from various federal agencies to regular meetings. Among the participants was Professor Robert C. Weaver of North Carolina A&M College, a knowledgeable political scientist who later succeeded Foreman as coordinator of the group. Eugene K. Jones, who was especially well informed about the problems of urban blacks, represented the Urban League. He also advised the Department of Commerce. Robert L. Vann, a laywer in the Department of Justice, often spoke knowingly of civil rights issues. Henry Hunt, who worked in the Farm Credit Administration, sought to keep the difficulties of southern black tenant farmers before the administration, often with limited success. William R. Hastie, one of the most distinguished black lawyers in the nation, spoke from his vantage point as an assistant solicitor in the Department of the Interior. Ira De A. Reid, in the Social Security Administration, was an expert on black poverty. Perhaps the most dynamic member of the group was Mary McLeod Bethune, the college president active in the National Youth Administration who advocated education for blacks as a means of improving their economic situation. Roosevelt listened more intently to the suggestions of the black cabinet than he acted on their recommendations, but his administration was still the first to make an effort to establish regular channels of communication with the black community. And many black voters felt represented in the White House as they had not been before.

Many of the New Deal's economic policies did not significantly affect black Americans since most were employed at unskilled or menial jobs and most New Deal legislation was aimed at helping the middle class. The NRA did little to improve the economic condition of blacks, very few of whom were independent entrepreneurs. In fact, many codes contained clauses that permitted employers to pay lower wages to black than to white employees.

Black migrant farm workers in New Jersey, 1936. (*U.S. Farm Security Administration*)

In 1933 and 1934 the TVA was accused of following discriminatory policies in many of its activities. Only under intense pressure from the White House did the TVA directors increase the percentage of their black employees.

That New Deal farm policies seriously neglected southern black tenant farmers was one of the most serious charges leveled against Roosevelt. Norman Thomas, the Socialist party leader, was particularly vociferous in criticizing the New Deal on this issue. In fact, AAA programs in the South tended to displace rural black farm workers and tenants and leave them jobless; perhaps 200,000 blacks were forced into this predicament. As white landowners received AAA payments to take land out of production, they discharged their black workers and set sharecroppers adrift. At the same time, the aid rendered by the Department of Agriculture to black farmers was limited. Ninety-seven percent of black farmers lived in the South, but only 20 percent owned the land they farmed. The others were at the bottom of the agricultural ladder—wage hands, sharecroppers, and tenant farmers. Their average income was only three-fourths that of whites, ranging from $200 to $300 yearly. Since the AAA programs affected landowners primarily, many black farmers were left out of federal farm relief payments, receiving only small sums; nor were most black tenants eligible for long-term loans from the Farm Credit Administration. At best they benefited from short-term production credit. The National Association for the Advancement of Colored People (NAACP) at its 1934 convention noted that "nearly 6 million Negroes dependent upon agriculture have found no remedy for their intolerable condition."

In the same year, blacks and whites joined to form the Southern Tenant Farmers Union. One of its first demands was that rental and parity payments be made directly to tenants and sharecroppers by the federal government instead of being paid to landowners. In part responding to criticism, the Roosevelt administration sought to develop programs designed specifically to aid black farmers. Between 1936 and 1939, tenants received a larger share of AAA benefit payments. And the Farm Security Administration now made long-term, low-interest loans available to even the poorest farmers. Almost 1 million black and white farmers received loans to rehabilitate the lands they occupied. Experiments with the creation of subsistence homesteads in planned communities were more limited. Fourteen hundred black families were living on thirty-two homestead projects, or about one-fourth of the total projects administered by the Farm Security Administration in 1940. In short, New Deal farm programs were of genuine help to many black farmers, but they fell far short either in altering the structure of southern agriculture or in making substantial improvements in the conditions of southern black tenant farmers and farm workers.

The New Deal's relief and social welfare laws did aid many blacks, since they constituted an especially high percentage of the nation's poor and unemployed. Thus although blacks comprised 10 percent of the nation's population, they filled 18 percent of the WPA rolls. However, local authorities in the South often practiced discrimination against blacks. In Atlanta in 1935, WPA payments to blacks were significantly lower than those paid to whites. Similarly, southern officials largely excluded blacks from the Civilian Conservation Corps. Only under pressure from Harry Hopkins did the CCC gradually accept blacks equal to 10 percent of its enrollment, and even then, blacks were usually assigned to segregated quarters.

Although the Roosevelt administration made few deliberate efforts to diminish racial intolerance in the United States, it did set a tone that led to greater integration. Secretary of the Interior Harold Ickes was a particularly vehement opponent of race discrimination, having once served as president of the Chicago chapter of the NAACP. Ickes not only desegregated all cafeterias at Interior Department headquarters in Washington, D.C., but also, at his insistence, the PWA reserved one-half of its housing projects in the South for blacks. All construction contracts awarded by the PWA required the hiring of black workers; this set a precedent for other federal agencies.

First Lady Eleanor Roosevelt also actively supported the NAACP in public and conspicuously appeared at interracial social functions. She was instrumental in arranging a concert by black contralto Marian Anderson at the Lincoln Memorial in Washington in 1939 after the Daughters of the American Revolution had withdrawn permission for Anderson's use of Constitution Hall because of her race.

Still, the president refused to support publicly federal antilynching bills pending in Congress between 1933 and 1939. Ever conscious of the power of southern members of Congress in his own party, he refrained from antagonizing them too openly. Although sympathetic to antilynching legislation, he declined to make it a major issue. In 1938 a group of southerners filibustered an antilynching bill to death in the Senate. Although encouragement from the White House might have cleared the path for the legislation, Roosevelt preferred to remain silent.

The limitations of black influence on public affairs in the 1930s were partly due to conflicts within the black community itself. The majority of blacks were poor and uneducated as well as politically unorganized and weak.

The inability of black Americans to exert greater influence on the New Deal was due to a lack of organization. Blacks constituted neither a strong political group nor an economic interest group. In these years they lacked the internal unity, leadership, or skill with which to attain a degree of racial solidarity. As the prominent black leader A. Philip Randolph aptly declared at the time: "True liberation can be acquired and maintained only when the Negro people possess power; and power is the product and flower of organization—organization of the masses, the masses in the mills and mines, on the farms, in the factories." The Congress of Industrial Organizations

(CIO) in 1937 was beginning to organize those laboring masses, black and white, but the benefits for blacks would not be visible until after World War II.

Serious internal conflict in the NAACP lessened its impact. The executive secretary of the organization during the New Deal was Walter White, an urbane individual who believed strongly in integration through use of the courts and through active public relations. His leadership was sharply challenged by Dr. William E. B. Du Bois, a shy and thoughtful scholar who believed in militant black nationalism and self-help rather than black reliance on the white community. Du Bois felt that White was unsuited to provide leadership for the black masses. Du Bois's resignation in 1934 as editor of *The Crisis*, the organization's journal, and from the NAACP a year later, seriously weakened the association's influence within and without.

Native Americans

As one of the most disadvantaged groups in American society, Native Americans also looked to the New Deal for help and guidance. The annual income of their families rarely exceeded $100; their infant mortality rate was the highest of any group in the United States, and their adult life span was the shortest; and their level of education—fewer than five years on the average—was the lowest of any racial group in the nation. The Depression plunged Native Americans into additional misery. Moreover, until 1933, federal policy was to integrate Native Americans into mainstream American society, even though the Native Americans resisted this and thought it destructive to their own culture.

Although Roosevelt had little firsthand knowledge of Native Americans and their conditions, he was sympathetic to their special problems. Moreover, Roosevelt placed great trust in Harold Ickes, who had been intensely interested in the impact of national policies on Native Americans for many decades. Before being offered a cabinet post, Ickes had hoped for an appointment as commissioner of the Bureau of Indian Affairs. As secretary of the interior, he turned to John S. Collier, a close friend who had long been a champion of Native American causes. Collier, born in Atlanta, spent much of his early life as a social worker. Soon after World War I he became involved with Native American problems and served as executive secretary of the American Indian Defense Association, a group concerned with gaining more rights for Native Americans. In addition, he edited *American Indian Life*, an important journal dedicated to the discussion of issues relating to Native Americans. During the 1920s, Collier became convinced that the federal government's integration policies had failed. He believed that Native Americans needed autonomy and self-determination to survive. During Collier's tenure as commissioner of the Bureau of Indian Affairs (1933–1945), his policy was to encourage cultural pluralism and cultural nationalism among Native Americans wherever practicable. To be sure, announcing such a declared goal was easier than carrying it out. Nevertheless, policy toward Native Americans under the New Deal was designed to encourage greater self-reliance.

Collier had ambitious plans to make Native Americans economically independent. He hoped to secure additional lands for many of the tribes through grants from federal and state governments, court actions, and private efforts. Such additional lands, he felt, would provide a firm economic foundation that would improve their agricultural self-sufficiency. Among the Navajos, for example, he attempted to improve soil conservation by discouraging overgrazing by cattle, but since ownership of stock was a status symbol for the Navajos, this policy clashed with their cultural values.

In an effort to encourage Native Americans to engage in business ventures on the reservations, Collier fostered the organization of credit unions and provided federal funds for local self-help ventures. Under his direction the Bureau of Indian Affairs encouraged tribes to make credit available to individuals or groups interested in forming businesses. At the same time, the bureau placed greater emphasis on hiring Native Americans for its own staff. More than one-fourth of its 5,235 employees during the New Deal were Native Americans.

Collier experienced only limited success. The problem of unemployment remained serious throughout the Depression. Of the many New Deal agencies in operation, the Civilian Conservation Corps particularly appealed to young Native Americans; many of its conservation projects were well suited to their interests and skills. More than 80,000 youths participated in CCC work in fifteen western states, where their income provided a welcome supplement to their needy families on the reservations. Even so, unemployment among Native Americans was three times the national average.

In another effort to make Native Americans self-sufficient and independent, the bureau encouraged tribes to establish formal councils or some formal hierarchy of officials to administer policies on a local level. Since such formal political institutions were alien to some cultures, these efforts were not always successful. Nevertheless, the New Deal era saw the establishment of formal tribal councils and a greater emphasis on self-government than in previous years.

Under Collier the bureau also made a concerted effort to encourage Native Americans' cultural awareness and independence. In contrast to the policy of previous administrations, which had sought to extirpate Native American culture in order to hasten integration, the Roosevelt administration sought to stimulate cultural pride. Since Collier appreciated native religion, art, languages, traditions, and ceremonials, he hoped to preserve them without interference by the federal government or by mainstream society. Under him the bureau's policies were designed to achieve these ends. Tribes were urged to celebrate their own traditions and festivals, artists to work in their native styles and to display their work, and all to speak their native languages.

Collier also attempted to reverse the previous policy of separating children from their parents by sending them away to boarding schools. Spending their teenage years away from the reservation weakened young people's ties to family and lessened their interest in their own culture. The bureau began to build day schools on reservations so that these youngsters could secure the education they needed to cope with mainstream American society while also being exposed to their own culture in their parents' homes. Since Native Americans were themselves sharply divided over the merits and disadvantages of integration, Collier's educational plans were not always popular.

The Bureau of Indian Affairs actively supported various congressional measures designed to institutionalize Collier's approach to federal management of Native American matters. The Johnson-O'Malley Act of 1934 created the bureaucratic machinery to provide for closer cooperation between federal and state officials engaged in the administration of these policies. This act also clarified the nature of Native Americans' civil rights. More controversial was the Wheeler-Howard Act of 1934, which granted extensive rights of self-government to various tribes while diminishing the authority of private traders and missionaries, the Bureau of Indian Affairs, and state and local governments. Some large tribes, such as the Navajos, rejected the measure because of their hostility to the federal livestock reduction program. Although limited in its application, the Wheeler-Howard Act helped to crystallize self-sufficiency as one component of federal policy.

Hispanic Americans

Hispanic Americans were not as self-conscious a group in the 1930s as they were to become several decades later. Their problems were similar to those of other minorities—poverty, a high rate of joblessness, and feelings of political impotence. To a considerable extent, the majority of Hispanic American voters supported Roosevelt in the belief that they benefited from the New Deal. Since many Hispanic Americans had little earning power, they looked favorably on New Deal social welfare policies. In Texas, New Mexico, and California, they constituted a significant number of workers in the Civilian Conservation Corps, the Federal Emergency Relief Administration, and the Works Progress Administration. Like other poor Americans, they welcomed social security. Although Hispanic Americans had traditionally voted for Republican candidates before 1930, they now came into Democratic party ranks in large numbers. To some extent, after 1934 particularly, this was due to the political shrewdness of Dennis Chávez of New Mexico, the only U.S. senator of Hispanic background. President Roosevelt frequently turned to Chávez as a spokesman for the Hispanic community. Chávez showed himself to be both skillful and aggressive in funneling relief and other federal funds into areas with significant Hispanic populations.

The Mexican population of the United States increased greatly during the Depression; perhaps as many as 1 million Mexicans arrived, seeking to escape rural poverty in Mexico, poverty far more wretched than that in the United States. Although many of these immigrants—a large portion of whom entered illegally—remained in the Southwest, significant numbers migrated to Kansas, Illinois, and Michigan. Uneducated and unskilled, many became migrant farm workers. Often they labored for wages lower than those demanded by native-born American workers, thus incurring hostility and prejudice. In the Midwest they worked in meat-packing plants and on railroad gangs; in Pennsylvania they joined the ranks of unskilled steelworkers. Many of the *barrios* in American cities were founded or greatly expanded by the stream of Mexican immigrants who came during the Great Depression. Local jurisdictions such as Los Angeles County, as well as federal authorities, annually deported tens of thousands of Mexicans who had entered as illegal aliens. Derogatorily called "wetbacks," these were temporary migratory field workers who came to help with the harvesting of vast crops in California and Texas but did not always return home as their alien status required.

A small trickle of Puerto Ricans came to New York City and a few other large American cities during the Depression, the advance guard of a large Puerto Rican migration to the United States just after World War II. Seeking escape from the poverty of their native land, they also found few opportunities in Depression-ridden America. Lacking special skills, education, or facility in the English language, many found that they had escaped from one cycle of poverty to another. Their coming added still another ethnic group to the Hispanic American peoples of the United States.

The New Deal Record

The New Deal's record on minorities was mixed. Reflective of Roosevelt's political style, the New Deal offered minorities less than they desired but more than they had been given by previous administrations. The New Deal was a shrewd combination of the theoretically desirable and the politically feasible.

From an organizational perspective, minority groups were encouraged to organize more effectively under the New Deal in order to influence the political process. Minority group members occupied a fair number of important government positions. Black Americans, more conscious of their political power, channeled their demands more effectively through the black cabinet. Native Americans were encouraged in their strivings for greater self-determination in the hope that as a group, rather than as individuals, they could exercise more influence in shaping their own destinies. Hispanic Americans were similarly encouraged to use the political process to advance their own special interests. The New Deal gave an impetus to the efforts of minorities to participate more fully in the mainstream of American life by encouraging self-awareness and the formation of interest group organizations that could influence public policies.

CHAPTER 9

American Culture during the Great Depression

1933–1939

The Depression shook the values of many Americans, who looked deeper into themselves in the search for an explanation of what had gone wrong. Was democracy possibly not the all-encompassing panacea it had appeared to be? Not surprisingly, some American intellectuals rejected many of their political traditions and briefly flirted with Marxism. Others criticized the system without rejecting the fundamental tenets of American democracy. For the masses, though, the search for an American identity also produced a nationalistic mood, a positive reaffirmation of American values even as the Depression revealed serious shortcomings. These attitudes and values were reflected in the work of writers, musicians, and entertainers of the era.

Religion during the Depression

As Americans became increasingly preoccupied with the Depression in the 1930s, public concern with religion became less pronounced than it had been. That was not to say that religious beliefs weakened. Most religions confined themselves to their particular interests rather than becoming involved in heated debates over public issues.

Protestant churches, especially fundamentalist denominations, grew steadily during the decade as millions sought solace from the crisis in greater spiritual fulfillment. In California, for example, the Reverend "Fighting Bob" Shuler built one of the largest congregations in the nation by urging Christians to renew and strengthen their identities by coming closer to the Gospels. Others entered politics, like the Reverend Gerald L. K. Smith, who campaigned actively for Huey Long. This was also a golden age for Protestant theology, as some of the most distinguished Protestant philosophers of the twentieth century—men like Paul Tillich, Karl Barth, and Reinhold Niebuhr—debated the great issues of faith. In a series of books, Niebuhr challenged the liberal orientation of American Protestantism. For more than forty years these liberals had stressed the essential goodness of humankind and the need for good works to achieve that perfection. The Social Gospel movement had embodied many of these beliefs. Niebuhr and his followers, in stark contrast, stressed human depravity and the necessity for spiritual perfection and orthodox Christian doctrine in the search for salvation. According to the religious press during the decade, Protestant churches dealt less than before with domestic issues but devoted considerable energies to pacifism and the peace movement. This not only strengthened isolationist views but also provided an outlet for idealism and disillusionment with World War I. Many young people, especially on college campuses, were caught up in the activities of the peace movement, in which the Protestant churches played an important role.

During the 1930s, Catholic churches consolidated their position, particularly in ethnic European neighborhoods—Irish, Italian, Polish, and others. Symbolically, Cardinal Francis J. Spellman, of Irish descent, succeeded to the archdiocese of New York in 1939, and Cardinal George Mundelein, of German ancestry, presided over large ethnic constituencies in Chicago. But Catholic churches were more preoccupied with strengthening the faith of their parishioners than in taking an active role in commenting on contemporary Depression problems. The Catholic religious press was reticent and subdued concerning the economic crisis and generally refrained from direct criticism or praise of the New Deal. In fact, leading church officials found an activist priest like Father Charles E. Coughlin a distinct embarrassment, and by 1937 they had succeeded in silencing him.

American Jews were divided in the 1930s and, like other religious groups, could not speak with a unified voice on public issues. Liberalism was a major trend in Judaism as Reform and Conservative sects sought to modernize the religious orthodoxy that many immigrants had brought from Eastern European ghettos. But other divisions surfaced in the Depression. Jews of German origin, who had come to the United States before the 1870s, differed—as "old" Americans—culturally, socially, and economically from the much larger number of poorer Jews of Eastern European background who had come between 1890 and 1914. In addition, the American Jewish community was divided in regard to Adolf Hitler's persecution of Jews in Germany. While on the one hand seeking to help their coreligionists escape from Germany, on the other hand they felt too insecure about their own status in the United States to advocate a massive emigration of the persecuted to the New World. Although many Jews as individuals supported the New Deal, the Jewish community could not speak with one voice on public issues.

The major religious groups during the Depression thus concentrated on strengthening the sense of identity of their members. Except for the peace movement, they refrained from involvement in the main public questions of the day. In that sense secular and religious concerns became increasingly separated.

American Writers and the Depression

American writers during the 1930s lacked the dazzle of their predecessors in the 1920s. They also wrote fewer outstanding novels, plays, or poetry and poured much energy into literary criticism. Nonfiction flowered, particularly forms that explained or attempted to explain what had happened to cause the Depression.

If the Depression resulted in reduced sales of books, the trend toward mass marketing continued. The Book-of-the-Month Club was organized in 1936 to stimulate large-scale distribution of hardcover volumes. At the same time, cost-conscious publishers were beginning to develop the new paperback format for books originally appearing in hard covers. Paperback books, an economy during the Depression, did not take a significant share of the market until after World War II, however.

The quality of many novels appearing during the Great Depression was mostly undistinguished. Various writers of Marxist orientation made a vigorous if not very successful effort to create a genuinely proletarian literature. They hoped it would serve as a prelude to the revolutionary class struggle, which, they were sure, was imminent in the United States. Thus novels were used to arouse the revolutionary consciousness of the masses. Many works dealt with class conflict and capitalist exploitation of workers and the poor. Meyer Levin in *The Old Bunch*, Michael Gold in *Jews without Money*, and Grace Lumpkin in *To Make My Bread* and *A Sign for Cain* examined these themes. Unfortunately, the structure of their plots was so poorly conceived and their style was so turgid that these novels—designed, ironically, to appeal to the masses—attracted few readers. Some of the architects of the would-be American proletarian novel received such adverse criticism that they abandoned their efforts. In contrast, established writers who embraced a Marxist orientation had greater success. The nation's leading black writer, Richard Wright, condemned racism in American society in his profoundly moving *Native Son*. Erskine Caldwell bitingly depicted southern rural poverty and the system that produced it in *God's Little Acre*. James T. Farrell, using Chicago as a setting in his popular *Studs Lonigan* series, told the story of a young man's degeneration during the Great Depression and described how the capitalist system had spawned it. John Dos Passos wrote the trilogy *U.S.A.* as a Marxist condemnation of American society. Although these works attracted attention from literary critics and from the reading public, they were not as widely acclaimed as the novels of Willa Cather, Theodore Dreiser, Sinclair Lewis, or F. Scott Fitzgerald in the previous decade, and did little to raise the political consciousness of Americans or serve as instruments of class struggle.

Other novelists were sharply critical of American life without paying tribute to another ideology. *Butterfield 8* and *Appointment in Samarra* by John O'Hara were bitingly realistic. As might be expected from a former newspaperman and reporter, O'Hara was a chronicler of facts, particularly of the disruptive and destructive influence of the economic crisis on the values, attitudes, and behavior of the middle class in American society. Similarly, James M. Cain in *The Postman Always Rings Twice* recorded the terror and fear inspired by this decade of crisis. In *You Can't Go Home Again,* Thomas Wolfe mirrored the bewilderment of his generation in the face of the collapse of the more secure and settled world of their youth.

Unquestionably the single American novel that best recorded the mood of the American people in the throes of the Great Depression was John Steinbeck's masterpiece, *The Grapes of Wrath.* Like most works that define a generation, this book could not be classified as belonging to any particular literary genre. Steinbeck was a realistic and critical observer of the American scene, but he also endowed his characters with a romanticism that made them representative of the values and feelings shared by millions. In this fictional account of the Joads, a migrant farm family fleeing the dust bowl of Oklahoma for the fertile fields of California, Steinbeck recorded the hopes and the dreams, as well as the tribulations and sufferings, of countless Americans during the Great Depression. Beset with defeat, the Joads never abandon their humanity or their hopes for a better future—and this, in a way, epitomized the contemporary American spirit.

Historical romance, as one might expect, provided an obvious avenue of escape during the Depression. The single most popular book of the decade was Margaret Mitchell's *Gone with the Wind,* a novel of epic proportions that chronicled the lives of uprooted southerners during the Civil War and Reconstruction. The parallel was too much for most Americans to resist and helps to explain its enormous popularity.

The major poets in the United States during the 1930s rallied to the defense of American society by celebrating the values that characterized its past development. Carl Sandburg fortified his reputation as America's troubadour with "The People, Yes," a reaffirmation of democratic ideals. With similar eloquence Archibald MacLeish in the poem "Panic" captured American courage and optimism during the Depression. Stephen Vincent Benet and Edna St. Vincent Millay looked deep into the American past to provide inspiration for their own generation. Other notable and innovative poets included Robert Frost, Marianne Moore, e e cummings, Langston Hughes, and Hart Crane. The message transmitted by some of these, like Frost, was that Americans could take pride in the vision and the stamina of their forebears that could sustain their hopes in their own time of troubles.

The critics used the Depression to pierce what they considered the bourgeois veneer of American writing. Granville Hicks in *The Great Tradition* and V. F. Calverton in *The Liberation of American Literature* discussed America's literary past as a reflection of capitalism and its false values. To them literature was a reflection of politics. Marxist media such as the *New Masses* and the *Daily Worker* reiterated these themes tirelessly. Other critics rejected the association of values with literature altogether. These were the so-called New Critics such as John C. Ransom, R. P. Blackmur, Allen Tate, and Kenneth Burke, who revolted against mass society and democracy. The New Critics explained that literature was the product of an intellectual elite that had the technical skill to divorce form and content. Between these poles were critics who wrote of the history of American literature as a reflection of the humane values that constituted the foundations of American democracy. Van Wyk Brooks, in the book *The Flowering of New England*, took this view.

History and biography were especially popular during the Depression. As Americans became aware of other crises in their past and how they were dealt with, they could put the Depression in better historical perspective. Widely read historians included James Truslow Adams, who wrote about the Puritans in *The Epic of America*, and Charles A. Beard, who wrote *The Idea of National Interest*, which explored the origins of American foreign policy. Ralph H. Gabriel in *The Course of American Democratic Thought* explored the origins and development of democratic ideas in America.

Interest in biography reflected the intense desire of many Americans to draw inspiration and guidance from great men and women of the past. Carl Van Doren's book *Benjamin Franklin* enjoyed enormous popularity, as did Marquis James's books about Andrew Jackson. One of the widely acclaimed masterpieces of the decade was the four-volume study of Abraham Lincoln written by Carl Sandburg. Former journalist Douglas S. Freeman wrote an equally moving biography of Robert E. Lee. Allan Nevins published numerous impressive biographies, including *Grover Cleveland: A Study in Courage*.

Popular books about economics and sociology were read with great interest during the New Deal era. One of the writers who sought to explain contemporary technological and economic changes was journalist Stuart Chase, who in his book *Men and Machines* pleaded for a more centralized and more rational economic system. Marxist-oriented writers such as Lewis Corey, author of *The Decline of American Capitalism*, documented what they perceived to be the collapse of the American economy. Thurman Arnold, a law professor at Yale, in *The Folklore of Capitalism* enlightened Americans about the great differences that existed between the myths and the realities of their economic system.

During the Great Depression, American writers consciously used their craft to comment on the crisis and its impact. Only the Marxist left viewed literature as a weapon in the ideological struggle that they were waging against American democracy. The social critics and romanticists also reflected the influence of economic crisis. Indeed, the impact of the Depression on American culture was as penetrating as on the economy.

The Theater in Economic Crisis

The Depression had a devastating effect on theater in America. As audiences dwindled, theaters were forced to close, bringing large-scale unemployment to thousands whose livelihood was in some way linked to the performing arts. On Broadway in 1932, two-thirds of the New York theater houses went into bankruptcy, and more than three-fourths of the plays closed because so few people could afford to attend. Among those to survive was George Gershwin's satirical musical *Of Thee I Sing*, which lampooned national politics, especially the presidency. Clifford Odets, a talented leftist playwright, wrote *Waiting for Lefty*, a critique of contemporary American society and its economic values. Other leading dramatists of the decade included Lillian Hellman, whose best-known play was *The Little Foxes;* Robert Sherwood, author of *Idiot's Delight*, who appealed to Americans with pacifist or isolationist leanings through his sardonic indictment of war; and Maxwell Anderson, who wrote *Both Your Houses*, an attempt to dramatize the conflict between realism and idealism among New Dealers.

One unforeseen result of the Depression was its stimulation of amateur theater; more than 1,000 local amateur theater groups sprang up during the 1930s.

The American musical play continued to enjoy popularity in this period. George Gershwin composed *The Swing Symphony* (1937) and *Shall We Dance?* (1938); Richard Rodgers and Lorenz Hart set Americans singing to melodies from *Babes in Arms* (1937), *The Boys from Syracuse* (1938), and *Pal Joey* (1940). Some of the most memorable songs of the decade came from the pen of the urbanely sophisticated Cole Porter, whose haunting melodies made musicals such as *Red, Hot, and Blue* (1936), *Leave It to Me* (1938), and *Du Barry Was a Lady* (1939) great successes.

Depression Art

Like writers, American painters were sufficiently moved by the experiences of the Depression to reflect it in their works. Artists whose work dealt with social protest included William Gropper, a Marxist sympathizer who painted angry satires of capitalism and the individuals who represented it. His paint-ing *The Senate* sought to convey his feelings about the hypocrisy, corruption, and selfishness he thought existed in government. His views were shared by another struggling young artist of this era, Jack Levine, whose distaste for the American system was evident in many of his canvases. *Feast of Pure Reason* and *The Syndicate* conveyed his hatred of capitalists with startling savagery. Other artists who worked in this style include Peter Bloom and George Grosz. Among the best known of the social protesters was Ben Shahn, who satirized American politics and his view of its hollowness in such works as *Huey Long, Crowd Listening*, and *East Side Soap Box*.

Another group concerned with the portrayal of American society was the romantic realists. Edward Hopper, one of the most popular painters of this genre, keenly reflected the loneliness and alienation experienced by millions of city dwellers. *Room in Brooklyn* was characteristic of his paintings on these themes, and *Cold Storage Plant* conveyed his feelings about how humans were dwarfed by industrialization. *New York Movie House* caught a mood of loneliness in a crowded city. While Hopper documented the growth of the urban scene, Charles Burchfield concerned himself with the decline of rural America in such paintings as *Old Farm House, November Evening*, and *Edge of Town*.

Regionalists were considerably more optimistic in their approach to American life as they celebrated the positive virtues of the American past. Thomas Hart Benton was one of the most prolific in this group. Colorful rather than profound, his works such as *Arts of the West, Cotton Pickers, Country Dance*, and *Cradling Wheat* were vignettes of Americana. Grant Wood brought a highly precise style to his art, reflected in *Churning* and *Parson Weems's Fable*. John S. Curry captured the grandeur of the American landscape in paintings such as *Spring Showers, Sunrise*, and *Corn*. The regionalists used images from the American past to quiet the doubts their contemporaries expressed about the present.

The impact of the Depression on American culture was to stimulate a reexamination of the values that formed it. Writers, dramatists, and artists probed positive as well as negative characteristics of life in the United States. In the process, Americans came to know themselves better than before and to discover aspects of their heritage of which they had not been aware earlier.

Music during the Depression

Although the Depression muted innovation in American music, the decade witnessed increasing maturity in the music world. As in literature and art, the economic crisis spurred a surge of nationalistic feelings as well as regional pride among musicians. Dubbed the American Wave, it reflected a revitalized concern by composers regarding their relation to society. Musicians, as well as other performers, found that the recently developed mass media— radio, recordings, and motion pictures—provided them with vast new audiences in their own country, whereas earlier they had had to rely on the more appreciative Europeans.

A musical trend toward regionalism and a celebration of historical traditions was reflected in such works as Aaron Copland's tone poem *El Salon Mexico* (1936), which drew on the traditions of the Southwest. This was true also of his popular ballet *Billy the Kid* (1938), and his musical scores for such films as *Of Mice and Men* (1939) and *Our Town* (1940) also used regional themes. Other American composers were inspired by the nation's past. Ross Lee Finney was influenced by colonial hymns, while William Schuman used children's calls (rhymes) for his *American Festival Overture*. A profound appreciation of American folk traditions was also expressed by Virgil Thompson, Roy Harris, and Marc Blitzstein. Thompson's opera *Four Saints in Three Acts*, written with librettist Gertrude Stein, enjoyed an enthusiastic reception from the critics. Harris's overture *When Johnny Comes Marching Home Again* (1934) was a reaffirmation of traditional American patriotism. His *Folksong Symphony* (1940) skillfully wove popular American tunes into a full orchestral work. Douglas Moore, a composer and professor of music at Columbia University, received acclaim for his folk opera *The Devil and Daniel Webster* (1939), which reflected a preoccupation with America's past. At the Eastman School of Music in Rochester, New York, Howard Hanson experimented with American themes in symphonic orchestrations.

American music was greatly enriched by many talented refugees who fled Nazi oppression. Some of the world's greatest composers immigrated to the United States, including Igor Stravinski, Arnold Schönberg, Paul Hindemith, Béla Bartók, Kurt Weill, and Darius Milhaud. They introduced a cosmopolitan sophistication into American music that it had lacked before, and they broke down some of the cultural isolation that had long characterized the American musical scene and did much to make the United States a new leader in the international world of music.

Major symphony orchestras such as the Philadelphia Orchestra under Leopold Stokowski and Eugene Ormandy, the New York Philharmonic under Arturo Toscanini (to 1936), and the Chicago Symphony under Frederick Stock achieved worldwide recognition. In 1937, Toscanini built his own orchestra, the NBC Symphony, into a first-class ensemble whose Saturday afternoon radio broadcasts brought fine symphonic music into millions of homes. Such talented singers as Rosa Ponselle, Lawrence Tibbett, Gladys Swarthout, and Risë Stevens were on the roster of the Metropolitan Opera House in New York City, which had previously relied mainly on European talent.

Popular music in the 1930s took on a lighter tone than the brash jazz of the preceding decade. Americans sought music made for dancing rather than contemplative listening. The jazz of the 1920s gave way to the more easygoing "swing" of the 1930s. Most likely the term *swing* derived from Duke Ellington's 1932 recording *It Don't Mean a Thing If It Ain't Got That Swing.* Small jazz combos were replaced in popularity by big bands. By 1935, Benny Goodman had established himself as the King of Swing and was rivaled in popularity by Glenn Miller, Tommy Dorsey, Artie Shaw, and Harry James. At the same time, "sweet" music bands such as those of Guy Lombardo and Wayne King attracted a wide following, as did a soothing crooner, Bing Crosby, the decade's most popular singing star. These entertainers enjoyed unprecedented popularity, since national broadcasting brought them audiences numbering in the tens of millions.

Ethnic and regional consciousness stimulated by the Depression also was reflected in the realm of music. Jazz and the blues became increasingly noticeable in the 1920s through the music of black artists like W. C. Handy, Bessie Smith, Ma Rainey, Robert Johnson, and Charlie Patton. Black spirituals, which gained a wide audience during the Depression, were especially popularized by talented black artists such as Marian Anderson and Paul Robeson. Regionalism found expression in the great popularity of country-western music, developed by Bob Wills and his band, who were inspired by southern and western folk themes. The Depression era saw great vitality in American folk music. Woody Guthrie, among others, gave expression in song to the burdens of common people during the decade.

The Growth of Film

Hollywood continued its growth as the movie capital of the world. If the 1920s were the golden age of the silent film, the 1930s saw the spectacular rise of sound movies. Films were the great escape; as mentioned earlier, each week more than 60 million Americans went to the movies. Some went to forget their problems and the grim reality of their Depression-dominated lives; others went simply to escape nasty weather. Inside a theater, the moviegoer encountered a world very different from the reality of Depression-wracked America.

Hollywood, as anthropologist Hortense Powdermaker noted, was America's dream factory. Spectacular musicals such as Busby Berkeley's *No, No, Nannette* and *Broadway Melody of 1935* carried their audiences into an elegant, sophisticated dream world where all was well. Fred Astaire and Ginger Rogers danced their way into the hearts of millions through films such as *Flying Down to Rio, Top Hat, Roberta,* and *Shall We Dance?* Judy Garland became one of Hollywood's brightest stars in her memorable role as Dorothy in *The Wizard of Oz.* Situation comedies such as *It Happened One Night,* with Cary Grant and Claudette Colbert, and *Mr. Smith Goes to*

Washington, starring James Stewart, provided pleasant entertainment. Actresses like Lucille Ball, Jean Arthur, Rosalind Russell, and Katharine Hepburn appeared in many of these lighthearted films. Historical romances also enjoyed great vogue. The greatest success in this genre was undoubtedly *Gone with the Wind*, starring Clark Gable and Vivien Leigh—it broke all existing attendance records. Swashbuckling sagas such as *The Three Musketeers* made actors such as Erroll Flynn and Douglas Fairbanks, Jr., national heroes. Gangster movies starring James Cagney, Humphrey Bogart, George Raft, and Edward G. Robinson likewise provided escape from the routine of daily life during the Depression.

Whatever the genre, films provided an easy escape from daily cares for many Americans, and the world created by Hollywood contrasted starkly with the real America of the 1930s. According to Hollywood, the "good guys" always won, and "bad guys" always lost; individuals who were poor ultimately became rich; virtue triumphed over evil; and the just were inevitably rewarded. How could this fail to appeal to Americans at this time?

The New Deal and Cultural Life

Contributors to American culture in the Depression decade suffered as much from unemployment as others, perhaps even more. Work opportunities for writers, artists, actors, musicians, and teachers were extremely limited in the 1930s. President Roosevelt early became aware of the dilemma. Under the influence of Harry Hopkins, he approved special programs in the Works Progress Administration to provide temporary employment for people in some way engaged in the arts. The result was significant federal support for cultural activities, including the Federal Writers Project, the Federal Theater Project, the Federal Dance Project, the Federal Music Project, and the Federal Art Project. Initially, the projects had been designed to provide temporary relief; they met, however, with great success and enabled many Americans to discover themselves and their local or national heritage.

The Federal Writers Project was an ambitious enterprise designed to provide work relief for struggling writers. To organize a highly individualistic group of people such as writers in cooperative projects was no easy task, and Henry Alsberg, the director of the Writers Project, experienced many anxious moments. During the half-dozen years that it was in operation, the project produced almost 1,000 publications. Most notable, perhaps, were the fifty-one state and territorial guidebooks written by teams of writers working under a state director. The guidebooks combined history, folklore, anthropology, geography, and other aspects of the life in a particular state or region. In addition to guidebooks for the states, the writers prepared publica-

Criticizing New Deal spending: a *Washington Star* cartoon that appeared on April 22, 1936. *(The Washington Star)*

tions for cities. They wrote 150 books for a Life in America series that included such titles as *The Italians of New York* and *The Hopi*.

The WPA also engaged in the collection and classification of long-neglected historical records. These included Spanish land-grant archives in New Mexico and Arizona and shipping records from colonial New England and municipal archives in colonial New York. Although a few famous writers such as Conrad Aiken worked on the project, most of its staff was young and not well known at the time. Some, such as John Cheever and Richard Wright, achieved fame in later years.

Considered daring in its day, the Federal Theater Project provided employment not only for needy actors but for directors, set designers, costume designers, and stage hands as well. The project proved to be highly innovative and managed to present hundreds of productions each year without charge to the public, including circuses, vaudeville, musical comedy, classics, dance theater, and drama. Blacks, who previously had been largely excluded from the legitimate stage, were welcomed. An all-black company performed Shakespeare's *Macbeth*, for example, under WPA sponsorship. It was estimated that more than 30 million Americans attended one or another of these federally sponsored theater attractions.

Unemployed musicians also found the WPA Music Project a haven. In large cities as well as in small towns, the WPA organized community orchestras to perform everything from symphonic music, opera, and chamber music to popular pieces. Los Angeles—where the number of unemployed musicians was especially high—had at least six symphony orchestras in 1937. In some communities WPA musicians offered free music lessons to interested persons. The project encouraged young composers such as William Schuman and provided hearings and critiques that aided their development as artists. The activities of the Music Project were diverse and also included collecting and cataloging local American music. In the South and in Appalachia, in particular, previously unrecorded songs were collected and preserved.

Former museum director Holger Cahill supervised the Federal Arts Project, which provided relief to thousands of artists and sculptors. A few of the participants, among them, Jackson Pollock, Willem de Kooning, and Stuart Davis, won fame in later years. In hundreds of communities, WPA artists taught painting, crafts, sculpture, clay modeling, and carving. Others painted murals in public buildings, many of which still exist today. Despite varying levels of quality, all the murals reflect a quite vigorous native American tradition.

The WPA also provided temporary relief for teachers. Particularly in California, the WPA offered adult education classes and pioneered various vocational training programs. It sponsored correspondence and home study courses and special classes for workers' education. Unemployed teachers on the WPA roster staffed new nursery schools that cared for children of low-income families. Dietitians also used their special talents under the WPA. Researchers were put to work for the cause of historic preservation; restoration was done on California missions, Civil War battlefields in the South, and colonial forts in New England and New York.

As the most encompassing event in the lives of most Americans during the 1930s, the Depression was bound to have a lasting effect on American culture. The net result of cultural activities stimulated by the Depression and the New Deal was to heighten the consciousness of the American people about their heritage. Millions of Americans first became conscious of local folklore, regional art and music, past traditions, and democratic values through cultural activities that were a direct product of the commonly shared experiences generated by the economic crisis. The Depression also hastened the formal organization of cultural activities. The New

Deal heightened the consciousness of writers, artists, and musicians as groups and, as in the WPA, provided a place for them in the broader framework of national policies. Moreover, the New Deal stimulated the organization of voluntary groups engaged in cultural activities. In this sense the New Deal organized popular culture and gave it a more prominent place in the structure of American life.

C H A P T E R   1 0

The Search for Order
in Foreign Policy

1933–1941

 While Roosevelt struggled with domestic issues throughout his first two terms, foreign affairs took an increasingly greater portion of his time and energy in his later terms. During this period Americans were watching the collapse of the world order, the fall of democratic governments throughout Europe, and the rise of Japan in Asia.

The Depression and Foreign Policy

Understandably, the Great Depression created many diplomatic problems for Americans. Instability in the international economy contributed to depressed economic conditions in the United States and to mass unemployment. The precipitous decline of American exports overseas cost thousands of jobs in the United States. Violent fluctuations in foreign currencies affected U.S. gold reserves and disrupted import and export trade. Withdrawal of foreign investments in 1929 and 1930 added to panic selling and the collapse of securities markets. The impact of the Depression, however, was not solely economic. A troubled economy worldwide led to the collapse of democratic governments in Europe and the rise of militarism, rearmament, and territorial expansion. These actions challenged Americans in conflicting ways. On the one hand, Americans viewed the rise of dictatorships as a threat to their own democratic values. On the other hand, disillusionment over American participation in World War I was widespread, and pacifist sentiment, particularly among young people, was strong. The seeming failure of President Wilson's plans for a stable world order left many Americans

109

bitter and disappointed. They felt passionately that the United States should not immerse itself too deeply in the treacherous currents of world politics.

Isolation thus became the keynote of U.S. foreign policy during Roosevelt's first term in the White House. In recent years historians such as William Appleman Williams who lean toward a New Left view have argued that even in the Depression era, Americans were more involved in world affairs than they realized. Such involvement is relative, however. In comparison to Cold War diplomacy between 1945 and 1970, Roosevelt's policies in the 1930s appear to reflect the nation's desire for nonintervention. His policy was to steer clear of European and Asian embroilments while consolidating American influence in the Western Hemisphere. In Congress the desire to retreat into isolationism was perhaps even stronger. Meanwhile, various antiwar organizations such as the Veterans of Future Wars and the Fellowship of Reconciliation sprang up and gained strength.

Soon after assuming the presidency, Roosevelt was forced to make a decision concerning American cooperation with other nations in respect to international tariff policies and currency stabilization. Months before he left office, the internationally minded Herbert Hoover had indicated American willingness to work with the British and French to solve the economic problems related to the Depression. In spring 1933, the major European industrial nations were planning a conference in London for July, at which their representatives were expected to work out detailed programs to help the world economy. Roosevelt was beset with conflicting advice concerning American involvement in the London Economic Conference. On one side, Secretary of State Cordell Hull, long an advocate of free trade, urged him to lower tariff and other trade barriers. On the other, though, Brains Truster Raymond Moley insisted that Roosevelt would jeopardize many of his domestic economic recovery measures if he made new international commitments. The choice seemed to be between a nationalist or an internationalist approach to economic recovery. Faced with this difficult choice, Roosevelt wavered. He sent Hull to head the official American delegation at the conference, but soon after Hull arrived in London, Roosevelt was persuaded by Moley's arguments, and on July 3, he sent his "bombshell" message to the conference, in which he declared his opposition to American participation in international efforts to regulate currencies or trade. Hull was stunned but abided by the decision. Roosevelt's message effectively derailed the conference and further efforts to conclude international economic agreements in 1933. Without the cooperation of the United States, such attempts were futile.

To some extent the impression of many Europeans that the United States was retreating into greater isolation was mitigated by American recognition of the Soviet Union in November 1933. Disturbed by Japan's invasion of Manchuria, Roosevelt cast a more benevolent eye on the USSR as a potential ally. Despite considerable criticism at home, the president extended official United States recognition to the Soviet Union, and in return, the Communist government promised to pay war debts owed to Americans and to abate its propaganda in the United States, two promises it did not keep.

Growing Isolationist Sentiments

During 1934, American isolationist feeling was whipped into virtual hysteria by the investigations of the Nye Committee. Established by Congress to explore the causes of American entry into World War I, the committee, headed by isolationist Senator Gerald P. Nye of North Dakota, focused on munitions manufacturers. Operating under the assumption that wars were caused by economic forces, the committee charged that the United States had been tricked into World War I by munitions makers. Although the evidence Nye and his staff collected hardly warranted such a conclusion, the committee's work had an enormous impact on the American public and stiffened isolationist resolve.

Partly because of the work of the Nye Committee, Congress responded aggressively to preclude further American involvement in European affairs. In 1935 it approved the Pitman Resolution, which prohibited exports of American arms to war-torn areas, like Ethiopia. The resolution also prohibited American merchant vessels from carrying munitions into such areas and withheld protection from Americans who traveled on ships belonging to belligerents. In 1936 and 1937, Congress enacted additional neutrality acts to strengthen its resolve of noninvolvement in Ethiopia and the Spanish Civil War. The Neutrality Act of 1936 prohibited loans to belligerent parties; the act of 1937 introduced an arms embargo but contained a cash-and-carry clause whereby belligerents who could pay for arms and who could transport them would be permitted to make arms purchases in the United States. Unfortunately, the impact of these acts was not what Congress had hoped. They benefited aggressor nations by making it more difficult for attacked nations to secure arms. In a sense the legislation only delayed the day of reckoning when Americans had to decide whether or not to join other democratic nations in opposing totalitarian expansion.

The disinclination of Americans to become too closely involved with European affairs was also reflected in the administration's refugee policies. As the Nazis stepped up their persecution of Jews and other minorities, a steady trickle of German Jews sought refuge in countries around the world. Although many besought the United States to allow them entry, Congress refused to modify the existing quota, which allowed only a total of 150,000 immigrants to enter the country each year. President Roosevelt was sympathetic to their plight but hesitant to take overt action. Furthermore, some State Department employees, such as Assistant Secretary Breckinridge Long, had anti-Semitic leanings. As a result, while about 120,000 German Jewish refugees were permitted to enter the United States between 1933 and 1941, millions more found the doors closed and eventually perished in Nazi death camps.

Americans' isolationist mood was also revealed in Roosevelt's diplomacy in the Far East. After more than a decade of discussion, Congress agreed to grant independence to the Philippines, ceded to the United States by Spain after the Spanish-American War in 1898. American sugar producers in particular strongly favored independence because Philippine sugar competed with their own product. And as long as the Philippines were part of the United States, American tariff duties did not apply. The Tydings-McDuffie Act of 1934 provided for Philippine independence after a ten-year period of transition.

Meanwhile, the continued Japanese invasion of China posed real problems for the United States. In 1933, Japanese armies marched into the five northern provinces of China—in direct violation of the Open Door agreements, the Nine-Power Pact of 1921, and the Kellogg-Briand Pact of 1927. Like Hoover, Roosevelt felt constrained to watch helplessly. His own absorption in the problems of domestic depression as well as the strong prevailing mood of isolation severely limited his alternatives.

On July 7, 1937, the Japanese intensified and broadened their invasion, and in the midst of a full-scale military attack against China, Japanese war planes sank the American gunboat *Panay* off Shanghai. Even in the face of this action, the majority of Americans were still opposed to any overt action by their government. A Gallup poll reported that more than 70 percent of Americans opposed any intervention. And more than a two-thirds majority in Congress voted against imposing any sanctions against the Japanese. In fact, most Americans breathed easier when they learned that the Japanese government had apologized and offered to pay damages for the *Panay*.

Paradoxically, though, the desire to remain aloof from the problems of Europe and Asia led the United States to seek more collaboration with other countries in the Western Hemisphere. With his talent for appropriate phrases, Roosevelt called this new idea the Good Neighbor policy. American concern for national security and solidarity against communism was obviously one motivation, but another was the desire to expand foreign markets during the Depression years. To fulfill this policy, Roosevelt took on the role of diplomat as he sought to dampen strong anti-American feelings throughout South America that were in part a product of U.S. interventionist policies in the decade following the Spanish-American War.

Like so many of Roosevelt's programs, the Good Neighbor policy embraced a many-sided approach. Economic cooperation was one facet. Congressional action on tariffs was another. In 1934, Congress approved the Reciprocal Trade Agreements Act, which allowed the president to negotiate treaties to reduce American tariffs for nations that made reciprocal reductions in return. Within two years, Roosevelt had concluded thirteen such agreements, many with countries in South America. During the same period, U.S. exports rose more than 14 percent. The Reciprocal Trade Agreements Act proved to be one of the most successful of the New Deal's foreign policies. Also in 1934, the United States established the Export-Import Bank, which made loans to South American countries seeking to stabilize their currencies.

At the same time, Roosevelt took special care to impress Latin Americans with the desire of the United States not to intervene in their affairs. At the Inter-American Conference at Montevideo, Uruguay, in 1933, the United States supported a declaration pledging nonintervention among Western Hemisphere states. The president underscored this policy by supporting the abrogation of the Platt Amendment, which had given the United States the right to intervene in the affairs of Cuba. In a treaty with Panama in 1936,

The Good Neighbor Policy in action: Franklin D. Roosevelt at the 1936 Inter-American Conference in Buenos Aires, Argentina. (*Acme*)

American negotiators gave up similar privileges. The president withdrew Marines from Haiti in 1934 and joined with representatives of twenty other governments in South America to ratify a Protocol of Non-Intervention at the Inter-American Conference in Buenos Aires, Argentina, in 1936. Roosevelt's personal appearance at this meeting underscored the importance he attached to fostering close ties and goodwill with Latin American countries.

To embellish its image as the friendly giant to the north, the United States also exerted an active influence as mediator of conflicts in Latin America; for example, American officials played a role in settling strife between Peru and Columbia in 1933. Roosevelt assiduously refrained from intervening in the Cuban revolution of 1933 and exercised great self-restraint in refusing to intervene when Mexico expropriated American oil companies during the 1930s. When Germany, Italy, and Japan entered into the Axis Alliance in 1939, nations of the Western Hemisphere adopted the Convention for Collective Security. This provided for mutual consultation in case of attack and brought the United States closer to its neighboring nations than it had been in many years.

The Gathering War Clouds

By 1937, however, Roosevelt had begun to doubt the effectiveness of American diplomacy in limiting Axis expansion. In 1936, Adolf Hitler had marched his troops into the Rhineland, which had been declared a buffer zone after World War I. In 1938 he occupied the Czech Sudetenland and annexed Austria as well.

Two years earlier, Hitler's Axis partner, Benito Mussolini, had conquered Ethiopia. In Spain both Hitler and Mussolini provided active military support for their would-be fellow dictator, General Francisco Franco, who was fighting a civil war to overthrow the elected republican government. Fascist politicians were also influential in Hungary and Romania.

Due mostly to the worsening international situation, Roosevelt's second administration witnessed increasingly heated debate between noninterventionists and interventionists concerning the course of American foreign policy. A strong isolationist policy prevailed. If the president himself had doubts about isolationism, he was careful to keep them to himself. He proceeded with characteristic caution, seemingly anxious not to alienate public opinion, but between 1937 and 1940, Roosevelt took an increasingly firm stand against German and Japanese expansion in Europe and the Far East, respectively.

This departure from nonintervention was first heralded in what became known as Roosevelt's Quarantine Address, delivered in Chicago on October 5, 1937. Prompted by the recently accelerated Japanese advance into China, Roosevelt called for the quarantining of aggressor nations by the international community. Possibly he was sounding out public opinion to determine whether or not isolationist sentiment was weakening, but certainly the tone of the address—and the fiery manner in which he delivered it—was firmer than any of his previous presidential foreign policy statements:

> The political situation in the world, which of late has been growing progressively worse, is such as to cause grave concern and anxiety to all the peoples and nations who wish to live in peace and amity with their neighbors. . . . The peace, the freedom, the security of 90 percent of the population of the world is being jeopardized by the remaining 10 percent who are threatening a breakdown of all international order and law. Surely the 90 percent . . . must find some way to make their will prevail. . . . It seems to be unfortunately true that the epidemic of world lawlessness is spreading. And mark this well! When an epidemic of physical disease starts to spread, the community approves and joins in a quarantine of the patients in order to protect the health of the community against the spread of the disease.

Such a quarantine against aggressor nations was his prescription for maintaining peace in the increasingly precarious international order.

The worsening international situation also aroused alarm in Congress. In consultation with the president, the lawmakers reluctantly voted to embark on a military preparedness program. Throughout the Depression, Congress had made only minimal appropriations for the armed forces. Between 1933 and 1937, appropriations had averaged only about $180 million annually. The navy—a favorite since Roosevelt had served as its assistant secretary in 1913—fared much better than the army, which numbered no more than 110,000 officers and men. In fact, the army was so poverty-striken that its men were forced to drill with wooden rifles. The Military Appropriations Act of 1938 changed all this as Congress voted $1 billion to expand the armed forces. A strong America, Roosevelt declared, would be the best deterrent against a would-be aggressor:

> The American nation is committed to peace and the principal reason for the existence of our armed forces is to guarantee our peace. The army of the United States is one of the smallest in the world. However, . . . its efficiency is steadily improving.

Amid American rearmament preparations in 1938 and 1939, the political situation in Europe worsened. At the Munich Conference of 1938, British Prime Minister Neville Chamberlain and French Premier Edward Daladier abjectly surrendered to Hitler's demand for German annexation of all of Czechoslovakia. In March 1939, German troops invaded Czechoslovakia while its British and French allies stood impotently by. In Spain, Franco won a decisive victory over the Republicans and established a harsh fascist dictatorship. Mussolini was preparing to move Italian troops into Albania and Greece, to give himself a foothold in the Balkans. And in September 1939,

Nazi troops attacked Poland, which they subdued and occupied within a month. The invasion of Poland left England and France little choice but to resist, and on September 1, 1939, World War II officially began.

Most Americans were still hopeful that the outbreak of war in Europe would not lead to significant changes in the Roosevelt administration's policy of nonintervention. Only in later years did Americans come to realize that the war doomed isolationism in U.S. diplomacy. Throughout the 1930s, the Depression was a major influence on foreign relations. Disillusionment after World War I had strengthened the isolationist mood, but the Depression led Americans to be even more concerned with domestic than with foreign problems. The increasing helplessness of the League of Nations during the 1930s, as well as the outbreak of armed hostilities in Europe, Africa, and the Far East, only intensified the resolve for nonintervention. Involvement of the United States in international crises was considered to be as detrimental to the national interest in the 1930s as U.S. intervention supposedly had been in the First World War. As President Roosevelt often said, the great enemy that Americans had to fight was the Depression. The year 1939 found the United States in a rapidly changing world. The Nazi menace to Western civilization was replacing the Depression as the overriding issue in American public life. American policymakers found themselves devoting more time to foreign affairs than to domestic issues.

CHAPTER 11

America's Road to War

1939–1941

 Although eventual American participation in the global conflict appeared likely, most Americans still hoped to avoid it. That question was resolved by Japan's attack on Pearl Harbor, on December 7, 1941. By then most Americans were more prepared for war—psychologically as well as militarily—than they had been two years earlier. Between 1939 and 1941 the problems of the nation—and its mood—changed dramatically.

World War II in Europe

In 1939, in a brilliant display of military skill and power, the Germans had conducted a *Blitzkrieg* ("lightning war") that caused the Poles to surrender within a month as the French and British stood by. That same year the Germans signed a friendship pact with the Soviet Union that appeared to eliminate possible Russian opposition in the east. The German army stationed on the Franco-German border remained inactive during the winter of 1939–1940. Indeed, some observers concluded rather prematurely that this *Sitzkrieg* ("sit-down war") was phony.

Unfortunately, a series of German advances in spring 1940 indicated unmistakably that the conflict was anything but phony. Powerful German armies subdued Norway and Denmark in April. Within weeks of the Scandinavian operation, German forces swept into Belgium, the Netherlands, and France, quickly crushing all opposition and occupying all three countries. To the dismay of the Americans, France surrendered on June 12, 1940, leaving only the British to carry on the struggle against the Germans. Wherever the Nazis extended their New Order, they established an unprecedented and barbaric reign of terror. Concentration and forced labor camps, executions of civilians, extreme brutality, and massive looting became the hallmarks of

117

German occupation. Now that Hitler was, in effect, the master of Europe, his earlier promises to extend his New Order to the rest of the world were taken more seriously.

Hitler was at this time planning the invasion of England. At one time his plans were set for 1940, but the action was postponed until the following year. In the fall of 1940 the German air force, the Luftwaffe, began the Battle of Britain. Large-scale bombing attacks preceded what was to be a direct invasion. On almost every night between September 1940 and March 1941, hundreds of German planes swept over Great Britain, raining thousands of bombs on British cities in an attempt to demoralize the civilian population. Yet the English people maintained high morale and stubbornly defied the German onslaught.

Hitler changed his mind about invading England when he decided to go after his most hated foe, the Soviet Union. Before he began a Russian campaign in 1941, however, he came to the aid of the Italians, who were suffering serious reverses at the hands of Albanian guerrillas and the Greek army. Hitler sent German forces into the Balkans and within a few months had subdued Yugoslavia, Greece, Hungary, Romania, and Bulgaria, while simultaneously challenging the British in North Africa.

In June more than forty German divisions began a major invasion of the Soviet Union. Within a few months they had penetrated deep into its interior and were almost within sight of Moscow.

By the end of 1941, Germany appeared on the road to world domination, having conquered most of Europe in less than two years and having penetrated the depths of the Soviet Union. Americans could not help but be concerned about their own fate.

Preparedness: Mobilizing America's Resources

President Roosevelt was keenly sensitive to the dangers that Nazi world domination held for the United States. Late in 1938 he sent Bernard Baruch, financier and former director of the War Industries Board who had supervised America's economic mobilization effort during World War I, on a fact-finding mission. He brought back alarming news. Germany appeared invincible, Baruch reported. Its rearmament program had made it the strongest military power in the world. In 1938 the German air force could boast of 3,353 planes, compared to 1,900 for the Soviet Union—and only 1,600 for the United States. Baruch urged a rapid buildup of American military might as the best possible deterrent to attack.

With his worst fears thus confirmed, Roosevelt asked Congress to increase defense appropriations. Baruch advocated expenditures on a scale exceeding $3 billion annually—a sum also advocated by the influential assistant secretary of war, Louis Johnson. Isolationists in Congress still opposed any but the most minimal expenditures. Roosevelt once again took a middle ground between the two extremes.

A modest rearmament effort was begun, although Roosevelt spoke strongly to Congress about the need to rearm:

> We have learned that survival cannot be guaranteed by arming after the attack begins, . . . that long before any overt military act, aggression begins with preliminaries of propaganda. . . . All about us rage undeclared wars— military and economic. All about us grow more deadly armaments— military and economic. All about us are threats of new aggression—military and economic.
>
> The world has grown so small, and weapons of attack so swift, that no nation can be safe in its will to peace so long as any other single powerful nation refuses to settle its grievances at the council table. We . . . must have armed forces and defenses strong enough to ward off sudden attack against strategic positions and key facilities.

In response, Congress appropriated $525 million to be divided among the army, the navy, and the fledgling air force. In addition, the president was authorized to stockpile essential materials. The Stockpile Act of 1939 allocated $125 million for this purpose. Meanwhile, the Educational Orders Act the same year was designed to bring about greater coordination between military planners and their industrial suppliers. This measure authorized expenditures of $2 billion yearly to enable the War Department to familiarize key contractors with particular kinds of munitions and other supplies needed. Louis Johnson sponsored scores of conferences at which he acquainted manufacturers in diverse industries with specific problems expected in large-scale industrial mobilization.

Since the industrial potential of the nation in case of war was unknown, Roosevelt also created a new agency, the War Resources Board, established in August 1939 as a civilian advisory commission to the Army-Navy Munitions Board. Its purpose was to develop a comprehensive industrial mobilization plan. Headed by Edward R. Stettinius, president of the U.S. Steel Corporation, the board included executives such as Walter Gifford of the American Telephone and Telegraph Company, John Pratt of General Motors, and Robert Wood of Sears, Roebuck and Company. Roosevelt had known Stettinius's father during World War I and felt a special fondness for his son. Although staffed by impressive business leaders, the board did little more than file a report on how industrial mobilization could be achieved. In part its ineffectiveness was due to Roosevelt's desire to maintain direct personal supervision of major portions of the defense program. To facilitate his objective, he issued an executive order on September 8, 1939, creating the Office of Emergency Management, to be set up within the White House. This allowed Roosevelt to centralize members of his staff who worked on various phases of mobilization. In addition, he selected General George C. Marshall as the army's new chief of staff. Marshall was known to be eager to cooperate with the president and Congress and was also sympathetic to strengthening the armed forces. To ensure coordination of military and civilian policies, the president issued a military order requiring the chiefs of staff, the Aeronautics Board, and the Army-Navy Munitions Board to report directly to him rather than to respective cabinet members. Such reorganization effectively enabled Roosevelt to supervise all aspects of defense policy and facilitated coordination between civilian and military officials. Most important, Roosevelt was able to create any emergency agencies needed for national security. By 1939, then, the president had begun the process of creating an organizational structure to harness the nation's military and industrial potential in case of war.

Yet Roosevelt shrank from adopting any sweeping comprehensive plan for industrial mobilization. Throughout 1939 and 1940, Bernard Baruch urged him to accept a detailed blueprint for centralized industrial mobilization such as one he had devised during World War I. And although Roosevelt professed to be sympathetic to Baruch, he was, in fact, as temperamentally opposed to an abstract scheme for mobilization as he was to abstract ideologies. He also hoped to avoid a push for intervention, opposed by so many Americans, until after the presidential election in November 1940. Moreover, his political sense persuaded him that he alone should retain the major reins of power over civilian as well as military mobilization. Consequently, the preparedness program between 1939 and 1941 was as piecemeal and experimental as the New Deal was from 1933 to 1935. Unfortunately, this resulted in waste and duplication that hampered rearmament in 1939 and 1940. Yet it allowed the administration to be flexible and to deal with new or unforeseen needs. Moreover, it permitted a wide range of interest groups in the nation to have a voice in shaping the defense program. Such participation aroused an enthusiasm and high morale among Americans that a more rigid plan might have been unable to tap.

Production of military goods increased somewhat in the United States during the first year of the war. Americans delivered 2,300 planes to the Allies, as well as small quantities of tanks and other weapons. Even so, some of Roosevelt's critics—Charles E. Lindbergh among them—accused him of being a warmonger.

The fall of France in 1940 prior to the American election provided the shock that convinced an increasing number of Americans to support an acceleration of the defense program. In June and July 1940, Congress readily acceded to President Roosevelt's request for additional funds to rearm the nation by appropriating more than $8 billion. Congress also authorized a one-year military draft. At the same time, Roosevelt broadened the political complexion of his cabinet by appointing two prominent Republicans to key posi-tions. As his secretary of war he chose Henry L. Stimson, who had directed the Department of State under Herbert Hoover. To head the Navy Depart-ment he selected Frank Knox, a Chicago newspaper publisher who had been the Republican vice-presidential candidate in 1936. A Gallup poll at the time indicated that at least one-half of the American public approved of these measures, reflecting a gradual shift of public opinion away from isolation.

Roosevelt now also sought to accelerate the pace of industrial produc-tion. During the first half of 1940, many industries had lagged behind in the shift to manufacture war supplies. To some extent this was due to the adminis-tration's lack of leadership in guiding business and agriculture, but it was also due to serious shortages of essential materials such as aviation gasoline, electric power, and railway freight cars. Thus in May 1940, Roosevelt fell back on the World War I experience and appointed the Council of National Defense, composed mostly of cabinet members. He appointed William S. Knudsen, president of General Motors, chairman and instructed him to produce 50,000 planes. Almost immediately, Knudsen began to award large defense contracts that averaged about $1.5 billion monthly. Meanwhile, Con-gress authorized the Reconstruction Finance Corporation to finance the building of new war plants and to stockpile supplies such as rubber and scarce metals.

Shortages continued to hamper various industries, leading Roosevelt to take still more emergency measures. He also established a priorities board attached to the Council of National Defense; it had authority to require manufacturers to place war orders before civilian production orders. He created the Office of Production Management to allocate scarce goods and raw materials and to schedule military requirements. William S. Knudsen and Sidney Hillman, a labor leader prominent in the CIO, were appointed codirectors. To control inflation as well as to ration scarce civilian goods, the president established the Office of Price Administration—largely to protect consumers. During the second half of 1940, therefore, American industry began to hum; it entered a production boom such as the nation had not witnessed for over a decade. By the end of the year, 17,000 planes, 9,000 tanks, and 17,000 heavy guns had rolled off assembly lines.

In the middle of this industrial push and the deteriorating world situa-tion, the major political parties assembled in the summer of 1940 to select their presidential candidates. The Republicans met first, just two days after the French surrendered to Germany. In a crisis atmosphere, staunch isola-tionists such as Senators Robert Taft of Ohio, Burton Wheeler of Montana, and Hiram Johnson of California, who opposed American aid to the Allies, fought to a deadlock with internationalists like Senator Arthur H. Vanden-berg of Michigan and Governor Thomas E. Dewey of New York. In a series of surprise moves, the internationalists won control of the convention and nominated Wendell Willkie, a relatively unknown figure. A Democrat until 1933, Willkie was president of one of the South's major public utility corporations, Commonwealth and Southern. Like Roosevelt, Willkie was sympathetic to the Allied cause and, in fact, privately believed that American involvement in the war might be difficult to avoid.

Among the Democrats, speculation was rife that Roosevelt would accept the nomination for a third time, breaking the two-term precedent. Roosevelt had said little about his political intentions, yet he did not encourage other candidates or do anything to restrain his supporters. When the Democrats met in July 1940, Roosevelt sent them a message that implied that he would accept the nomination if it were offered—a gesture that was in itself sufficient to start a Roosevelt bandwagon. Although he lost the support of some leading Democrats, such as his former manager James A. Farley, the convention nominated him with great enthusiasm.

The campaign was bitter. Willkie attacked Roosevelt for being power-hungry. He criticized the slowness and haphazardness of Roosevelt's defense program. Although an active interventionist himself, Willkie, in the last weeks before the election, accused Roosevelt of being a warmonger. Roosevelt did not respond to Willkie's charges until late in the campaign. Then he reiterated his record and his experience, leaving it to his partisans to tell the voters that they should not swap horses in midstream in a time of world crisis. That strategy worked, for in 1940, Roosevelt received 27 million votes, compared to 22 million for Willkie.

By the end of 1940, the nation's defense program was finally gathering momentum. During the first year of the European war, the president had not established a clearly defined mobilization plan. Always eager to protect his political position, he shrank from decisive action—in particular, he was anxious to offend neither the isolationists nor the noninterventionists. Only after the fall of France in June 1940 did Roosevelt communicate his alarm to the nation and solicit support for a large-scale national defense program. Then, confident of the approval of a majority of the American people, he embarked on a more determined course by pledging maximum aid—short of war—to the Allies.

From Isolation to Intervention

The fall of France brought World War II closer to America. Any illusions that Americans might have harbored concerning Nazi intentions about world conquest or about the strength of the Allies were rudely shattered by the spectacular German victories. England alone stood between the United States and the Nazi juggernaut—and the British showed signs of weakening.

Americans were now forced to confront the realities of the war as it affected their own national interest.

The reversal in the United States' position was publicized by the president in a commencement speech at the University of Virginia on June 10, 1940, as France fell, when he said:

> Some indeed still hold to the now somewhat obvious delusion that we of the United States can safely permit the United States to become a lone island, a lone island in a world dominated by the philosophy of force.
>
> Such an island may be the dream of those who still talk and vote as isolationists. Such an island represents to me and to the overwhelming majority of the Americans today a helpless nightmare of a people without freedom. Yes, the nightmare of a people lodged in prison, handcuffed, hungry, and fed through the bars from day to day by the contemptuous, unpitying masters of other continents.
>
> Let us not hesitate—all of us—to proclaim certain truths. Overwhelmingly, we as a nation . . . are convinced that military and naval victory of the gods of force and hate would endanger the institutions of democracy in the Western world—and that, equally, therefore, the whole of our sympathies lie with those nations that are giving the lifeblood of combat against those forces.
>
> In our unity . . . we will pursue two obvious and simultaneous courses; we will extend to the opponents of force the material resources of this nation, and at the same time we will harness and speed up the use of those resources in order that we ourselves in the Americas may have equipment and training equal to the task of any emergency and every defense.

The collapse of France had created a threat to American security in the Caribbean too. The French possessions of Martinique and Guadeloupe were in strategic locations and might possibly be occupied by Germans. To counter this danger, the Roosevelt administration called for a meeting of pan-American foreign ministers to take place in Havana in late July 1940. This conference displayed surprising unanimity, for large numbers of German settlers and their descendants in Argentina, Brazil, and Chile had cultivated considerable pro-German sentiment in South America. In the Declaration of Havana the participating nations declared that they would consider an attack on any American country an attack on all. A commission was established to take temporary control of any European possessions in the Western Hemisphere to guard against possible incursions by the Axis.

During the spring and summer of 1940, British Prime Minister Winston Churchill was importuning Roosevelt to transfer some U.S. naval vessels to desperately needed convoy duty in the North Atlantic. When Churchill first broached the question, Roosevelt was decidedly against the idea, although Churchill argued that England had lost one-third of its fleet of 100 destroyers and that those remaining were needed to repel the expected German invasion from the east. "We must ask therefore, as a matter of life or death," wrote Churchill, "to be reinforced with these destroyers." Roosevelt hesitated to act without congressional approval. In July, the British ambassador to the United States, Lord Lothian, offered the United States the rights to military bases in Newfoundland, Bermuda, and Trinidad in return for aid. The idea of a trade had great appeal to Roosevelt. Through his friend William Allen White, a well-known newspaper editor from Kansas, he sounded out the Republican challenger Wendell Willkie on his attitude toward the proposal. Willkie agreed not to make it an issue. Meanwhile, a group of distinguished lawyers advised the president that he did not require congressional approval for a destroyer transfer, and in early fall Roosevelt transferred fifty antiquated World War I destroyers to Great Britain in return for eight American military bases in the New World. Public reaction to the transaction was mostly favorable, in part because Roosevelt had cultivated it carefully during the preceding months.

While Americans were going to the polls in the fall of 1940, the English were huddling in bomb shelters and wondering about the impending bankruptcy of their government. Great Britain had spent $4.5 billion of its $6.5 billion in dollar reserves and lacked funds to pay for further large-scale purchases of military supplies in the United States. Prime Minister Churchill chose to present his case dramatically. As Roosevelt was vacationing in the Caribbean on a navy cruiser in early December, a seaplane approached the vessel, bearing an urgent message from Churchill. "My dear Mr. President," he wrote.

> As we reach the end of this year, I feel you will expect me to lay before you the prospects for 1941. I do so with candour and confidence, because it seems to me that the vast majority of American citizens have recorded their conviction that the safety of the United States, as well as the future of our two Democracies and the kind of civilization for which they stand, is bound up with the survival and independence of the British Commonwealth of Nations. . . . [But] the moment approaches when we shall no longer be able to pay cash for shipping and other supplies. . . . Regard this letter not as an appeal for aid but as a statement of minimum action to achieve our common purpose.

Churchill urged Roosevelt to provide supplies the British so desperately needed but for which they could no longer pay.

Roosevelt considered the appeal and then formulated a plan of action. After he returned to Washington and consulted with his aides, he revealed his scheme for what became known as the Lend-Lease Program. At a press conference he told reporters:

What I'm trying to do is to eliminate the dollar sign, . . . get rid of the silly, foolish old dollar sign. Well, let me give you an illustration: Suppose my neighbor's home catches on fire, and I have a length of garden hose four or five hundred feet away. If he can take my garden hose and connect it with his hydrant, I may help him to put out his fire. Now what do I do? I don't say to him before that operation, "Neighbor, my garden hose cost me $15; you have to pay me $15 for it." What is the transaction that goes on? I don't want $15—I want my garden hose back after the fire is over. All right, if it goes through the fire all right, intact . . . he gives it back to me and thanks me very much for the use of it.

On December 29, 1940, Roosevelt spoke to Americans directly in a Fireside Chat. "The United States," he said, "must be the great arsenal of democracy." He asked Congress for authority to send war supplies to England in return for goods and services rather than for dollars. His pleas fell on sympathetic ears, and within two months Congress had appropriated $7 billion for operation of the Lend-Lease Program. In return for supplies, the British also made additional air and naval bases available to the United States off the Canadian coast and in the British West Indies.

The Havana declaration, together with Roosevelt's commencement address at the University of Virginia and the adoption of Lend-Lease, transformed the United States from a neutral into a partisan, albeit nonbelligerent, nation. This new diplomatic status was developed further by Roosevelt's authorization of limited American naval action in the first half of 1941. By then an increasing number of Americans had begun to realize that Britain was America's first line of defense. If Britain were defeated, no doubt the United States would be left to face Nazi Germany alone. American public opinion was shifting in favor of intervention. Since Roosevelt kept a close watch on opinions expressed in the popular press, he felt more assured in modifying the nation's neutral stance. In view of the great shipping losses the British suffered in the Atlantic at the hands of German submarines, in March 1941, Roosevelt authorized American shipyards to repair British vessels. In addition, he ordered the transfer of ten Coast Guard cutters to the Royal Navy for convoy duty. And he extended the American Neutrality Patrol almost 2,000 miles into the Atlantic. The U.S. Navy was ordered to locate German submarines but not to attack them.

By the middle of 1941, Roosevelt had extended American nonbelligerency further. Fleets of Nazi submarines were roaming in the North Atlantic, sinking British vessels at an alarming rate of two ships daily and endangering the American supply route to England. With the United States now committed to the defense of Great Britain, the president felt compelled to take additional steps to ensure the continued flow of aid to the embattled British. That lifeline seemed threatened by a German declaration in March 1941 extending the Atlantic war zone to include Iceland as well as the Denmark Strait between Iceland and Greenland. The practical effect of this measure was that German submarines and surface vessels would roam Atlantic waters less than 1,000 miles from American shores. Roosevelt considered the German action for several months before making retaliatory moves. In July 1941 he announced that U.S. Marines would occupy Iceland to prevent its possible seizure by Germany and to ensure the defense of the Western Hemisphere. These measures made the United States a *de facto* ally of the British.

Although Roosevelt and Churchill were in almost daily contact in 1940 and 1941, the two leaders had not met personally. Roosevelt recalled having seen Churchill briefly during World War I, but the British leader could not remember the occasion. Consequently, in July 1941, Harry Hopkins went to London to arrange a secret meeting. Within a few weeks Churchill embarked on one of the Royal Navy's finest battleships bound for Argentia, off Newfoundland. Roosevelt was steaming to the rendezvous on the U.S. Navy cruiser *Augusta*. The two men met aboard the American ship on August 9, 1941. Churchill hoped to secure some kind of commitment from the United States to participate in the war, but Roosevelt refused to bind his nation in this way. The military advisers who accompanied the two men did discuss loose plans for Anglo-American cooperation at some future time, if circumstances warranted.

The outcome of this meeting was the Atlantic Charter, a joint declaration concerning common aims. This document embodied an Anglo-American vision for organization of the postwar world. That world was to be ordered according to principles based on self-determination of nations. The charter also reiterated Anglo-American adherence to the Four Freedoms, which Roosevelt had enunciated in his annual message to Congress earlier that year—freedom from want, freedom from fear, freedom of speech, and freedom of religion. When the contents of the Atlantic Charter were made public a week after the meeting, Americans responded positively. In the context of growing support for his diplomacy, the president extended Lend-Lease aid to the Soviet Union a few months later.

By fall 1941, the United States was involved in an undeclared naval war. On September 4, 1941, a German submarine had attacked the U.S. destroyer *Greer* off Iceland. President Roosevelt reacted by ordering U.S. naval vessels to shoot on sight any German or Italian vessels they encountered in the North Atlantic. A few weeks later Congress approved the arming of American merchant ships.

Throughout 1940 and 1941, Roosevelt's shift to a diplomacy tending to intervention came under fire from various groups and individuals. Staunch isolationists such as Senator Burton Wheeler belittled the supposed threat from the Axis powers and castigated Roosevelt as a warmonger. Some Americans, such as Charles Lindbergh, also did not regard fascism as a threat to the United States and opposed Roosevelt's policies of aiding the Allies. There were ethnic isolationists such as Americans of German or Irish descent, antimilitarists, left-wingers, and communists. Early in 1941 the opponents of intervention activated the America First Committee with Robert E. Wood of Sears, Roebuck as its chairman. Through an active public relations campaign and lobbying in Congress, the committee brought its views before the American public, although international events increasingly weakened its influence.

Advocates of intervention felt that Roosevelt was too slow and too cautious in extending aid to the Allies. Led by William ˉAllen White, they organized the Committee to Defend America by Aiding the Allies to counter the influence of isolationists and to prod the administration into closer collaboration with France and Britain. Despite these organizations, neither the isolationists nor the interventionists swayed large numbers of Americans as effectively as the rapidly changing military situation in Europe and the Far East. The majority of Americans, however, were still holding out hope that direct participation in the war by the United States might not be necessary.

While Roosevelt had his hands full in dealing with the European crisis after 1939, American relations with Japan were also deteriorating. Despite protests by the United States, The Japanese continued their invasion of China, begun in 1937. One of the Japanese government's major objectives during this period was an alliance with Nazi Germany, which promised to facilitate Japan's further expansion in Asia. After tortuous negotiations, Japan concluded the Tri-Partite Agreement with Germany and Italy in 1940. Japan recognized German and Italian dominance in Europe, and the European powers agreed to recognize Japanese influence in East Asia. They also promised to aid the Japanese if they were attacked by a neutral power. Such an alliance was clearly a challenge to the United States, since American insistence on Japanese recognition of the Open Door policy and the independence of China was a cloak for allowing the United States to maintain a dominant position in East Asia and to limit Japanese expansion there. The goals of the United States and Japan were now on a collision course.

On hearing of British recognition of Japanese conquests in China, in July 1939, Roosevelt warned Japan that he might impose embargoes on the export of raw materials such as steel, iron, and petroleum. Initially, the response of the Japanese government was restrained, but in the spring of 1940, Nazi victories in Europe emboldened the Japanese. A more militant government headed by Prime Minister Fumimaro Konoye came to power in July. Its military leaders decided that the time was ripe to seize French Indochina and the Dutch East Indies, now that Japan had become an Axis partner. That such moves would further antagonize the United States was clear. When the Japanese made incursions into Indochina in July and December, Roosevelt reacted by placing embargoes on the export of aviation gasoline, scrap metals, and other vital materials to Japan. Furious, the Japanese were willing to bide their time in order to bolster their military prowess.

Within the framework of their respective aspirations, the leaders of neither the United States nor Japan felt in 1941 that they could make significant concessions. During April and May, the Konoye government offered various proposals to Washington, including the suggestion that the United States and Japan enter into a neutrality pact. Among other things, such a pact would have allowed the Japanese to seize British, French, and Dutch possessions in Asia. They also suggested a personal meeting between President Roosevelt and Prime Minister Konoye to attempt to settle their differences.

After the German invasion of the Soviet Union in June 1941, the Japanese became bolder and occupied the southern portion of French Indochina. Roosevelt was furious. In July 1941 he closed the Panama Canal to Japanese shipping, impounded Japanese funds in the United States, and extended the embargo to include additional raw materials. Both sides were now taking firmer and more intransigent positions from which retreat was increasingly difficult. Konoye invited Roosevelt to a conference to discuss mutual problems, but the president, heeding the advice of his secretary of state, Cordell Hull, declined to attend unless the Japanese first recognized China's independence. This unwillingness to compromise strengthened the position of militarists in Japan, and in September 1941 they began to make secret war preparations. In October the aggressive militarist Admiral Hideki Tojo became the new prime minister. Although negotiations continued throughout October and November, rigid and opposing positions of Admiral Tojo and Secretary Hull doomed them to failure.

During the last week of November 1941, American intelligence sources surmised that Japanese military leaders were preparing for an attack on either American or Allied possessions. The Departments of the Army and the Navy sent warnings to commanders in the Pacific indicating that Japanese troop and naval movements suggested possible attacks on Guam or the Philippines. No one knew precisely where the Japanese might strike, especially since American intelligence operations were still uncoordinated and frequently channeled confused information to various agencies in Washington. Since many American military men expected an attack on British territories in Singapore or Malaya, they were not overly concerned about other areas. In Hawaii, Admiral Husband E. Kimmel concentrated the Pacific fleet at Pearl Harbor, Hawaii, largely to minimize sabotage. General Walter C. Short rather casually dispersed his forces in the Hawaiian Islands. Thus the United States was caught off guard when a Japanese carrier task force loosed the first wave of 189 planes on American naval vessels and on airfields at Pearl Harbor. Neither this nor a second wave of 171 planes met significant opposition as they attacked the American fleet. All eight U.S. battleships in Oahu harbor were disabled, three cruisers and three destroyers were blown out of the water, and virtually all American planes on the ground were destroyed. Other Japanese forces were simultaneously attacking the Philippines, Hong Kong, Thailand, Malaya, and Wake and Midway islands. Only after the attack did the world receive the news that Japan had declared war on the United States and Great Britain.

On December 8, 1941, President Roosevelt appeared before a tense Congress to ask for a declaration of war against Japan:

> Yesterday, December 7, 1941—a date which will live in infamy—the United States of America was suddenly and deliberately attacked by naval and air forces of the empire of Japan.
>
> As Commander-in-Chief of the Army and Navy, I have directed that all measures be taken for our defense, that always will our whole nation remember the character of the onslaught against us.
>
> No matter how long it may take us to overcome this premeditated invasion, the American people in their righteous might, will win through to absolute victory.
>
> With confidence in our armed forces, with the unbounding determination of our people, we will gain the inevitable triumph, so help us God.

Within a few days Germany and Italy also declared war on the United States. Americans were now engaged in another worldwide conflict.

Disaster at Pearl Harbor: the airfield after the Japanese raid, December 7, 1941. (*Official U.S. Navy Photo*)

Despite the desire of an overwhelming majority of the American people to remain aloof from the war in Europe, by 1941 the United States was once again embroiled in a major conflict. Between 1939 and 1941, circumstances narrowed the alternatives open to American policymakers. Keeping close tabs on public opinion, President Roosevelt had followed a restrained neutrality until June 1940. The fall of France, however, shocked Americans into an acute awareness of what a Nazi victory in Western Europe would mean and led them to support a policy of extensive aid. By the time of Pearl Harbor, the reasons for United States' entry into the war were clear to most Americans. Nazi and Japanese policies were restricting American commercial expansion in Europe and the Far East. The proliferation of Nazi and other totalitarian governments constituted an increasing threat to democracy in the United States and elsewhere. Ultimately, the ideals of freedom and of the Judeo-Christian ethic were being challenged by Nazi doctrines of racial superiority and barbarism. World War II was not fought primarily because of disputes over territory, economic concessions, or political rivalries, although these played a role. From the American point of view, the conflict was generated by the clash of two radically differing ideologies and lifestyles. This became a war for survival.

CHAPTER 12

Restructuring the World Order

Military and Diplomatic Policies 1941–1945

 World War II transformed Roosevelt into a world leader. Although many domestic issues remained unsettled, the nation's major problems between 1941 and 1945 revolved around the war. As commander in chief, Roosevelt assumed the heavy burdens of directing military as well as diplomatic policies at the highest level. It was his responsibility to supervise the military buildup and to determine the most effective deployment of America's might. It was also his task to formulate foreign policy goals and to conduct delicate negotiations with neutral nations as well as with wartime allies.

The attack on Pearl Harbor plunged the United States into global war. Americans were compelled to fight five wars simultaneously. The war in the Pacific—in the Philippines, New Guinea, Midway, and Guam—was foremost in the minds of most Americans right after Pearl Harbor. At the same time, however, a fierce naval war raged in the North Atlantic, where German submarines exacted a costly toll on American and Allied shipping. Within a year Americans also became involved in the campaign against the Germans in North Africa—and soon thereafter played a major role in the invasion of Italy. Once the United States and the Allies entered France in 1944 to strike at the Germans directly, Americans also became involved in a major military operation in western and central Europe.

Roosevelt's Military Policies

The supervision of these extensive military operations was a herculean task. Roosevelt performed the arduous duties of commander in chief with the same relish with which he had wielded executive powers during the New Deal. He sought to balance military, political, and economic considerations with the exigencies of the world situation. Such balancing required the artful handling of military and civilian individuals and groups. The juggling of these myriad divergent interests placed great pressures on the president, yet outwardly he continued to be calm and affable.

Roosevelt's personality profoundly affected his performance during the war. A connoisseur of power, he relished the extraordinary expansion of his authority as he assumed his constitutional duties as commander in chief. Secretary of State Hull later noted that Roosevelt took special pride in this role and, indeed, at state dinners in the White House preferred to be introduced as commander in chief rather than as president. During World War I, Roosevelt had been deeply frustrated by his inability to participate in active service in France since he was serving as assistant secretary of the navy; in World War II, he hoped to participate fully in military planning. He wanted to act as coordinator, mediator, and compromiser. Despite this, Roosevelt maintained his usual independence. In 1942 he overrode the advice of most of his military commanders, who favored greater emphasis on the war against Japan. Instead he authorized large-scale American involvement in the Allied invasion of North Africa. Roosevelt also insisted on the *unconditional* surrender of the Axis powers, although some of his critics argued that it could prolong German resistance. In opposition to British Prime Minister Winston Churchill, Roosevelt favored the opening of a second front in France rather than in the Balkans. Churchill feared that this would open central and eastern Europe to Soviet influence.

Roosevelt's first priority, however, was a quick military victory, and he felt that a new French front was the way to achieve it. Unlike the British or the Russians, he was less inclined to give primacy to long-range political objectives to be attained after the fighting stopped. Mostly, he and other Americans wanted and expected a quick end to the war.

Roosevelt maintained close relationships with his military leaders. His personal contacts with Chief of Staff General George C. Marshall were as cordial as those with Admiral of the Fleet Harold King and Air Force General Hap Arnold. If he had relatively few serious policy disagreements with these men, this was largely because of the mutual respect they felt. There was little turnover in the American high command during wartime.

Without question, Roosevelt's wartime mobilization guided the evolution of a military-industrial complex whose influence was to persist and even increase after World War II. Effective mobilization required a closely coordinated effort among business, industry, and military and government officials. Such cooperation was characteristic of President Wilson's economic mobilization in World War I, in which Roosevelt himself had played an integral role. During the war, close relations between business and government multiplied. Entire cities such as Knoxville, Tennessee; Los Alamos, New Mexico; and Hanford, Washington, became largely dependent on national security expenditures. In this fashion, the war years fostered the growth of the military-industrial complex in the United States. Unwittingly perhaps, President Roosevelt created the organizational structure in which this network of relationships between individuals in industry, the military, and government was to flourish. As the chief executive himself noted in 1943, Dr. New Deal had retired to become Dr. Win the War.

World War II mobilization resulted in the establishment of the largest American military force in the nation's history. By 1944 the army had mobilized more than 12 million men and women into an awesome striking force. The navy was at peak strength, consisting of more than 3.4 million men and women, the largest naval force in the world. And the air force, with fewer than 300 planes in 1939, had more than 260,000 aircraft just five years later.

The War Fronts, 1941–1945

The price of victory was far greater than most Americans expected it would be at the time of Pearl Harbor. Indeed, the first year of the war was characterized mainly by retreat. Only in 1943 were American and Allied forces able to mount offensives, and not until 1944 was military triumph over Germany and Japan in sight.

The military situation early in 1942 was grim. In the Pacific, the Japanese appeared to be sweeping all before them. They overran the oil-rich Netherlands East Indies, fortified the jungles of New Guinea, occupied Burma, and took control of hundreds of small islands in the central and southern Pacific, including the Gilbert and Marshall islands, Guam, Wake Island, and Singapore. In well-executed campaigns, the Japanese defeated American forces in the Philippines. Outnumbered and isolated from supplies, American army and naval units fought a valiant but losing battle under Generals Douglas MacArthur and Nicholas B. Wainwright. By May 1942 the Japanese had broken American resistance on the islands. They forced their prisoners to submit to the grueling Bataan Death March, which ended in their confinement in prison camps, and gloated over General Wainwright's surrender. On the seas, Japanese naval squadrons destroyed an Allied fleet at the Battle of the Java Sea (March 1, 1942). In subsequent naval engagements—the Battle of the Coral Sea (May 7, 1942) and the Battle of Midway (June 3, 1942)—American forces were able to contain the Japanese tide and to inflict losses. The stunning first year of the Pacific war dispelled the illusion of some Americans that defeat of the Japanese would be quick and easy.

At the same time, the United States Navy was preoccupied with the menace of German submarines in the Atlantic. During most of 1942 packs of U-boats roamed along the American sea lanes to England, sinking about three ships daily—or more than 1,000 vessels yearly. The rate of ship destruction was at least three times as great as the ability of United States shipyards to replace them. And as the flow of American supplies to England increased in 1942, the navy found itself short of escort vessels to protect the long Allied convoys across the ocean. Throughout 1942 the navy and the shipbuilders and repairers grappled with this serious crisis in the North Atlantic.

In Europe and the Middle East, Nazi forces advanced relentlessly. German armies penetrated deep into the interior of the Soviet Union. Throughout occupied France, the Low Countries, and Norway and Denmark, the Germans solidified their military stronghold. In the Middle East, the German Afrika Korps under German General Erwin Rommel drove back Allied armies and threatened to seize the Suez Canal—the British lifeline for oil and other essential supplies.

The tide of battle turned slowly in 1943 and 1944, when the United States and the Allies, bolstered by the American production effort, started to take the offensive. Beginning in August 1943, the navy and the marines began costly campaigns to recapture the Pacific from well-entrenched, determined Japanese forces. A campaign to oust the Japanese from the Aleutian Islands in the northern Pacific began in August 1943; that November, U.S. Marines fought bitterly to recapture the Gilbert Islands; February 1944 found them assaulting the Marshall Islands, on hundreds of tiny atolls in the region, and in the steamy hot jungles of New Guinea. Meanwhile, the U.S. Navy developed various methods to combat the German submarines in the Atlantic. By use of special air patrols and newly developed radar devices, detection became easier. The navy sunk 237 German submarines in 1943. And American shipyards were now producing vast quantities of ships and escort vessels to provide protection for convoys. By 1943, United States shipping losses had been cut to less than 1 percent of traffic in the Atlantic.

Elsewhere, the Allied position had also improved. In Europe, American and British air forces carried out massive bombing attacks on German industrial areas in an effort to cripple war production. Throughout 1943 and 1944, fleets of 1,000 to 1,500 Allied bombers dotted the German skies, raining a hail of destruction on factories, railroads, and, inevitably, civilian areas in Germany. In the east the Soviet army revealed unusual strength and courage by routing the Germans during the siege of Stalingrad, now called Volgograd (November 1942 to February 1943). Not only were the Soviets able to defend the city, but they also seized the initiative to begin a long, persistent campaign to drive the Germans out of the Soviet Union. At the same time,

American, British and Free French forces were mounting an offensive in North Africa, where they destroyed General Rommel's army and ended the German threat to the Suez Canal (October 1942 to May 1943). Next they crossed the Mediterranean to Sicily and then invaded Italy directly. By the summer of 1943, the Italians had withdrawn from the war, although strong German resistance in northern Italy continued.

The mood of the Allies became more optimistic in early 1944. The defeat of the Axis was in the future, but the military initiative had clearly shifted to the Allies. On June 6, 1944, American and British forces under Supreme Allied Commander General Dwight D. Eisenhower launched the long awaited D-Day from England, a massive invasion across the English Channel to open a major second front in France. More than 2 million Americans waded ashore on the Normandy beachhead and marched into the interior of France. Amid much jubilation, the Allies captured Paris on August 25, 1944, and then turned east toward Germany. Around Christmas, German resistance grew unexpectedly fiercer and more effective. At the Battle of the Bulge in Belgium in December 1944, the Allies narrowly missed being driven back by the still-powerful German army. Meanwhile, the Soviet army broke German lines and by January 1945 was speeding across Poland toward the German border. In spring 1945 the Soviet armies began their invasion of Germany from the east while the American and Allied army converged from the west. General Eisenhower restrained his forces and ordered General George S. Patton to draw back from Prague, Czechoslovakia, so that the victorious Soviets could be first to enter Berlin. Recognizing imminent defeat, Hitler and his closest confidants presumably committed suicide in an underground bunker in the city just a few days before the invasion of Berlin. Most of the other leaders of Nazi Germany were in flight. The Soviets occupied Poland, Czechoslovakia, and eastern Germany. On May 7, 1945, a temporary German government under Admiral Karl Doenitz surrendered unconditionally. Americans wildly celebrated Victory in Europe (VE) Day.

The defeat of Germany enabled the United States to shift a major part of its military force to the Far East. After the recapture of the Philippines in May 1944, the consolidation of supply lines, and establishment of air bases, American strength steadily grew in the Pacific. But Chief of Staff General George C. Marshall and Pacific Commander General Douglas MacArthur believed that U.S. strategy required the capture of the island approaches to Japan and eventually a direct invasion of Japan itself. In view of strong Japanese resistance, they expected the war to continue for at least a year or longer after victory in Europe, and they feared that their planned assaults would entail the loss of perhaps a million American lives. In 1944 they began a series of destructive air raids on Japan in which hundreds of American planes rained bombs on Japanese industrial areas and cities.

As Japanese hopes for victory faded, their resistance became more ferocious. Even after much of the remaining Japanese navy was destroyed in October 1944 in the Battle of Leyte Gulf, the Japanese navy began a major counteroffensive designed to weaken the U.S. position in the Philippines. The U.S. Third and Seventh Fleets under Admirals Bull Halsey and Thomas C. Kincaid were ready for them. In a series of elaborate maneuvers, the U.S. Navy sank three battleships and ten cruisers while sustaining only light losses. In China, in Burma, and on countless small islands in the Pacific, Japanese soldiers fought bitterly to the death—both theirs and that of their assailants. The Americans captured Iwo Jima in February 1945 and Okinawa in March. Both islands were strategically located to serve as bomber bases and as potential stepping stones for an invasion of the Japanese mainland. Their capture by U.S. Marines resulted in the downfall of the Japanese militarist regime of Admiral Tojo. Yet the war continued, and many American leaders feared that it would be long and difficult.

Roosevelt's World War II Diplomacy

World War II altered the course of American diplomacy. Whereas the national mood between 1919 and 1939 had leaned toward isolation, by 1945 wartime experience had convinced a majority of Americans that world leadership, collaboration with other powers, and foreign intervention provided the surest and most practical road to a lasting postwar peace. The necessities and vicissitudes of the postwar era helped to produce this metamorphosis in United States diplomacy as much as Roosevelt's leadership of the Allies.

Early in the war, Roosevelt became convinced that the United States would have to take the initiative in preventing neutral nations from joining the Axis cause. Thus he embarked on an active campaign to woo Vichy France, Spain, and Portugal. Vichy France, the southern area of the country initially unoccupied by the Germans, was still nevertheless under German influence, but its government controlled the bulk of the French navy as well as important military bases in Algeria and North Africa. The authority of this collaborationist regime—headed by Marshal Henri Pétain—was openly challenged by the anti-Nazi, Free French government-in-exile headquartered in London. General Charles de Gaulle was its spokesman. Roosevelt's sympathies lay clearly with the latter, but he was anxious to prevent German seizure of France's fleet and its North African possessions. Consequently, Roosevelt recognized the pro-German Vichy regime and, under the Murphy-Weygand Agreement of 1940, authorized American aid for it. His action aroused bitter hostility from General de Gaulle and a great many critics, but Roosevelt achieved his goal of preventing Nazi expansion in French North Africa, thus facilitating the Allied offensive in that region during the fall of 1942.

This same kind of pragmatism colored Roosevelt's policy toward Spain.

General Francisco Franco was an avowed Nazi sympathizer. Roosevelt knew that Spain's strategic location, especially its proximity to Gibraltar and its safe access to the Mediterranean Sea, was essential to Allied military operations in that region, so he labored to keep Spain from joining the Axis powers. His prime instrument was economic. A poor nation, Spain desperately needed lucrative export markets. The United States arranged to purchase a variety of Spanish exports, including more than 90 percent of its tungsten. In return, the Spanish received sorely needed American petroleum supplies. Such economic diplomacy, combined with the declining fortunes of the Nazis, persuaded General Franco to maintain a discreet neutrality, which was of inestimable benefit to the Allied cause. Secretary of State Hull cultivated the neutrality of the Portuguese government by offering economic aid in exchange for strategic American air bases in the Azores, located in the South Atlantic.

American policy toward the neutrals after 1941 was certainly not isolationist; rather, Roosevelt emphasized close collaboration to maintain a neutrality that was of prime benefit to the United States.

In 1942 the United States took the lead in fashioning a Grand Alliance against the Axis. Soon after Pearl Harbor, Roosevelt announced the formation of the United Nations, to be composed of countries opposed to Axis expansion. In the Declaration of the United Nations on January 1, 1942, these nations endorsed the principles of the Atlantic Charter and pledged themselves not to conclude a separate peace. By establishing this new alliance, Roosevelt hoped to replace the defunct League of Nations and to lay the groundwork for the creation of a more effectively structured organization to maintain international order in the postwar era.

The United States developed its closest friendship with the British. In 1942, Roosevelt and Churchill established the Combined Chiefs of Staff, which included the ranking military commanders of each nation. In their many meetings they jointly decided on military strategy, planned campaigns, and allocated supplies and resources. Despite conflicts and differences of opinion, the Combined Chiefs were remarkably effective in coordinating their joint ventures. The work of the many international committees achieved a high level of successful coordination, a marked contrast to the limited collaboration during World War I.

A large part of the American-British alliance was due to the cordial personal relationship between Roosevelt and Churchill. Although the two men had their differences—most notably over self-determination for British colonies—these were transcended by their bonds of common interest. Both men realized that close cooperation was in the best interest of their respective nations. Both shared a sense of history, of the common fate of the English-speaking peoples, and of the Anglo-American tradition of democracy. And as Roosevelt admired English culture, so Churchill's American-born mother made him especially sensitive to American traditions. These ties were reflected in Churchill's address to Congress on December 26, 1941:

> You do not, I am certain, underrate the severity of the ordeal to which you and we still have to be subjected. The forces ranged against us are enormous. They are bitter. They are ruthless. . . . They will stop at nothing. . . . We have, therefore, without doubt, a time of tribulation before us. . . . Many disappointments and unpleasant surprises await us.
>
> We have indeed to be thankful that so much time has been granted us. If Germany had tried to invade the British Isles after the French collapse in June 1940 and if Japan had declared war on the British Empire and the United States at about the same time, no one can say what disasters and agonies might not have been our lot. But now, at the end of December 1941, our transformation from easygoing peace to total war efficiency has made very great progress. . . .
>
> Now that we are together, now that we are linked in a righteous comradeship of arms, now that our two considerable nations, each in perfect unity, have joined all their life energies in a common resolve, a new scene opens upon which a steady light will glow and brighten. . . . Here we are together defending all that to free men is dear.
>
> It is not given to us to peer into the mysteries of the future. Still I avow my hope and faith . . . that in the days to come the British and American people will for their own safety and for the good of all walk together in majesty, in justice, and in peace.

Throughout the war the two leaders were in close communication, often on a daily basis. Churchill would send cables through the American embassy in London around 2 A.M. The embassy would then send these directly to the White House through special coding machines so that Roosevelt could read them before he went to bed. And when Churchill awoke the next morning, he would often find a response waiting from Roosevelt.

American relations with the Soviets were not as close as with the British. The mutual distrust that arose from the differing political stances of the Americans and the Soviets was tempered but not wholly removed by wartime exigencies requiring close collaboration. The Soviet government muted its Communist propaganda against the Western nations and paid lip service to the Atlantic Charter, and the Roosevelt administration authorized large-scale Lend-Lease aid for the Soviets. During the war the United States sent more than $11 billion in supplies to the USSR through the Pacific port of Vladivostok. This aid was significant in enabling Soviet armies to repel the Nazi onslaught. Roosevelt also cultivated a closer personal relationship with Soviet Premier Joseph Stalin.

Roosevelt felt that a harmonious working collaboration between the United States and the Soviet Union was absolutely essential to a lasting postwar peace. Churchill often expressed his distrust of Roosevelt's assumption—and of Soviet motives as well—earning him Roosevelt's annoyance and Stalin's ire. The uneasy relation between the Soviets and the Western powers, however, was a working part of the Grand Alliance.

In the Far East, Roosevelt hoped to solidify American wartime alliances by providing extensive support for Nationalist China, led by General Chiang Kai-shek. The Nationalist Chinese had been fighting the Japanese since 1937 with only moderate success, and after 1941 the United States sought to stiffen their resistance. Thus Roosevelt authorized more than $4 billion in Lend-Lease aid to Nationalist China and also extended more than $100 million in loans. In addition, the United States sent military advisers to train the Chinese army. The two nations signed various treaties in 1943, under which the United States gave up its extraterritorial rights in China while at the same time lifting the ban on Chinese immigrants that had been in effect since 1924. Although in theory Nationalist China ranked as one of the major powers in the Grand Alliance, in fact the weakness of the Chiang Kai-shek regime led the country to play a secondary role.

World War II also provided Roosevelt with a further opportunity to solidify his Good Neighbor policy toward Latin American nations and to bring them into the Alliance against the Axis. At the Inter-American Conference at Rio de Janeiro in 1942, the nations of the Western Hemisphere, except Argentina and Chile, agreed to break diplomatic relations with the Axis. Eventually they all declared war on Germany. Meanwhile, the United States secured military bases in Brazil, Cuba, Ecuador, and Panama.

Despite a strong spirit of collaboration and goodwill among the members of the Grand Alliance, invariably they also had their differences, which generated international conferences at the highest level. Soon after the Allied invasion of North Africa in January 1942, British, American, and Free French leaders felt the need to confer on the next steps in their military strategy. They arranged to meet in Casablanca, Morocco. Roosevelt, Churchill, de Gaulle, and chief military advisers deliberated on the issues before them. After considerable discussion, they agreed that Allied forces should next launch an assault on Italy. In addition, they accepted Roosevelt's proposal to demand unconditional surrender from the Axis.

When the Soviet government began the slow and arduous task of driving the Nazis from inside its borders, Stalin became more insistent on the opening of a second front in the West to relieve the pressure on his forces. The issue was fraught with many complexities, and it caused a divergence of views among the Allies. The United States and the Soviet Union favored an assault through France; the British wanted to attack through the Balkans. To resolve this and lesser issues, Roosevelt, Churchill, and Stalin planned a conference. They met in November 1943 at Teheran, Iran (Stalin had insisted that he could not venture far from Moscow). On their way to Teheran,

The Big Three at Teheran, Iran: Franklin D. Roosevelt, Winston Churchill, and Joseph Stalin, 1943. (*U.S. Army Signal Corps*)

Roosevelt and Churchill stopped in Cairo to meet with Chiang and de Gaulle to discuss the next phase in the war against Germany and Japan. Then the leaders of the Big Three met for the first time in Teheran. Amid much pomp and ceremony, they discussed some of the major issues of wartime strategy. Roosevelt and Stalin prevailed over the dubious Churchill to agree that a second front must be opened within the coming year. They also discussed the political future of Germany and Soviet eagerness to enter the war in the Pacific. On his return, Roosevelt reported to Congress:

> I have recently returned from extensive journeyings in the region of the Mediterranean and as far as the borders of Russia. . . . At Cairo and Teheran we devoted ourselves not only to military matters; . . . we devoted ourselves also to the consideration of the future, to plans for the kind of world which alone can justify all the sacrifices of this war. It was well worth traveling thousands of miles over land and sea to bring about this personal meeting with Chiang Kai-shek and Winston Churchill and Marshal Stalin.
>
> I believe, and I think I can say, the other three great nations we are fighting so magnificently to gain peace are in complete agreement that we must be prepared to keep the peace by force. If the people of Germany and Japan are made to realize thoroughly that the world is not going to let them

break out again, it is possible and, I hope, probable, that they will abandon the philosophy of aggression.

Roosevelt was encouraged by his first meeting with Stalin to believe that he and the Soviet leader could work together not only to shape wartime strategy but also to lay the foundations for a postwar peace. Churchill, in contrast, came away from Teheran with a greater mistrust than ever of the Soviet leader.

Although Teheran had allowed the three leaders to take measure of each other, many issues remained unresolved. Soon after the presidential election of 1944, therefore, Roosevelt made plans to meet with Churchill and Stalin again, this time at Yalta, a Black Sea resort. With military victory almost in sight, the Big Three grappled with even thornier problems of postwar politics. Stalin was intent on expanding Soviet influence in central and eastern Europe as well as in the Far East. The Western statesmen wanted to ensure self-determination and democratic governments for these areas. After exploring each other's views in some detail, a series of compromises was set. Germany was not dismembered but was divided into four zones of occupation. Poland, where communists were vying with anticommunists for control, was to hold national elections, albeit under the watchful eye of the occupying Soviet army. The Soviet Union agreed to declare war on Japan at the right moment—despite doubts by some American military leaders that such action was necessary. Roosevelt took pride in persuading the Soviets to participate in the organization of the United Nations, with details to be worked out at a San Francisco conference in June 1945.

The decisions at Yalta have been argued at length over the years. Some historians believed that Roosevelt yielded too much to Stalin and thus gave the Soviets hegemony in eastern Europe. Others felt that he had succeeded in laying the groundwork for closer collaboration between the United States and the Soviet Union. The Yalta agreements constituted a bundle of compromises that seemed functional at the time but were not fully satisfactory to any participant. More important for the United States, Yalta signaled the end of peacetime isolationism and a new postwar era of collaboration among nations.

CHAPTER 13

Mobilizing for War

Expansion of the
Organizational Society
1941–1945

 American involvement in World War II greatly hastened the development of a more highly organized society in the United States. Already the crisis of the Depression had brought greater centralization in government, the economy, and social and cultural life. The war accelerated this trend.

Rarely had the American people shown such self-discipline and unity as they did during World War II. They entrusted the direction of most wartime activities to a vastly expanded federal bureaucracy; they gave wholehearted support to centralization in the American economy to achieve maximum production; they relaxed prejudices against minority groups and women for the sake of wartime unity, and they even organized their cultural activities to boost their morale. More than any previous conflict, World War II prompted an unprecedented national effort to mobilize materials and human resources for the common effort.

War and American Bureaucracy

Federal organization in wartime was haphazard. Roosevelt organized and reorganized countless agencies. He showed little concern for their overlapping functions. Even on an organization chart, many of the agencies made little sense to planners accustomed to the well-defined delegation of authority. Yet the cumbersome organizational machine Roosevelt created worked well, mostly because it harnessed the potential abilities of millions of Americans. Roosevelt himself was perhaps more concerned with stimulating a massive mobilization effort by the entire nation than with any administrative rationale that would explain the activity. Thus the establishment and consolidation of particular wartime agencies tended to be haphazard, the product of short-range pressures rather than long-range planning.

Once the United States formally entered the war, Roosevelt undertook more comprehensive federal direction of the national economy. In January 1942 he created the War Production Board (WPB) to supervise production and distribution of a wide range of industrial products. To direct the new agency, Roosevelt appointed Donald Nelson, who hailed from Hannibal, Missouri. Shortly after graduation from the state university as a chemist in 1912, he joined Sears, Roebuck and Company and began a long and steady climb up its corporate ladder. By 1939 he was executive vice-president of Sears and one of the most knowledgeable retailers in the nation.

The WPB had a stormy life, full of frustrations and conflicts. Its broad powers touched on most phases of American business. Indeed, many of its critics charged that it was dominated by large corporations that received favored treatment. At the same time, Nelson was extremely sensitive to the demands of military leaders, who often played a major role in determining production priorities, even to the detriment of the civilian sector. Because of the frenzied efforts and intensive pressures to which the WPB was subject, confusion became one of its marked characteristics. Since Roosevelt did not grant the WPB authority to control prices, Nelson had to work with other agencies in the federal bureaucracy. His authority was often challenged. That was especially true of the Office of Price Administration (OPA), to which the president delegated authority over prices in January 1942. Administratively, it was cumbersome for the chief executive to grant one agency the power to allocate production priorities and another the power to regulate prices. But Roosevelt felt that the existence of creative tensions between competing agencies added to their overall effectiveness. From 1942 to 1944 the OPA was under the direction of Chester Bowles, a dynamic and controversial leader. The scion of an old New England family, Bowles had graduated from Yale University in 1924 and had become a journalist. In 1929 he organized his own advertising agency, Benton and Bowles, which in the course of the next decade grew to be one of the most prominent. Roosevelt knew that few men had a more intimate knowledge of consumers, business, and merchandising than Chester Bowles. The OPA's primary function was to set price ceilings for thousands of nonagricultural goods and to retard inflationary pressures to protect consumers. Since the WPB was seeking to placate manufacturers and producers in an effort to stimulate maximum production, its recommendations for ceiling prices were usually much higher than those stipulated by the OPA. Thus the two agencies frequently came into conflict.

On October 3, 1942, Roosevelt created still another agency, the Office of Economic Stabilization (OES), directed by James F. Byrnes. A former governor of South Carolina, a U.S. senator, and a U.S. Supreme Court justice, Byrnes was a moderate and conciliatory patrician whose great prestige in Washington made him an imposing figure. In an effort to unravel production snarls and imbalances and to settle conflicts between the WPB and the Department of War, the OES concentrated on rigid control of supplies of three strategic raw materials: steel, aluminum, and copper. Through stringent oversight of production, Byrnes was able to regulate the flow of finished products. In addition, he had authority over labor recruitment and wage levels. Despite intense pressures from farm, labor, and industrial groups, Byrnes was successful in holding down inflation.

Byrnes was soon second only to Roosevelt in authority to direct the nation's war mobilization effort. Late in 1944, as quarrels within the WPB rendered it ineffective, Byrnes gained even more power when he became director of a new agency, the Office of War Mobilization and Reconversion. His responsibilities now included postwar planning, particularly the job of guiding the economy from wartime to peacetime status. Aware that President Wilson's refusal to plan for peace in 1919 and 1920 had in part precipitated the Depression, President Roosevelt was anxious in 1944 and 1945 to avoid a repetition of that sad chapter in the nation's history.

The administration did not engage in the blatant censorship or hatemongering that had been characteristic of World War I, but it exercised some wartime control over the media. To a considerable extent this control was possible because of the credibility of the newspeople who took on these major responsibilities. At the time of Pearl Harbor, the president asked Byron Price, a news editor for the Associated Press, to become director of an office of censorship. Its main function was to examine all letters or communications between the United States and foreign nations. Price also issued the Code of Wartime Practices for publishers and broadcasters, which banned news concerning troop movements or war casualties.

Roosevelt assigned propaganda responsibilities to the Office of War Information (OWI), which he created in 1942. One of the nation's most respected radio news commentators, Elmer Davis, served as its director. He was able to attract to the agency a sizable number of advertising executives who showed great skill in cultivating patriotism at home through radio broadcasts, pamphlets, and posters. At the same time, the OWI beamed broadcasts overseas to sustain resistance movements in German-occupied territories.

Unlike most major powers, the United States entered World War II without a central agency responsible for collecting and disseminating intelligence reports or for coordinating espionage. In fact, the confusion at Pearl Harbor was caused in part by the absence of a central clearinghouse for intelligence information. Soon afterward, President Roosevelt established the Office of Strategic Services (OSS) and appointed career army officer

General James J. Donovan its director. The OSS became the nation's first official intelligence agency. In addition to enlisting its own operatives and sources of information in the United States and elsewhere, the OSS organized the intelligence activities of scores of other federal agencies and the armed services.

One of the most significant extensions of federal authority was in the field of science. Although the national government had encouraged various forms of scientific endeavor over the years, it had not undertaken a comprehensive program. War urgencies led Roosevelt to organize a unified national effort. In June 1940, in the midst of the rearmament effort, the president yielded to the pleas of leading scientists to create the National Defense Research Committee, which matched government needs with available scientific resources. A year later Roosevelt established the Office of Scientific Research and Development (OSRD), endowed with direct authority to sponsor scientific research useful to national security. He chose Vannevar Bush, a leading scientist who had served as president of Johns Hopkins University, as its director. By coordinating scientists and scientific projects and by initiating new inquiries, the OSRD made many significant contributions to the war effort. Among its most brilliant breakthroughs was the development of radar and sonar devices, which proved essential in the victory over Nazi submarines in the Atlantic and in aerial warfare. Invention of the proximity fuse, a miniature radio set in a shell that detonated it by proximity to a target, ushered in the age of guided missiles. The OSRD also made great advances in the development of blood plasma, which greatly reduced battlefield casualties. In World War I, nine out of ten wounded in combat succumbed to injuries, but in World War II, the ratio was reversed and only one out of ten died from battle wounds. Great progress was also made in the development of insecticides such as DDT, which eased the burdens of Americans fighting in the Pacific, who often found unfamiliar insects almost as deadly as the Japanese.

But the most complicated scientific enterprise sponsored by the OSRD was the fabrication of an atomic bomb. Early in 1939, German scientists had accomplished nuclear fission, which made it possible to consider eventual production of a powerful bomb. Aware of German advances, scientists in the United States, notably physicists Enrico Fermi and Albert Einstein, persuaded the administration to sponsor its own atomic program. The OSRD assumed responsibility for this program in 1941. Known as the Manhattan Project, its director, Major General Leslie Groves, embarked on a far-flung program to coordinate scientific talent. Thousands of scientists in the United States and around the world cooperated in the development of the bomb. Much research was accomplished in Chicago; Berkeley, California; and Los Alamos, New Mexico. Plutonium materials for the bomb were manufactured in Oak Ridge, Tennessee, and Hanford, Washington. The vast effort came to fruition in July 1945, when scientists at Los Alamos, working feverishly under the prodding of their director, the brilliant physicist Dr. J. Robert Oppenheimer, finally assembled an atomic bomb. On July 16, 1945, they successfully detonated the first atomic blast in world history at Alamogordo, New Mexico. In the opinion of some historians, the atomic bomb shortened the Pacific war.

Despite intense rivalries and conflicts within the agencies in Washington, they successfully managed the extraordinarily complex problems of national mobilization. Roosevelt's persuasive leadership was the cement that held his disparate administrators and their agencies together while the war experience accelerated the trend toward greater bureaucratic control over many phases of the nation's life. Decision making by individuals was often supplanted by decision making on the part of public agencies. And to sustain themselves, the officials of these agencies often sought to expand their powers and their size.

War and the Economy

The direction of domestic mobilization gave government a more central role in directing the national economy. World War II saw the development of the military-industrial complex and the subsequent close alliance between government officials and executives of large corporations. Industry executives went to work for the federal government without compensation except a token dollar annually (and became known as "dollar-a-year men"), and federal officials often secured high-paying jobs in private industry after leaving government service. The alliance led to a phenomenal production record. Aircraft manufacturing production in 1943 was twice what it had been the previous year (see Table 13-1). The individual income of Americans in-

Table 13-1
U.S. Aircraft Production, 1940–1945

Year	Aircraft Production
1940	3,807
1941	19,433
1942	47,836
1943	85,898
1944	96,318
1945	46,001

Source: Wesley Frank Craven et al. (eds.), *The Army Air Forces in World War II* (Chicago, 1955), vol. 6, p. 352.

creased correspondingly from $77.6 billion in 1940 to $161.0 billion in 1945 (see Table 13-2). The gross national product (GNP) rose from $60 billion in 1940 to $170 billion in 1945. And the national debt skyrocketed (see Table 13-3). At the end of the war, most Americans felt that the Depression—which the New Deal had been unable to shake off—seemed like a bad dream.

The war hastened further concentration of American industry. Fifty-six of the largest companies in the United States received three-fourths of all the federal war contracts. The ten biggest ones garnered almost one-third of the $175 billion awarded in war contracts. To a considerable degree, technological and economic necessity dictated these choices, for planes, tanks, and guns could not be manufactured efficiently by small companies; huge plants employing thousands of workers on assembly lines were more efficient for such production.

Table 13-2
Total National Income, 1939–1945

Year	Total National Income (in billions of dollars)
1939	70.8
1940	77.6
1941	96.9
1942	122.2
1943	149.4
1944	160.7
1945	161.0

Source: *Historical Statistics of the United States.*

Table 13-3
National Debt, 1939–1945

Year	National Debt (in billions of dollars)
1939	42.9
1940	42.9
1941	48.9
1942	72.4
1943	136.6
1944	201.0
1945	258.6

Source: *Historical Statistics of the United States.*

Aviation and automobile manufacturers built more than 300,000 airplanes, 88,140 tanks, and 3,000 merchant ships. Some increased their output significantly. That was the case with aluminum production. Before 1940 the Aluminum Company of America (Alcoa) had held a virtual monopoly on its product. Increasing war demands, however, made its total production so painfully inadequate that Roosevelt ordered a crash program to increase production. Congress authorized more than $300 million for construction of new plants in the Columbia River valley of the Pacific Northwest, where the Bonneville and Grand Coulee federal power projects would furnish cheap electricity. Other plants were built near the Tennessee Valley Authority, operated by Alcoa and new competitors like Reynolds and Kaiser.

Production increases were also achieved when thousands of businesses shifted from civilian to war manufactures. A canning company shifted to the fabrication of parts for merchant ships; a manufacturer of mechanical pencils made bomb parts; a bedding manufacturer turned to mosquito nets; a soft drink bottler loaded shells with explosives. As manufacturers suspended the production of civilian goods, they were able to boost supplies of wartime products in a relatively short period.

Although the government's share of the nation's capital goods had rarely exceeded 10 percent during the first four decades of the twentieth century, between 1941 and 1945 this proportion doubled, largely because the Roosevelt administration used public funds to build and equip new manufacturing plants in the United States. After the war, many large corporations were allowed to purchase these facilities for a fraction of their original cost.

Of the new major industries stimulated by the war, synthetic rubber was prominent. When the Japanese captured the Dutch East Indies in 1941, they cut off a major source of America's supply of natural rubber. In this emergency President Roosevelt ordered a crash program to produce a synthetic substitute. Through funds granted by the Reconstruction Finance Corporation, the federal government poured more than $400 million into the construction of new facilities. By 1944, factories produced more than 800,000 tons of synthetic rubber, making the United States virtually self-sufficient for most of its civilian and military needs for this product.

The war fostered more efficient organization of industry and its use of new techniques. A striking illustration was the career of Henry J. Kaiser, a former contractor and builder who in 1941 was attracted to the shipbuilding industry. Scoffing at the methods of older companies in the industry, Kaiser introduced mass production methods, with revolutionary results. In 1940 it took Todd Shipyards more than 300 days to produce a single merchant vessel; in 1942 Kaiser reduced that time to eighty days, and in 1944 his yards set a record by completing a 10,000-ton liberty ship in just seventeen days. Kaiser achieved his remarkable records by using prefabricated materials,

Building ships during World War II: the Kaiser shipyards in Portland, Oregon, 1942. (*U.S. Navy photo*)

closely coordinating diverse processes, and motivating his workers with high pay and attractive fringe benefits.

Harnessing the nation's labor power to wartime needs strengthened the role of organizations such as labor unions. After 1939, the booming war industries drew on the pool of unemployed left by the Depression, and American workers enjoyed rising wages despite federal efforts to freeze salaries for the first time in a decade. By 1942 the once elusive goal of full employment had been reached. At the end of the war, more than 53 million were employed, including teenagers, women, the aged, and minorities previously excluded by discrimination. At the same time, the number of workers organized in unions also rose appreciably, from 7 million to 15 million. Thanks to the generally cooperative spirit of the nation, less than 1 percent of working time was lost due to strikes. The American worker, like the entrepreneur and the farmer, found that large organizations had become vital instruments for achieving the twin goals of economic security and employment.

Federal financial policies did much to stimulate the phenomenal economic expansion that characterized the American war effort. Federal agencies subsidized the efforts of millions of employers and employees engaged in the war effort. Altogether, the treasury pumped $320 billion into the economy, thus lifting the nation out of the Depression and into a new era of prosperity and full employment. At the same time, these expenditures led federal officials to make their methods of tax collection more efficient. Congress imposed an excess-profits tax on business, whereby extraordinarily high profits reverted to the treasury. To avoid a possible postwar depression, though, federal regulations permitted companies to claim refunds on wartime tax payments to cover possible losses in the future. Another innovation was the payroll deduction; by withholding taxes at the source, the Internal Revenue Service increased efficiency and lowered collection costs. Through tax policies, as well as through mandatory ceiling prices imposed by the Office of Price Administration, the federal government was able to contain wartime inflation. During the war years, price increases did not exceed an average rate of 5 percent annually.

What the war experience revealed to the American people was that the federal government, if necessary, could effectively manage the economy. It could stimulate production, facilitate full employment, create a higher standard of living, and still keep the nation solvent. That role, many Americans felt, should be continued after the war, lest the nation again sink into depression and mass unemployment.

Many Americans realized that full employment and prosperity were due largely to extensive federal expenditures related to the war effort. This seemed to provide the evidence that proponents of Keynesian economic theories needed to persuade their doubters. Lord John Maynard Keynes, a British economist, advocated deficit spending by governments in time of depression and manipulation of taxes and interest rates to generate economic prosperity. The solution to depression and unemployment seemed at hand. Did the war not prove the theory? This belief buoyed both Democrats and Republicans and led government at every level to hire trained economists. Indeed, during the war and thereafter, economists played an increasingly important role in American society and the formation of public policy.

Agriculture also rose to the challenge. Farmers increased their production by almost one-third, providing food not only for domestic consumption and the nation's armed forces but also for American allies, especially Great Britain and the Soviet Union. Their achievement was especially remarkable in view of the fact that the farm population had declined by 17 percent between 1940 and 1945 as farmers went to cities to take lucrative jobs in industry. Moreover, farm labor was woefully inadequate. If high production quotas were met by farmers, it was due not only to increased individual effort but also to increasing mechanization. The use of a machine such as the mechanical cotton picker and of new chemicals and insecticides reduced staffing needs. Farm size also increased as larger units absorbed smaller or less efficient operations.

America's phenomenal production record in manufacturing, farming, and labor was admired throughout the world. It made Americans aware of the enormous potential in human and material resources that had gone unused during the bitter years of the Depression. Rightly or wrongly, Americans came to perceive that full employment and maximum production were somehow closely related to increased government activity in an economy in which large corporations played a major role. The federal government could, the World War II experience revealed, provide needed investment capital and regulate levels of consumer demand so as to maintain full employment. This belief strengthened the faith of millions of Americans in the role of big government, big business, agriculture, and labor unions in dealing with the nation's major problems. Americans thus entered the postwar era with a positive, if somewhat naive, belief in the efficacy of an organizational society.

Politics in Wartime

The war did not lead to a suspension of political activities. After Pearl Harbor, the national chairmen of the Democratic and the Republican parties announced that they would keep politics out of the war, but political processes continued to operate. Opponents of the New Deal feared that the president would expand reforms under the guise of wartime necessity, and supporters of the president often appealed to patriotism in order to gain political advantages. The number of voters declined during the war, in part because persons in the armed forces sometimes found it difficult to obtain absentee ballots, and highly paid war workers were disinclined to take time off to vote. Then, too, since so many Americans moved about and changed residences, they often did not meet local residency requirements for voting.

The trend toward conservatism that had begun as a reaction to the New Deal continued to gather strength during the war. Many New Deal policies were suspended in the heat of war, in part because of the pressures of a conservative coalition in Congress composed of southern Democrats and Republicans. This coalition began to gather strength in 1938 and continued to attract followers during the war. In the congressional elections of 1942, the Republicans won 209 seats in the House, just short of the majority of 218. Essentially, the conservatives opposed the increasingly centralized and government-dominated society, which, New Dealers argued, was necessary to cope with crises such as depressions and wars. Conservatives winced at price controls, rationing, and increased federal regulations, and they opposed expansion of social security, public housing programs, or federal health insurance. Still, the coalition was hesitant to repeal the bulk of New Deal legislation, and indeed, in the presidential election of 1944, Republican candidate Governor Thomas E. Dewey of New York promised to retain the New Deal but pledged himself to administer it more effectively.

Many leaders of American business held key positions in administrative agencies and were in a position to affect public policies significantly. Congress had suspended the antitrust laws, exempted insurance companies from federal regulation, and framed tax laws that were especially attractive to big business. Temporary New Deal programs that restricted business, such as the PWA, the WPA, the CCC, the NYA, and the National Resources Planning Board, were ended.

The activities of labor unions were restricted by the lawmakers, in part, due to the activities of the new coalition. The Connally-Smith Act gave the president power to seize factories or mines, prohibited strike activity by union leaders in plants seized by the federal government, and forbade political contributions by labor unions. Critics of labor also had a greater voice than during peaceful times. Even the administration opposed across-the-board wage increases, fearing their inflationary effect. Still, Roosevelt's proposal to limit salaries at the upper levels to $25,000 yearly met with steely opposition in Congress.

The congressional coalition did not act in the field of civil rights, except to oppose the repeal of poll taxes, which were required in parts of the country when citizens exercised their right to vote.

The war introduced new issues into politics—issues dealing with mobilization, military strategy, and foreign affairs. Thus it weakened the consensus of the urban coalition that had been the backbone of the New Deal. Roosevelt conceded in 1942, "The weaknesses and many of the social inequalities as of 1932 have been repaired or removed, and the job now is, first and foremost, to win the war."

The new conservative coalition was active not only in Congress but in the federal bureaucracy as well. Many of the New Deal lawyers, social workers, and economists who had come to Washington to staff federal agencies during the New Deal departed. Some retired, some went with the waning of reform, and some were forced out by political opponents. In their place came conservative lawyers, business people, engineers, and technicians. As the influence of Edward R. Stettinius, James V. Forrestal, and Henry L. Stimson increased, that of individuals such as Henry A. Wallace, Rexford G. Tugwell, and Aubrey Williams declined. In the Depression, the public image of business and business people had been distinctly unfavorable, but in the heat of war, business people occupied vital positions of power in the mobilization program, and their prestige grew enormously. The business executive once again became one of the nation's heroes.

Although the issue was rarely mentioned in campaign rhetoric, the war inexorably speeded up the regimentation of American life that had begun to accelerate under the New Deal. To many Americans it seemed that the manifold problems of a complex technological society required specialized experts and rigorous organization. Wartime exigencies greatly expanded the power and influence of bureaucracy. All this seemed necessary and even good, yet many Americans grew to resent the growth of government influence, even though they felt helpless to stem its tide. Some of these feelings of frustration were reflected by Congressman Martin Dies, chairman of the House Un-American Activities Committee, in 1943 when he asked his colleagues to "guard jealously and zealously the rights and prerogatives of this body [or else] the real power and function of government will not be exercised in this chamber, but . . . by bureaucracy." Another manifestation of these feelings was the establishment of the Special Investigative Committee into the War Program, chaired by Senator Harry S Truman of Missouri. Beginning in 1941, the Truman Committee investigated most phases of the mobilization program, ferreting out waste, inefficiency, and corruption. One of its prime aims was to supervise the reorganization of American society as it girded for total war. The committee proved to be extremely valuable and saved taxpayers millions of dollars. It was praised by both Democrats and Republicans and made Senator Truman a nationally known political figure.

As the presidential election of 1944 approached, speculation concerning Roosevelt understandably increased, but Roosevelt remained silent about his intentions. Only a week before the meeting of the Democratic convention, however, he announced that he would accept a nomination for a fourth term if it were offered. "All that is within me cries out to go back to my home on the Hudson River," he said. "But as a good soldier . . . I will accept and serve." Although the convention was ready to nominate him for a fourth term, the party's professionals resolutely opposed the renomination of Henry A. Wallace as vice-president. Most considered him impractical and too radical. After considerable negotiations, Truman was chosen to be the president's running mate in 1944. The party platform pledged continuation of the New Deal and international cooperation.

Among the Republicans, Thomas Dewey was an early favorite. Wendell Willkie had lost the support of party leaders, in part because of his public approval of many of Roosevelt's policies. Dewey easily won the Republican nomination on the first ballot, and he chose Senator John W. Bricker of Ohio as his running mate. The platform proposed no major changes in domestic or foreign policies.

The campaign was a contest of personalities more than issues. Rumors that Roosevelt's health was failing persisted, although he made strenuous campaign tours throughout the nation. The rigors of electioneering did, in fact, tax the president's strength. Roosevelt was elected to an unprecedented fourth term. The final returns showed over 25 million votes for Roosevelt and

22 million for Dewey. Americans appeared reluctant to change leaders in the final phases of the war. The election seemed to reveal broad consensus on domestic and foreign policies and the increased political strength of urban areas. This consensus and the mood of the nation were the result of the war.

Cultural Changes

In many parts of the nation, schools were overcrowded and understaffed. Children in congested industrial areas often attended school for only half a day. Some schools, particularly elementary schools in rural areas, were without teachers. The proliferation of well-paying jobs tempted many youngsters to leave school to enter the labor force. The number of working teenagers rose from 1 to 3 million between 1940 and 1944, and more than 1 million dropped out of school to go to work. Even young children between the ages of 7 and 12 worked part-time—as delivery or errand runners, pinsetters in bowling alleys, or helpers in retail stores—sometimes in violation of child labor laws.

The nation's high schools sought to meet wartime demands and to counteract the dropout problem by broadening their curricula to include language courses, world history, and vocational training programs in war-related skills such as welding and aircraft mechanics. Some schools attempted to solve the dropout problem by offering late afternoon or evening classes. Meanwhile, the armed forces denuded colleges of students as well as faculty. Most institutions maintained only a fraction of their prewar enrollments, and many enrolled mostly women. The precarious existence of colleges led the army and navy to use them for special training programs for service personnel, stressing language skills, social sciences, and humanities.

Exposure to higher education and the world whetted the desires of many Americans who had been unable to afford advanced education before the war. Such desires were enough to persuade Congress to enact the GI Bill of Rights in June 1944. Every ex–service person was entitled to paid education or training at any level for one year plus up to four additional years, equal to the time spent in the armed forces. The bill also authorized unemployment payments for veterans, job referral services, medical care, pensions, and reemployment rights. It gave "emphatic notice to the men and women in the armed forces," Roosevelt said, "that the American people do not intend to let them down." Congress also hoped that the GI Bill would help prevent another depression after the war, caused by the mustering out of more than 10 million members of the armed forces and the inevitable slowing down of the postwar economy. The GI Bill, together with the various federal programs in education, would transform the nation's colleges and universities into centers for national scientific research and vocational instruction after the war.

The war also spurred tendencies toward a more formal organization of American culture, particularly in the mass media. The publishing industry had been propelled toward a greater emphasis on mass production by the armed forces' need for vast quantities of inexpensive reading materials. To relieve the boredom of American military personnel stationed in remote areas, the U.S. Government Printing Office published Armed Services Editions, reprints of thousands of books in paperback. These books rolled off the presses in large numbers—more than 350 million—and introduced innumerable Americans to paperback books. Armed forces publications such as *Stars and Stripes* and the army humor magazine *Yank* gave experience in publishing mass circulation magazines to many future stars of postwar journalism. Propaganda—whether in war films such as *Guadalcanal Diary* and *Wake Island* or in radio broadcasts beamed by the Office of War Information—provided experience for thousands of individuals who entered the advertising industry after the war and contributed to the advertising boom in the affluent society of the 1950s.

Hollywood made an all-out effort to turn its talents to the war effort. Skilled screenwriters composed scripts to meet the specifications of the Office of War Information, while famous directors of the caliber of Frank Capra devoted much of their time to war-oriented or propagandistic films. If the war did not actually inaugurate new developments in American culture, it did much to accelerate the trend toward an increasingly centralized and powerful mass media.

As few other events in the lives of most Americans would do, World War II greatly accelerated the growth of an organizational society in the United States, a society whose destiny was increasingly determined by government and other large organizations rather than by individuals. These developments did not trouble most Americans and would not become an issue for many years.

CHAPTER 14

The South and the West during World War II

World War II affected Americans everywhere in the United States, but it had a particularly striking impact on the South and the West. These were the most underdeveloped regions of the nation, lagging behind other sections in economic development, standard of living, and educational facilities. The South had never fully recovered from its defeat and devastation during the Civil War. In the 1930s it was still struggling to regain the momentum it had lost in that bitter conflict. The trans-Mississippi West, in contrast, was the most recently settled part of the continental United States, scarcely 100 years old in 1941, and thus far less developed than regions like New England or the Midwest. For different reasons, therefore, southerners and westerners shared a common colonial mentality. Many believed that their status in the Union was like that of colonies beholden to the mother country—in this case the older and wealthier Northeast. That area held most of the country's manufacturing establishments, served as its financial capital, and was the arbiter of its cultural life. Like tributaries, the South and the West sent their raw materials to the North for processing and manufacturing. That placed them in the grip of financiers and large corporations outside their own borders who exploited them for their own selfish interests and kept them dependent by perpetuating their raw-material economies.

But World War II disrupted this colonial relationship by accelerating the pace of change. By 1945 the South had finally begun to recover the ground it had lost in preceding years as the war diversified its economy and uprooted social relationships, including those between blacks and whites. In a similar manner, war mobilization lessened the colonial status of the West. It did a great deal to promote economic diversification, it brought a great increase of population and social diversity, it enriched the cultural life of the West, and it stimulated development of the sciences. Thus the war had a pronounced impact on both regions.

156

Throughout the 1930s, the American South had been perceived by many, even President Roosevelt himself, as the nation's major economic problem. As a region, it seemed mired in abject poverty. Its image was that of a declining rural region, with more than two-thirds of its people living in dire want. The southern states ranked lowest nationally in the general health levels of its population; its inhabitants had the lowest educational attainments, and its schools were the poorest in the nation. Dominating much of southern life was the issue of race, the segregation of blacks, which permeated the social structure. That issue also dominated southern politics. Systematic discrimination against blacks, known as Jim Crowism, was widespread, and the virtually unassailable Democratic party sought to preserve the prowhite status quo. Progress had been slow in the region for generations, and radical change seemed unlikely.

Yet in just four years World War II did much to transform the South, arouse it from its torpor, and provide it with a different image. Mobilization brought an increased measure of economic prosperity. It led to significant industrial expansion, diversification in agriculture, an expanding labor force, and an extensive network of new military installations. Federal funds now reached even into hitherto isolated communities. The war also resulted in a considerable increase of population, especially in towns and cities. Significant was the increasing ethnic diversity of newcomers. Until 1940, white southerners were largely of Anglo-Saxon Protestant background. But the war-induced immigration brought more people with diverse ethnic and cultural origins. These changes jolted the South out of its lethargy. For better or worse, they transformed it into a more dynamic, fast-paced urban civilization.

Economic Impact of the War on the South

Between 1941 and 1945, mobilization rejuvenated the southern economy. The federal government awarded more than $4 billion in war contracts to the South. Rearmament bolstered the steel industry, created an unprecedented boom in shipbuilding and textile manufacturing, and stimulated small factory enterprises. Expansion of the armed forces benefited southern cotton and tobacco growers as the demand for uniforms and cigarettes expanded enormously. Foodstuffs such as rice and sugar came to be in short supply. Hundreds of new military training camps also did much to stimulate new service industries. Meanwhile, the South benefited from increased demand for coal and petroleum products. Kentucky and West Virginia coal mines operated at capacity for the first time in a generation. Louisiana and Texas became the nation's leading oil producing states. That in turn led to a vast increase in refining facilities in the South, especially on the Gulf Coast. Such developments also provided a basis for an extensive new petrochemical industry in the region, much of it financed with federal funds during wartime. Petro-chemicals were essential for a burgeoning plastics industry. They also facili-tated the manufacture of synthetic rubber. More than half of the factories producing synthetic rubber between 1941 and 1945 were located around the Louisiana and Texas (near the Gulf) oil fields, and others were near Louis-ville, Kentucky. With all of these varied enterprises, the South gained 40 percent in industrial capacity during World War II. Total expenditures for war plants in the South exceeded $4.4 billion, and the federal government spent almost as much for new military facilities, especially in Texas, Louisi-ana, and Alabama.

Donald Nelson, the chairman of the War Production Board in 1944, summarized it well. "A bird's-eye view of large-scale Southern industry makes you feel that the South has rubbed Aladdin's lamp," he said. Accu-rately forecasting the future, he noted that in the next generation the founda-tions laid by the war would "bring the South into the vanguard of world industrial progress." The South had become home to the nation's largest powder and explosive plant, near Birmingham, Alabama; the largest repair and supply depot, in San Antonio, Texas; the largest bomber and modifica-tion facility, at Marietta, Georgia; and the largest chemical warfare plant, at Huntsville, Alabama. The war had brought a greater pace of industrialization to the South in four years than southerners had been able to achieve in many decades.

That was evident to many travelers to the wartime South who marveled at the transformation. For example, during the Depression, the steel facto-ries in Birmingham had operated at less than 40 percent of capacity because of shrinking markets; in wartime they were functioning at full capacity. The pall of smog and smoke that hung over the city was viewed by many of its inhabitants as a welcome sign of industrial vitality rather than as an ecological problem perceived by later generations.

Shipbuilding became a prime source of income for the South. Largely dormant between the wars, the southern ship construction industry experi-enced an unprecedented boom. Scores of southern communities now opened or expanded shipyards, which became major employers. One of the largest was the Newport News Shipbuilding and Dry Dock Company in Norfolk, Virginia, which built battleships and aircraft carriers. In Houston, Texas; Tampa, Florida; Pascagoula, Mississippi; Beaumont, Texas; and Wil-mington, North Carolina, the new shipyards hired tens of thousands of work-ers. Mobile, Alabama, was one of the most active in the industry, securing more than $300 million in contracts. The Alabama Dry Dock and Shipbuild-ing Company there employed more than 30,000 men and women, 5,000 of whom were black. In addition to the private yards, the U.S. Navy greatly expanded its own facilities in Norfolk, Virginia, and Charleston, South Caro-lina. Shipbuilding records in the South were not as spectacular as in the

West, but they were still notable. In May 1944 the black workers at the Alabama Dry Dock and Shipbuilding Company in Mobile completed a merchant ship, the *Tule Canyon*, in just seventy-nine days, a yard record. If Henry J. Kaiser was the hero of western shipbuilding, Andrew Jackson Higgins filled that role in the South. Higgins, a builder of small vessels, such as the famous PT boats, built these craft with extraordinary speed, usually in a span of two weeks per unit, particularly in his New Orleans and Norfolk yards. Altogether, the seventeen major shipyards in the South built one-fourth of all ships constructed in wartime, aggregating more than $6 billion in value.

Other industries benefited from war contracts. Airplane manufacturers now developed manufacturing in the South on a large scale. Consolidated Vultee established a major plant in Dallas, Texas, to produce B-24 bombers. In Marietta, Georgia, the Bell Aircraft Corporation turned out B-29 bombers. Giant assembly plants sprang up in New Orleans, Louisiana; Tulsa, Oklahoma; Nashville, Tennessee; Birmingham, Alabama; and Miami, Florida. Invariably the industry stimulated the expansion of aluminum fabrication. Arkansas was the nation's major source of bauxite, the raw material needed to manufacture aluminum. The federal government provided the funds for establishing extensive new processing facilities in Alabama, North Carolina, and Tennessee. Since some explosives were manufactured from cotton linters and wood cellulose, the federal government funded several new big plants in the South. The most important was the Du Pont Ordnance Works at Childers, Alabama, not far from Birmingham. Others included the Holston Works near Kingsport, Tennessee; the Redford Works not far from Richmond, Virginia; and the Volunteer Works in Chattanooga, Tennessee. The most important was the extensive new facility at Oak Ridge, Tennessee, dedicated to processing uranium for the manufacture of an atomic bomb. Between 1942 and 1945 it employed 110,000 people.

The war also generated an insatiable demand for coal and petroleum. Southern coal mines had been in a slump since World War I. The expanded demand, however, led to the reopening of old mines, creating thousands of new jobs. More spectacular growth took place in the petroleum industry, which had seen depressed conditions since 1929. Old wells in East Texas and Louisiana were reopened by anxious operators, and intensive drilling made these the nation's leading oil-producing states. Not only did the conflict increase the demand for lubricants, but the building of an air force of more than 250,000 planes necessitated the production of 100-octane aviation gasoline—a product that had not been refined much before 1940. Clearly, the popular prewar image of the South as an agricultural region was undergoing rapid change in wartime.

The mild climates of the South also made it a favorite staging area for the armed forces, which built scores of new training camps and air bases there.

Oil in the West: Amarillo, Texas. (*Edwards Studio*)

Huntsville, Alabama, for example, became one of the largest army air force installations in the United States. Since southerners had long prided themselves on their military traditions, local communities throughout the region greeted the coming of military facilities with great enthusiasm. The long coastlines of the southern states were well suited to housing major supply depots to service the European theater of war.

Southern farmers also geared up for the war. As in the West, a shortage of workers and agricultural machinery impeded southern producers. Conscription as well as higher-paying factory jobs created a dearth of willing farm workers. Southern farmers turned to various alternatives. Some used Italian and German prisoners of war or black migrants from Jamaica and the Bahamas. Quite a few converted to less labor-intensive crops, abandoning their traditional single-minded concentration on cotton. Instead, they turned to livestock or fruit and vegetable farming. Cotton was no longer king. Increased mechanization was another means of increasing production with a dwindling supply of workers. Wartime shortages of machinery limited this alternative. But more intensive use of tractors and the development of the automatic cotton picker lessened the traditional dependence on black labor.

Rice growers in Arkansas and along the Gulf Coast bought intricate combine harvesters, which consolidated operations and eliminated much hand labor. Thus the war did much to disrupt labor-intensive farming in the South, previously small-scale. Instead, agriculture became more of a large-scale operation heavily dependent on mechanization and diversified production.

War and Southern Society

Such far-reaching economic changes resulted in considerable social transformations. One of the most notable was rapid urbanization. Rarely had the South experienced such intensive population growth as during World War II. Atlanta, Charleston, New Orleans, Mobile, Birmingham, and many smaller towns were besieged with newcomers. Of forty-eight metropolitan areas in the South, thirty-nine experienced rapid growth. Savannah grew by 29 percent between 1940 and 1950, Charleston by 37 percent, Norfolk by 57 percent, and Mobile by 61 percent. Smaller cities had even larger increases. Such growth altered the ethnic composition of the South and, inevitably, the nature of race relations. Many of the newcomers came from the Northeast and the Midwest. They camped in hotels, trailer camps, and abandoned buildings. Since they usually paid no property taxes, southern cities faced real crises in providing necessary services—sanitation, trash collection, public transportation, public schools. Wartime conditions thus sowed the seeds of many urban problems faced by southern cities in ensuing decades.

Racial Tensions in the South

Wartime conditions heightened racial tensions in the region, reflected in rumor mongering, lynchings, and riots. In 1942, for example, rumors spread among southern whites that blacks were organizing "Eleanor Roosevelt Clubs" to boycott white employers of household help. Other whispering campaigns created panic when some southerners charged that blacks were buying ice picks to use in a violent uprising once southern white men went off to war. None of these rumors had any factual basis. But the number of lynchings between 1942 and 1945 increased. Mississippi once experienced three lynchings in a single week. More typical, however, were thousands of minor racial incidents as large numbers of rural southern whites now mingled with blacks in cities heavily involved with war production. And the presence of hundreds of thousands of blacks in the armed forces aroused apprehension among some whites, reflected in efforts to exclude blacks from white communities. When black soldiers on military leave tried to use recreational facilities, such as swimming pools or moving picture houses in small southern cities near their army camps, local white residents were often fearful and hostile. Not only did they refuse to admit blacks, there were instances where residents ordered the local police to harass or forcibly escort them out of town.

Blacks also experienced discrimination in civilian wartime employment opportunities. In the first years of the war, vocational training schools in the South refused to accept blacks who wished to enroll in classes that would have qualified them for job openings in war-related industries. Employers in such industries as ship and aircraft production avoided hiring blacks until the later stages of the war. When blacks were employed, they were usually forced to work in segregated production areas.

Eventually, wartime pressures tended to lessen race discrimination in the southern economy. The increasingly critical labor shortage was clearly a major influence in lowering discriminatory barriers. In addition, the war heightened consciousness of ideological differences between democratic and totalitarian societies, and the social policies of racist Germany lessened the enthusiasm of many southern whites for segregation. At the same time, the war encouraged many blacks to become more militant in demanding equal rights. As the southern economy lost some of its distinctive character and became more like that of the East and the Midwest, so too did its social composition approximate that of other regions. Traditionalists bemoaned the passing of southern distinctiveness, but the advocates of change welcomed a new future. As a distinguished southern historian, George B. Tindall noted:

> In 1945 the South emerged from the war . . . with more social change and more unfinished business than any other part of the country, with fewer sharecroppers but more pipefitters and welders, with less plowing and hoeing but more mowing and sowing, with less rural isolation and more urban sophistication, with nearly a million people in the ranks of organized labor, . . . with veterans returning from new experiences beyond the seven seas, and with a standard of living for the common man that was undreamt of in its prewar philosophy. The region was more an integral part of the Union and of the world than ever before.[1]

Economic Impact of the War on the West

As in the South, wartime mobilization left a deep imprint on the West. In part this was due to the sparsity of population in the area, for only 12 percent of the national total lived west of the Mississippi River in 1940. Major

---

[1]George B. Tindall, *The Emergence of the New South, 1913–1945* (Baton Rouge: Louisiana State University Press, 1967), p. 731.

changes therefore were felt more strongly here than in well-established older regions in the East. The war profoundly affected the economy and also social and cultural life. In many ways the war transformed what was a dependent colonial region before 1940—America's "third world"—into a dynamic pacesetter after 1945.

The war did much to lessen the economic dependence of the West on the industrial East. Until 1940 the West contained very few manufacturing plants but concentrated on shipping its raw materials—farm produce, petroleum, and minerals—to the East, which dominated manufactures and finance and treated the West like a colony. Domestic mobilization, however, did much to diversify the western economy and to make it more self-sufficient and independent. It stimulated the creation of new industries, boosted agricultural production, promoted new service industries, and vastly increased federal expenditures for military installations and research complexes. In four years it changed a region almost entirely dependent on the extraction of raw materials to one producing ships and airplanes, aluminum, magnesium, and steel. Moreover, every state in the West was now dotted with airfields, training camps, ordnance depots, and testing or repair centers, significant sources of income and employment. Such large-scale expansion had been unthinkable before the war.

The West Coast shipping industry was among the first to benefit from national rearmament. Between 1919 and 1939, shipyards there had not built even a single merchant ship. But between 1941 and 1945, the yards in California and the Pacific Northwest constructed more than 2,000 merchant vessels and large numbers of naval craft and employed more than 400,000 people annually. By the end of the war, the Pacific coast had accounted for almost half the ships built in wartime.

Shipyards in the West—in Los Angeles, the San Francisco Bay Area, Portland, and Seattle—enjoyed a special distinction for speed. Directed by brilliant managers such as Henry J. Kaiser and his son Edgar, they pioneered new methods of mass production that reduced the time needed to complete a ship. Whereas East Coast yards in 1941 still used craftsmen who lovingly fabricated a 10,000-ton vessel in about thirteen months, the Kaisers were able to build such a ship in less than four days. They also used innovative labor policies and actively recruited women and minorities. Not only did Kaiser employees receive generous wages, but the company also established day-care centers for children of employees and offered generous medical benefits.

The years between 1941 and 1945 also witnessed the rapid expansion of the aircraft industry in the West. Before 1940, aircraft manufacturers had operated on a small scale, producing fewer than 500 planes annually in the San Diego and Los Angeles areas. When President Roosevelt called for the production of 50,000 planes in 1940, few people believed that such goals could be met. But the federal government provided the funds for the establishment of new factories and offered attractive incentives to the private manufacturers in the West. These included the Boeing Company in Seattle and Douglas, Ryan, Lockheed, and Consolidated Vultee in southern California. Using assembly lines and mass production techniques, they built half of the 300,000 planes produced in the United States between 1941 and 1945. Moreover, they laid the foundations for a vast aerospace and missile industry that was to develop in the West during the postwar era.

Domestic mobilization spawned a new steel industry in the West. Before 1940, the West was forced to import almost all of its needed steel from the East since it had virtually no facilities of its own. But vast shipbuilding activities required closer sources in the region. Thus the federal government built a large new plant in Provo, Utah, which the United States Steel Corporation operated. Federal funds also made it possible for Henry J. Kaiser to build a steel mill in Fontana, California. Together these plants made the West less dependent on eastern steel producers and allowed it to provide more readily for its own needs.

Similarly, the war crisis led to the creation of an aluminum industry in the West. Before the conflict, all aluminum in the United States was manufactured by just one company, the Aluminum Company of America. In the initial stages of the war, that company was unable to meet the demand of aircraft producers in the West. So the federal government built seven new aluminum plants in the region, operated by Henry J. Kaiser and by Alcoa. The federal government also built the world's largest magnesium-producing facility near the sleepy little town of Las Vegas, Nevada. Magnesium was vital for the production not only of aircraft but also of deadly fire bombs.

As America's minerals storehouse, the West met almost all of the nation's needs. Arizona, Montana, and Colorado supplied most of the necessary copper; other western states provided minerals necessary for steel alloys. West Texas, Oklahoma, California, and other western states pumped much of the crude oil and derivatives that fueled American military forces and the vast civilian production complex.

Since much of World War II was fought in the Pacific, the West assumed great strategic importance between 1941 and 1945. The federal government built hundreds of air bases in the region because of year-round good flying weather and vast open spaces. The military services also established extensive testing areas for weapons, gases, and sophisticated rockets and missiles first developed during these years. To supply the far-flung battlefields in the Pacific, the War and Navy Departments created major ordnance depots throughout the West on an unprecedented scale. In addition, the federal government, for the first time a major patron of science, established large weapons research facilities such as the one at Los Alamos, New Mexico, which devoted itself to the production of the atomic bomb. That accelerated the growth of an extensive network of scientists and laboratories in the region. Rocket research was promoted at the California Institute of Technology in Pasadena and oceanic research at the Scripps Institute of Oceanography at La Jolla, California. When the war ended, the West had become the hub of important federally sponsored scientific research in a wide range of fields. It now had a scientific establishment, whereas there had been virtually none in 1940.

Social Changes in the West

Such extensive economic changes were bound to have social consequences. As in the South, the war accentuated the pace of urbanization in the West. Before 1940 this had been a sparsely populated region with few large urban areas. Domestic mobilization speeded the growth of cities, however. The older ones like Denver and Salt Lake City grew considerably. But smaller towns experienced much more spectacular growth. San Diego doubled its population to 450,000. Los Angeles gained 30 percent in four years, as did the San Francisco Bay Area; Portland, Oregon; and Seattle, Washington. Moreover, the crush of people created entirely new metropolitan areas, among them Tucson and Phoenix, Arizona; Las Vegas, Nevada; Albuquerque, New Mexico; and Colorado Springs, Colorado. The war transformed the once rural West into an urban society.

That society was increasingly multiethnic and multiracial. Before 1940, few black Americans had ventured westward, no more than about 40,000. But between 1940 and 1945, more than 250,000 went west to work in factories. Most settled in cities like Los Angeles, San Francisco, Seattle, and Portland. The shortage of labor also drew several hundred thousand Mexicans across the border. The *braceros,* who were guest workers, did much to alleviate the shortage of farm labor, and other Mexicans performed track maintenance for the western railroads.

The influence of the war on the West was manifold. It diversified the economy and brought a great influx of population. It introduced a greater measure of ethnic and racial diversity and made the West more of an urban civilization. It did much, also, to foster greater cultural maturity, particularly in the sciences. What might have taken a generation to accomplish in peacetime was compressed into four years of hectic wartime change.

More than other parts of the United States, the South and the West were most strikingly affected by the mobilization effort during the Second World War. They witnessed the transformation of their economies, the diversification of their social structures, and an increase in their political influence in national affairs. Nor were such changes temporary wartime phenomena. Rather, they laid the foundation for the development of these regions in the next decades by creating opportunities during those years of spectacular expansion. World War II established the framework for southern and western expansion in the next generation.

CHAPTER 15

Women and Minority Groups during World War II

 If the Second World War did not initiate totally new departures in the position of women and minorities in the United States, it did a great deal to accelerate the pace of change. In the lives of many women, the war opened new horizons, and they did not forget their experiences in later years. Mobilization emphasized the importance of women's work outside the home and their place in the labor force. It opened up a very wide range of occupations from which women had been excluded. Wartime needs also made new opportunities in vocational training and higher education accessible to women. The substantial movement of population to urban areas greatly increased the importance of suburbs and laid the foundations for new lifestyles that many women were to adopt in the next three decades. All of these influences altered existing patterns of female behavior as well as the expectations of both women and men and eventually altered national attitudes about the role of women in American society.

The movement for greater equality between women and men was reinforced by a nascent civil rights movement between 1941 and 1945. Members of minority groups were quick to realize that government programs in wartime could help them achieve many of their goals, particularly equality. The war gave minorities new job opportunities, and federal regulations requiring fair employment practices reduced discrimination. Service in the armed forces often opened the door to vocational training, travel, education, and other benefits. Minority group concentration in the cities led to stronger political representation by minorities and a new sense of political power. And the concentration of blacks, Hispanics, and other minorities in cities such as New York, Detroit, Chicago, and Los Angeles gave them a heightened sense of cultural identity.

Economic Impact of the War on Women

It was primarily the shortage of labor during World War II that forced Americans to reexamine the role of women in American society and some of the inequalities between the sexes. In particular, the assumption that the primary responsibility of women was to supervise the home was subjected to some scrutiny, although it was certainly not abandoned. Women's activities in the home, such as planting victory gardens and canning, contributed to the overall war effort and were not belittled. But women were also desperately needed in the work force, in industry, in agriculture, and in the professions. Active recruitment of women for the armed forces only dramatized this changing perception. And since the war drew attention to ideological conflicts and the United States' commitment to freedom and equality, it dramatized existing inequalities between men and women. Millions of women served in war agencies, in civil defense units, and as volunteers for the Red Cross or the United Service Organizations, which provided recreational activities for soldiers in uniform. Seeing the myriad contributions of women to the war effort, millions of Americans could not help but alter their images of women and the potential for women to succeed in hitherto untried fields.

Mobilization accelerated the movement of women into the labor force as jobs became available to them. Between 1940 and 1945, the number of working women increased from 12 million to 18.6 million, an increase of 55 percent. At the end of the war, women constituted more than one-third of the nation's labor force, up from 27 percent just five years earlier. What was distinctive also was the high percentage of married women working outside the home, about three-fourths of the new women workers. Most of these jobs were in shipyards, aircraft factories, and ordnance depots. Although it is true that many of these women in 1945 left their jobs to return to their earlier function as homemakers, a sizable number remained in the work force. In 1950 the percentage of women in the labor force, 29 percent, was higher than it had been a decade earlier.

In the initial stages of the war, neither employers nor government officials envisaged recruiting a significant number of women to the war effort. A survey of 12,512 war plants in January 1942 revealed that they expected to hire few female workers. In fact, at that same time, the War Department recommended that its contractors employ men before they turned to the available pool of women. Meanwhile, between 1940 and 1942 many women experienced considerable difficulties in gaining admission to special training programs that would provide them with new skills. Fewer than 5 percent of the workers admitted to the government-run Vocational Training for War Production Workers program were females, and private schools were equally restrictive, often excluding all blacks as well. To try to remedy the situation, the Women's Bureau of the Department of Labor issued scores of publications detailing the types of jobs that women could perform. But the labor shortage that developed in the spring of 1942 wrought a marvelous change of attitude. By the middle of 1942, most companies were willing to hire women for semiskilled and some managerial openings. As it turned out, women were to be America's secret weapon.

Many women found jobs in shipyards and heavy industries. In 1939 only 36 women were employed in ship construction. By the end of 1942, this number had grown to almost 200,000. That total quadrupled by 1945, when more than 2 million women worked in heavy industries. In the shipyards, women performed every conceivable job, from welding and assembling parts to riveting and operating heavy machinery such as cranes, as well as clerical duties. To accommodate women, employers often made special adjustments in work processes. Where brute strength had been required, as in the turning of a vise, they automated the operation, using pneumatic pressure that a woman could apply at the touch of a button. The simplification of work processes made it easier to train new, inexperienced workers in a short period of time. Throughout American industry, conveyor belts, automatic elevators, cranes, and push buttons replaced brute strength and made it possible for women to perform operations that once had been the exclusive domain of men. Such adjustment was not always easy for women, and many factories established counseling services to help them with personal and job-related problems.

The contribution of women was vital to the nation's aircraft production program. At various times during the war, women constituted almost one-half of the work force in the factories on the Pacific coast. When the Women's Bureau surveyed seven aircraft plants in April 1941, it found only 143 females employed. Within eighteen months the number had grown to 65,000. Nationwide, more than 400,000 women performed a wide range of tasks in aircraft production plants during the war. They assembled and tuned engines, fabricated wings, riveted parts, and engaged in all kinds of assembly. Some women also served as test pilots or ferried planes from factories to air bases. Women were also skilled in electrical work and installing intricate electrical and navigation systems on a wide variety of planes. The challenges were many, but women in the work force met them. As one female labor leader, Jennie Matyas, noted in 1943, women "are building up an entirely different social climate," and their activities "will become the regular thing to do after this [war]."

The federal government itself became a major employer of women in the civilian sector. It hired almost a million women between 1941 and 1944, about half of its new employees. The number of females in the civil service jumped from 200,000 in 1939 to 1 million in 1944, constituting 38 percent of all federal officeholders. These were by no means all clerical positions; they ranged into hundreds of classifications in which women assumed the positions vacated by men.

Women and Political Processes

At the same time, the federal government tried to alleviate some of the problems encountered by women who streamed into private industry. One approach was the establishment of equal pay scales for the sexes. Both the War Production Board and the War Manpower Commission followed an equal-pay policy, and by 1943 the National Labor Relations Board had applied the same standard in thousands of cases that came before it. Another problem was the high rate of turnover among women workers. Many found that the burdens of maintaining a home, caring for children, and holding down a full-time job were too much to bear. In California, such turnover was sometimes 100 percent annually. Federal officials were thus directly concerned with reducing the high rate of absenteeism among women (more than twice the rate of men), and dealing with the problems that contributed to it. These included inadequate housing near war plants, too few shopping facilities, lack of schools and health care, and perhaps most important, an insufficiency of child-care centers. By 1943 congressional investigators had visited some of the most congested production areas for a firsthand look at such conditions. As a result, the federal government built new housing projects, installed shopping and eating facilities in factories, and even provided laundry services. Under the Lanham Act of 1940 the federal government established some of the nation's first day-care centers for the children of mothers in the factories. The demand always outran the supply, although some employers like the Kaiser shipyards provided excellent child-support programs.

The changing status of women was reflected in the policies of the armed forces, which for the first time accepted female volunteers as enlisted personnel and officers. At least 300,000 women took advantage of these opportunities. About 140,000 served with the Women's Army Auxiliary Corps (WAACS), 100,000 with the navy (WAVES), 23,000 with the marines (MCWR), and 13,000 with the Coast Guard (SPARS). Another 60,000 volunteered for the Army Nurse Corps and 14,000 for the Navy Nurse Corps. Black nurses were not accepted into the armed services before 1941 and thereafter were allowed to minister only to black troops and prisoners of war. Women were not assigned to combat duty but relieved men for such assignments. Most of the women served in the United States, but about one-fourth were sent overseas. They provided clerical help, maintained communications and transportation, and performed a wide range of necessary and vital jobs. The first WAACS whom the army sent overseas arrived in North Africa and thereafter moved to the European and later the Pacific theaters of war.

Women at war: Women's Army Auxiliary Corps (WAAC) officer candidates taking their oaths. (*U.S. Army Signal Corps*)

In the Philippines in early 1942, the Japanese captured a sizable detachment of nurses, who endured great suffering as prisoners of war. As with men, black women in the WAACS were segregated and sent to all-black units. The navy did not accept any black women until close to the end of the war.

Social Strains on Women

With women working outside the home or in the armed forces, it was not surprising that strains on the American family developed during wartime. Juvenile delinquency increased, and rates of school truancy rose. Sexual promiscuity became more common among young people and was reflected in rapidly rising rates of venereal disease. Everywhere patriotic "V-girls," often teenagers, provided companionship for servicemen. And many teenage boys, attracted by high-paying wartime jobs, became school dropouts. The war thus provided numerous pressures that tended to disrupt family structures.

In fact, the war affected other aspects of marriage and family life. Although the marriage rate declined during the first half of the 1940s, it increased significantly during the second half of the decade as demobilization occurred. By that time greater financial stability also made marriages more feasible and boosted the low rates that had been typical during the Depression. At the same time, the rate of divorce increased considerably, especially among veterans, as hasty war marriages disintegrated. One out of every four such unions resulted in separation. This more common resort to divorce, and its increasing social acceptance, presaged future trends.

Wartime conditions provided women with more liberal access to educational opportunities and thus greater independence. The various new job opportunities appealed to many women and put greater pressure on colleges to broaden their educational curricula. As male college enrollment plummeted between 1941 and 1945, that of women grew from 600,000 in 1940 to 800,000 ten years later. Instead of restricting women to teaching and nursing as before, other fields, including journalism, medicine, and engineering, became available.

At least half of the male war veterans who attended college from 1945 to 1950, about 1.2 million of them, were married. These men brought their wives and children to the campuses, creating a pattern that was to be characteristic of campus life for the remainder of the century. Many of these women took advantage of their proximity to higher education after the years of motherhood when they returned to campuses as full-time students. Thus the wartime experiences established a tradition of continued schooling for women after marriage and enhanced their awareness of a broad range of possible vocational opportunities.

Wartime experiences quietly and unobtrusively fostered greater political awareness among women. Intensive lobbying by major women's groups such as the American Association of University Women and the National Federation of Business and Professional Women's Clubs resulted in some concrete gains. Four state legislatures mandated equal pay for women. Other states enacted laws to protect women from job discrimination. Thirteen states made women eligible for jury duty. Florida eliminated common law restrictions on married women. Eleven state legislatures approved the equal rights amendment. Voters sent more women than ever to represent them in state legislatures: from 144 in 1944, their numbers grew to 228 in 1945. In short, wartime conditions created a climate of opinion that was favorable to more active participation by women in politics and, indeed, in broader spheres of social and economic life.

World War II created many opportunities for women. It opened new job opportunities, permitted greater equality of pay, and expanded lifestyle options. The social status of women was modified, if only temporarily for some, by new educational horizons and by greater freedom in matters of sexual behavior, marriage, and divorce. And even if the war did not cause revolutionary changes in American politics, it broke down barriers to the full participation of women in the nation's political affairs.

Minorities during the War

Attracted by new economic opportunities, members of minority groups abandoned rural areas and migrated in large numbers to towns and cities. Black tenant farmers and field workers from the South, Hispanic-American migrant farm workers, and Native Americans flocked to factories. Once in an urban environment, they faced many new and unfamiliar problems. They competed with other groups for scarce housing and social services and often encountered overt or subtle discrimination. Despite the difficulties, most minorities found new opportunities in urban life, which they hoped would improve their status in American society.

Among the newcomers to the cities, black Americans were prominent. Drawn by the lure of well-paying factory jobs in the Midwest and the West, large numbers of rural blacks from the South migrated. They streamed to industrial cities such as Cleveland, Detroit, and Chicago. For the first time also, many blacks settled on the Pacific coast, where shipyards and aircraft factories badly needed labor. The shortage of workers broke down many of the racial barriers that had prevented blacks from finding jobs in industry. Altogether, perhaps as many as 1 million southern blacks moved to other regions during the war. The number of black war workers increased from 3 percent of the labor force in 1942 to 8 percent in 1945. The number of skilled black workers doubled.

As black Americans were uprooted by and contributed to the war effort, they sought more aggressively to diminish racial discrimination. The availability of war jobs also provided blacks with greater economic power than they had known before. The concentration of blacks in cities gave them a greater sense of political power, and more than 800,000 blacks served in the armed forces, which, though still segregated, opened up new hopes for social equality. Overseas assignments led many blacks to experience a new sense of dignity. Moreover, the wartime emphasis on brotherhood and equality in democratic societies as distinguished from the rampant racism of Germany caused many Americans embarrassment over the racial prejudices in their own society.

The war also hastened the organization of blacks into well-defined protest groups that could press their demands more effectively. Between 1941 and 1945, black Americans became increasingly militant in their advocacy of civil rights. In the summer of 1941, J. Philip Randolph founded the March on Washington movement. Randolph, president of the Brotherhood of Sleeping Car Porters, believed that massive protest rather than acquiescence would win blacks greater rights. As early as May 1941 he called on blacks to undertake "a thundering march . . . to shake up white America." Randolph hoped to mobilize the black man on the street and black tenant farmers rather than the black elite. Because he advocated direct action rather than traditional methods, such as court battles, the black press tended to be cool to his calls for action. President Roosevelt did not look favorably on the movement, for he feared that it would disrupt national unity and heighten racial tensions. Randolph agreed to cancel the protest march on Washington, which threatened to embarrass the administration, if the president would create a Fair Employment Practices Committee. This directive, which Roosevelt issued by executive order, instructed all federal agencies and federal defense contractors to end discrimination in hiring. (It did not, however, apply to the armed forces.) To enforce this new policy, the Fair Employment Practices Committee, which could hear complaints from aggrieved individuals or groups, was created. Although the agency lacked statutory authority, it effectively used the threat of withholding government contracts to break down discriminatory barriers against black workers. Greatly encouraged, in 1942 Randolph called on blacks to engage in mass marches on city halls to demand civil rights. His call went largely unheeded, as an increasingly large number of blacks found well-paying jobs in the booming war economy. In 1943 Randolph urged blacks to engage in civil disobedience to protest segregationist Jim Crow practices in the South and in the North. This was also the year of race riots in Detroit and New York City, and blacks as well as whites were fearful of further domestic violence.

A recognition that organization could heighten the effectiveness of black protests also underlay the formation of the Congress of Racial Equality (CORE) in 1942. The organization was inspired by the theories of nonviolent resistance developed by India's great leader, Mahatma Gandhi. As early as 1943, CORE sponsored sit-ins to integrate restaurants and movie theaters in major cities.

The National Association for the Advancement of Colored People (NAACP) and the Urban League continued to be the most important black organizations to espouse civil rights. Due to increasing prosperity and interest in racial equality, the NAACP was able to quadruple its membership between 1941 and 1945. This growth gave its leaders confidence that they could influence national politics and legislation to attain their goal of racial equality. Yet they sensed that winning the war superseded civil rights for the time being, and although both these organizations continued to advocate the achievement of racial justice via judicial action and publicity, they kept their demands more muted than was true of the proposed march on Washington or CORE sit-in activities.

Even so, the strivings of black Americans often created tensions that erupted into violence. Few cities were more directly affected than Detroit, Michigan. More than 500,000 people had come between 1940 and 1943 to take advantage of the thousands of newly created war jobs. At least 60,000 blacks were living in some of the worst housing in the nation. Local ethnic groups, including the Poles and the Irish, resented the newcomers, who, they felt, were causing rapid deterioration of the central city. A mere spark was needed to ignite hostilities, and that spark occurred on a hot, muggy Sunday evening, June 23, 1943. A group of teenagers—black and white—began a melee in a recreation park located near Paradise Valley, a predominantly black neighborhood. As rumors of rape, assault, and murder spread through black and white sections of the city, thousands of Detroiters poured into the streets bent on vengeance. Blacks attacked unsuspecting white workers just returning from the night shift or white motorists and pedestrians near black neighborhoods. Bands of whites attacked innocent black passengers on streetcars and buses. The Detroit police attempted to control looters and rooftop snipers in the black ghetto, with limited success. The next day the situation became even more menacing. When a large and angry crowd of whites milled around the edge of Paradise Valley, a frightened black began to shoot at them indiscriminately. Within hours thousands of rioters roamed the streets of the black neighborhood, looting, burning, and inflicting violence. When it became obvious that the police were unable to subdue the rioters, Governor Frank Murphy requested federal assistance. Six thousand National Guardsmen arrived in Detroit on Monday evening. They patrolled streets, and by the end of the week order had been restored. Twenty-five blacks and nine whites lost their lives in the riot, and nearly 1,000 individuals were injured.

Other cities also throbbed with tensions. Although the Harlem riot of 1943 in New York City was not as destructive as the Detroit riot, it reflected the same kind of racial antagonisms. It began on August 1, 1943, with an inaccurate rumor that a white policeman had killed a black serviceman. Thousands of blacks rampaged along 125th Street, Harlem's main thoroughfare. The New York police deputized 1,500 blacks to help restore order. Perhaps because many Harlem residents were unsympathetic to the rioters, their effective self-policing quickly contained the disturbances, but not before six blacks were killed and more than 300 were injured.

The winds of change that the war set into motion also reached into the communities of Native Americans. Since they were a rural people living in remote areas, the international crisis seemed very distant. Yet a sufficient number sensed a threat to their own independence if the Axis powers won. Thus Native Americans responded generously to the war effort. The Crow tribe in Montana, for example, offered all its resources to the government. In Santa Ana, New Mexico, Pueblo Indians went to their ancient shrine on December 8, 1941, and remained in prayer for one month. The Zuni Pueblo, though desperately poor, donated generously to Red Cross war appeals. The Indians of the Six Nations of the Iroquois Confederacy, in New York, as an independent nation even declared war on the Axis.

In addition, many Native Americans actively participated in the war effort. More than 29,000 served in the armed forces. A contingent of Navajos formed a special services unit, the Code Talkers, who used their language for secret communications that completely confounded the Japanese. In the Pacific, the marines used them extensively. Approximately 100,000 Native Americans migrated to cities to take war jobs. Most, however, remained on reservations but took advantage of jobs in their localities that became available because of a general labor shortage. More than 2,000 Navajos, for example, worked on the construction of the Fort Wingate Ordnance Depot near Gallup, New Mexico.

In various ways the war accelerated the culture shock that Native Americans were forced to cope with. Those who served in the armed forces, which did not segregate them, felt at loose ends at the completion of their service, unsure whether to return to their traditional ways or to adapt to the majority culture. Those who held war jobs found adjustment to urban living extremely difficult and were keenly conscious of their lack of skills or education. And many Native Americans who stayed on their lands, where they were desperately poor, suffered from the suspension of many federal and New Deal programs as the government placed winning the war above all other aims. The war threatened whatever progress had been made during the New Deal in achieving greater self-determination and sharpened the cultural conflict between mainstream American and Native American values.

Spanish-speaking Americans were influenced by wartime experiences in many ways. Most lived in the Southwest and the West, and significant numbers could be found also in the barrios of midwestern cities. Small farmers living in southern Colorado and northern New Mexico eked out a meager living on lands that they had occupied for many generations. In most areas Hispanic Americans were poor unskilled or semiskilled workers with little education and were subject to ethnic discrimination. The availability of jobs in the war economy opened new vistas for Hispanic Americans. In the rural villages of New Mexico, for example, one-half of the male population left to secure work in larger towns and cities. Many learned new trades under the auspices of the State Department of Vocational Education. Others secured jobs in industries that had not previously afforded them such opportunities.

The Mexican-American response to the war effort was enthusiastic. Often isolated in small villages or urban barrios, Mexican-Americans found military service a bridge to the outside world from which they had largely been excluded. Throughout the nation, Mexican-Americans volunteered for the armed forces in numbers much higher than warranted by their proportion in the population. New Mexico—with its large Spanish-speaking population—had the largest number of military volunteers per capita of any state in the nation. Many New Mexicans served in the Philippines in the 200th and 515th Coast Artillery. Seventeen Mexican-Americans earned the Congressional Medal of Honor. Of the fourteen Texans who were awarded the medal, five were Mexican-American. Among the war heroes of the Mexican-American community was Guy Gabaldon, who talked 1,000 Japanese into surrendering at the Battle of Saipan. José Martinez of Colorado had the distinction of being the first draftee to win the Congressional Medal of Honor.

In the first year of the war, discrimination against Hispanic Americans was widespread, whether in the copper mines of Arizona or in the shipyards and oil refineries on the Gulf and Pacific coasts. But as the labor shortage increased, many of these barriers fell, and Mexican-Americans were able to secure better-paying jobs. To relieve the shortage of farm labor, the United States government negotiated an agreement with Mexico, which provided for the import of *braceros*, as noted earlier.

In 1942, President Roosevelt appointed Carlos Castañeda of the University of Texas to the dual roles of special assistant on Latin American problems and assistant to the chairman of the Fair Employment Practices Committee. The Spanish-speaking People's Division was created in the Office of Inter-American Affairs. Under the direction of Carey McWilliams—a well-known writer who championed the cause of Mexican-Americans—this office sought to lessen discrimination against Hispanic Americans. Its influence, for example, led to a lessening of segregation in public schools, particularly in California and Texas. Texas established teacher training institutes during World War II to enable teachers to work with Spanish-speaking students.

War-generated tensions also affected Hispanics. In Los Angeles, groups of Mexican-American youths formed *Pachuco* gangs, known for their distinctive attire, which consisted of "zoot suits"—flashy suits characterized by jackets with large shoulder pads and with flared-knee trousers—long hair, broad-brimmed felt hats, and pocket knives. These gangs roamed the streets and engaged in acts of vandalism, sometimes attacking servicemen from nearby bases. Frequently rival gangs fought. In June 1943 a group of sailors from the Chávez Ravine Naval Base entered the East Los Angeles section where the gangs were concentrated. Without much police interference, they attacked the gangs as well as any blacks who were in sight. A large-scale riot involving more than 1,000 youths ensued, lasting two days before order could be restored. During the spring of 1943 similar smaller disturbances rocked San Diego, Long Beach, Chicago, Detroit, and Philadelphia.

The Tragedy of Japanese-Americans

Of all the victims of discrimination, the Japanese-Americans were treated to the most extreme form of racial prejudice. It is true that the treatment of aliens by the federal government in World War II contrasted favorably with the World War I experience. In 1919 and 1920, aliens had been harassed and imprisoned, and the federal government freely violated their civil rights. By contrast, from 1941 to 1945 the federal courts zealously guarded the civil liberties of aliens or opponents of the war. But Japanese nationals and Americans of Japanese ancestry (*nisei*), were an exception.

Soon after Pearl Harbor, Secretary of War Henry L. Stimson and the War Department urged President Roosevelt to remove about 120,000 Japanese—citizens as well as aliens—from the West Coast, where most of them resided. In part they were responding to the clamor of important public figures on the Pacific coast such as California's attorney general, Earl Warren, who later became a Supreme Court justice. Some westerners feared collaboration if there were a direct attack by Japanese naval forces. Others had disliked the Japanese-Americans for decades, resenting their lack of assimilation and their skills in farming, horticulture, and commerce. Pearl Harbor crystallized many of these fears and prejudices. "We believe that when we are dealing with the Caucasian race, we have methods that will test the loyalty of them," declared Earl Warren, "but when we deal with the Japanese, we are in an entirely different field, and we cannot form any opinion that we believe to be sound." As such pressures converged on the White House, in March 1942, President Roosevelt requested congressional authorization to order the evacuation of all Japanese-Americans from the Pacific coast.

By June the federal government had herded more than 100,000 Japanese-Americans into hastily erected detention camps in seven western states in the Rocky Mountain region. Most evacuees were allowed to bring only a few personal items and clothing. They were forced to abandon their homes, their businesses, and all other possessions. In the camps—administered by the War Relocation Authority—Japanese-Americans lived in large wooden barracks furnished with cots. They were provided with communal eating and recreational facilities. Many of the persons detained were bitter, for they were loyal Americans who had committed no offense. Their racial ancestry was the sole reason for their internment. Some sought legal recourse. In *Hirabayashi* v. *United States* (1943) the Supreme Court upheld the right of military officials to detain Japanese and Japanese-Americans. In December 1944, however, the Court noted in *ex parte Endo* that detention of loyal persons was illegal. As the wave of war hysteria subsided in 1943, the War Relocation Authority began a program of gradual release. In January 1945 all Japanese-Americans still interned were allowed to leave. The experience left deep emotional scars among those who underwent this traumatic experience and was yet another example of the deep-seated racial feelings of many Americans. In 1989, Congress formally recognized the injustice of the internments and agreed to pay monetary compensation to those involved and to their descendants. It was a belated acknowledgment of what had been a serious violation of Americans' civil rights.

President Roosevelt did not live to see victory over Japan. Worn down by his role as commander in chief, the 1944 election, and the Yalta Confer-

ence, he sought rest in late March at a favorite vacation retreat in Warm
Springs, Georgia. There, on April 12, 1945, while sitting for a portrait, he
suddenly collapsed of heart failure. He died within two hours. The nation
and much of the world mourned his passing, knowing that an epoch in the
American experience had come to an end.

Roosevelt's successor, Harry S Truman, continued to press the war
against Japan. American air raids on Japan intensified in the spring and
summer of 1945. Although rumors of Japanese desires to end the fighting
reached Washington, D.C., no substantial settlement had crystallized by
July 1945 when Truman met with Churchill and Stalin at Potsdam, Germany,
to discuss joint policies. On that occasion the new president warned Japan to
surrender. His demand, however, did not elicit an immediate response from
the Japanese. Truman gave this warning knowing that American scientists
had just developed the first atomic bomb. On July 28, 1945, Truman authorized its use, and nine days later an American plane dropped an atomic bomb
on Hiroshima, Japan. Its destructiveness was unprecedented. It leveled
most of the city and killed more than 80,000 persons. Three days later
American aircraft dropped another atomic bomb on Nagasaki. At the same
time, the Soviet Union declared war on Japan. In desperation, Japan surrendered unconditionally. On September 2, 1945, known as VJ Day, U.S. Army
General Douglas MacArthur received the Japanese delegation on the battle-
ship *Missouri* in Tokyo harbor. The global conflict was now officially over.
More than 292,000 Americans had lost their lives in the fighting, and 671,000
had sustained injuries. In terms of both lives and materials, the Second
World War was the costliest foreign conflict in the nation's history.

Though the nation paid dearly for waging this war, it had positive repercussions at home. As women and minority groups took advantage of new
economic opportunities, they developed greater self-awareness and self-
confidence, to flower more fully in future years. The ideological overtones of
the war as a struggle between freedom and totalitarianism focused attention
on the inequalities in American society and thus benefited movements for
greater equality. The increased urbanization of the nation in wartime also
served to stimulate the political cohesiveness of women and minority groups
and heightened their desire for more active political participation. The war
did much to lay the foundations for the feminist and civil rights movements
that gained momentum in the second half of the twentieth century.

C H A P T E R   1 6

Legacy of a
Crucial Era

1945–1991

In retrospect, it is clear that the period from 1929 to 1945 constitutes a distinct epoch in the history of America. This period witnessed a remarkable transformation of life in the United States as Americans strove to cope with problems of unprecedented magnitude in their own lives and in the life of the nation. The issues and policies that emerged preoccupied the country for four decades. Not until the middle of the 1980s did the patterns established during the New Deal and World War II start to disintegrate. The generation of men and women who grew to maturity between 1929 and 1945 never forgot the experiences of their youth in this crucial era. And as they assumed leadership positions during the next forty years—in foreign policy, in politics, in gender and race relations, in cultural, social, and myriad other phases of American life—the impress of this period did much to shape their view of the world and their problem-solving approach.

The names of many of these individuals quickly come to mind. Certainly presidents such as Truman, Eisenhower, Kennedy, Johnson, Reagan, and Bush shaped their policies in support of or in reaction to their experiences in the Depression and World War II years. Diplomats like Acheson, Dulles, Rusk, and Kissinger developed their programs against the background of events in the crucial era. Notable women such as Eleanor Roosevelt; Oveta Culp Hobby, who served in the Eisenhower administration; and Betty Friedan, an early feminist, formed their views in the context of these years, as did a wide range of writers such as James Jones, James G. Cozzens, and Truman Capote. Members of this generation did much to shape the contours of American life for four decades. By the 1980s, however, time was taking its toll and thinning their numbers. In their place new leaders arose, men and women born in the post–World War II era, the product of other influences.

180

Economic Legacy

The crucial era provided models for many of the economic policies of postwar America. One significant heritage was the concept of a government-managed economy, an economy in which the federal government played a major role in efforts to maintain prosperity and stability. Before 1929 most Americans had considered economic matters the responsibility of individuals and private enterprise. But as federal officials assumed increasingly greater burdens for the nation's economic welfare between 1929 and 1945, they transformed the attitudes of most Americans. By 1945 a majority of voters had come to agree that this was a prime public function. The Employment Act of 1946 institutionalized this belief by making full employment a federal responsibility and by establishing the Council of Economic Advisers to suggest economic policies to the president. Congress enacted this law by overwhelming majorities, and it received widespread bipartisan support in ensuing decades. Such consensus also met the methods to be used in achieving economic stability, methods that the Roosevelt administration had developed during the Depression and the war. These included large-scale deficit spending, unbalanced budgets, and an array of Federal Reserve Board policies to raise or lower interest rates so as to manipulate the pace of economic activity.

The crucial era also crystallized corporate capitalism in the United States. During the years from 1929 to 1945, Americans chose neither laissez-faire nor a completely government-controlled economic system. They opted for a middle way, a mixed economy characterized by private enterprise coexisting with an intricate network of federal, state, and local regulation. Some segments of this economy were characterized by oligopoly, control of entire industries by a few large corporations. Despite the fact that federal antitrust laws could be used to determine the balance in particular sectors, the 500 largest corporations in the United States in 1991 controlled about two-thirds of all corporate assets in the nation. This pattern of a mixed economy dominated by giant corporations first emerged during the crucial era and came to characterize American economic life during the second half of the twentieth century.

The crucial era saw the institutionalization of the regulatory state in the United States. During the Depression and the war, the Roosevelt administration developed an intricate network of federal regulatory controls over business, finance, agriculture, and labor that remained virtually intact until the 1980s. Even thereafter, New Deal agencies and their successors—such as the Securities and Exchange Commission, the National Labor Relations Board, the Tennessee Valley Authority, the Federal Power Commission, and the Federal Communications Commission—continued to regulate major segments of the economy and to make government a partner in management of the economy.

Military Legacy

The period between 1929 and 1945 was significant also in giving birth to a military-industrial complex in the United States. This was to become an increasingly prominent fixture in American life during the course of the century. Before 1929, military expenditures had always played a minor role in peacetime. But after 1941 such outlays came to be a major factor in national affairs, largely because of Cold War fears. Unlike the post–World War I decade, after 1945 the federal government did not close most of the military bases it opened during the war. Instead, it retained and expanded many of them. They became a regular fixture in thousands of communities throughout the United States and an integral part of the economy. The interchange of individuals between the military and civilian sectors, between the armed services and their suppliers, wove an intricate network of relationships that made the peacetime economy far more dependent on the military than it had ever been.

Such relationships were sustained because of a high level of military expenditures by the federal government, based on precedents developed during World War II. Before 1939, Congress had appropriated less than 1 percent of the gross national product (GNP) for military purposes. During World War II this ratio increased dramatically, exceeding 30 percent. But in 1945 peace did not bring a return to prewar levels of military expenditures. Many of the fears engendered by appeasement policies of the 1930s led Americans to continue a high level of appropriations for the military, ranging from 8 to 20 percent of GNP annually in the four decades after 1945. That resulted in a large standing army, navy, and air force on a scale such as the United States had never had before in peacetime. The federal government established a vast network of military bases, scientific research facilities for weapons, and testing centers. A large military establishment became a permanent fixture, a way of life, in post–World War II America, part of the heritage of the crucial era.

Civil Rights Legacy

The years from 1929 to 1945 provided a base for the civil rights movement of succeeding decades. Many conditions that grew out of wartime necessities served to support civil rights activism in later years. These included an expanded range of job opportunities originally created by labor shortages. The Fair Employment Practices Committee in 1941 established a precedent for the use of federal powers to lessen discriminatory barriers. Military service by blacks further stimulated the desire for equal treatment and equal opportunity. Having served their country well, many blacks felt that they had earned the right to respect and nondiscrimination. Racial consciousness was also reinforced by the wartime trend for black Americans to move to where the jobs were, the cities. Feelings of solidarity and self-worth were strengthened ideologically during the war as Americans emphasized the contrasts between democratic and totalitarian ideals and found their own shortcomings in race relations increasingly embarrassing. At the same time, the growth of independence movements in colonial empires in Africa during the 1940s and the rise of independent states there in the 1950s gave black Americans a stronger sense of identity and racial pride. In these and many other ways, events of the crucial era provided an agenda that civil rights advocates in the postwar decade hoped to implement more fully, an agenda emphasizing the abolition of discrimination, equal opportunities, and racial awareness, increasingly called black nationalism.

The period between 1929 and 1945 also inaugurated profound changes for Hispanics in the United States. The Great Depression accelerated their movement from rural areas into the cities, from agricultural pursuits to jobs in service and manufacturing industries. World War II accelerated the pace of these changes. The war also provided an opportunity for several hundred thousand young Hispanic men and women to serve in the armed forces. There they learned new skills and trades and also developed an increased sense of pride and ethnic awareness. The crucial era thus created a framework for changing Hispanic lifestyles that did much to set precedents for the next forty years. In the years after 1945, Hispanics increasingly became an urban people. In contrast to the years before 1929, a majority now lived in cities. The barrios of many large metropolitan areas in the United States— New York City, Chicago, Los Angeles, Denver, El Paso, Phoenix, Tucson, and Albuquerque—now came to contain a significant portion of the total population. Such urban concentrations not only heightened ethnic consciousness and cultural awareness but also stimulated the demand for more equal civil rights. At the same time, it fostered increased political involvement of Hispanics as they became an increasingly important voting bloc.

Native Americans could also look back on the years between 1929 and 1945 as some of the most significant in their history. The Native American policies of the New Deal had fostered greater cultural awareness and self-determination. The war service of Native Americans had fostered increased ethnic pride, provided job training for some, and broadened cultural and geographic horizons. These experiences conditioned the new generation of leaders in the generation after 1945. The GI Bill, which provided educational benefits for veterans, was especially important for Native Americans because until then most of them had been unable to afford a college education. Most of the prominent Native American educators and politicians between 1945 and 1990 were World War II veterans. The conflict also made Native Americans more insistent on winning civil and political rights because in some western states they were denied the right to vote and to hold office before 1945. Having served their nation well, these Americans rightly expected all of the perquisites of citizenship. The crucial era thus did much to set the agenda for the lives of many Native Americans during the second half of the twentieth century. It fostered their movement to the cities (where more than one-third lived by 1990), opened up new economic opportunities, and whetted their appetite for greater political and civil rights.

Historians are still debating to what extent the years between 1929 and 1945 were a spur to the feminist movement later in the century. Clearly, many factors were at work to bring about changes in the position of women in American society. Some of the conditions of the crucial era provided precedents. One of these was the lessening of job discrimination as women proved during World War II that they were capable of performing a wide range of tasks that had previously been exclusively the domain of men. If the memory of such experiences faded, it was not forgotten. And the service of women in the military establishment during wartime effectively dramatized the issue of equal rights and made it a responsibility of government.

Political Legacy

Many of the measures undertaken in the crucial era were to dominate American domestic politics until the 1980s. Certainly this was true of Franklin Roosevelt's domestic agenda. His successors in the White House, both Democrats and Republicans, were dedicated to the consolidation or expansion of many of the programs he had initiated. Thus Harry Truman presented his Fair Deal to the American people, advocating expansion of many New Deal programs such as social security, economic regulation of business, and subsidies for public housing and agriculture. Dwight Eisenhower, under the banner of Moderate Republicanism, consolidated many New Deal measures even when he did not expand their range. John Kennedy deliberately sought to imitate Roosevelt. He launched his own programs, which he boldly announced would lead America to New Frontiers. Although in fact Kennedy proposed little that was new, he promised a more vigorous implementation of social and economic policies first initiated during the New Deal. His successor, Lyndon Johnson, was an even greater admirer of Roosevelt. Johnson's greatest wish was to equal or exceed Roosevelt's accomplishments in domestic and foreign affairs. His Great Society programs were designed to extend the New Deal on a vast scale. Rather than devise original reforms, Johnson based most of his proposals on precedents first created between 1929 and 1945. As loyal Republicans, Richard Nixon and Gerald Ford did not openly pay homage to Roosevelt. Yet their programs were still largely within the framework of the crucial era, and they did little to undo New Deal ideas.

President Carter was not an avid politician, but his successor, Ronald Reagan, was a former New Deal Democrat who had voted for Roosevelt in the New Deal and World War II era. Although openly avowing a desire to reverse some New Deal measures, some historians believed that Reagan defined his own proposals against the backdrop of programs established in the crucial era.

The New Deal age also created patterns for political party alignments in the next generation. Between 1929 and 1945, Roosevelt fashioned a winning combination of interest groups within the Democratic party. They included ethnic groups and minorities in the big cities, middle-class Americans, organized labor, farmers, small business people, and many southerners. That combination proved to be a potent force in American politics until 1968, when it began to disintegrate. Southerners increasingly gravitated to the Republican party, as did a growing number of middle-class Americans. Meanwhile, labor and farm groups became weaker as their numbers shrank. As a result, in the two decades after 1968, Republicans dominated the White House, with the exception of the one-term Carter administration. Nevertheless, even in the 1970s and 1980s, the Democrats still hoped to maintain the major components of the Roosevelt coalition.

The crucial era did much to define the nature of the American presidency during the second half of the twentieth century. By greatly expanding the use of presidential powers so that they often overshadowed the legislative and judicial branches, Roosevelt created what later observers designated the imperial presidency. That became a model that his successors followed. Similarly, they adopted Roosevelt's use of the mass media to build a personal image. Roosevelt excelled at using the radio. Truman and Eisenhower continued that tradition, developing their own styles. By 1960 television had become sufficiently well established to be a powerful force in American politics. Kennedy manipulated it effectively in his debates with Richard Nixon during the presidential campaign of 1960 and made extensive use of media experts. The Kennedys fashioned the myth of Camelot—a noble young knight and his fair lady—that was not an accurate reflection of reality. But television became such an important factor in American politics that some critics in the 1970s and 1980s charged that it had made image more important than substance.

Perhaps the most significant political heritage left by the crucial era was the tradition of big government. The consensus that Roosevelt forged among the American people between 1933 and 1945 expressed faith in a federal government that was strong enough to cope with the problems that arose in a capitalist-oriented industrial society. Big government regulated and modulated the national economy, it was the foundation for the social welfare state, and it was the conservator of the natural environment. To carry out these responsibilities, Americans agreed, though reluctantly at times, that an ex-

Master of the air waves:Franklin D. Roosevelt delivering a Fireside Chat in 1936.
(*UPI/Acme*)

panded professional bureaucracy was needed. That came to be the fourth
branch of government in the United States. Thus the crucial era gave birth to
an organizational society dominated by private as well as public bureaucra-
cies in many aspects of American life.

Environmental Legacy

The crucial era contributed to a growing environmental consciousness in
later years. The Great Depression as well as World War II heightened national awareness about the end of American self-sufficiency and increasing
dependence on foreign supplies of minerals and petroleum. The increased
pace of resource use in wartime sharpened this awareness. Wartime activities accentuated water and air pollution, increased timber cutting, and led to
the neglect of peacetime conservation programs. The worsening of such
problems in the next two decades contributed to the surge of environmental

concerns that surfaced in the 1960s and led Congress to enact a variety of stringent environmental regulatory measures during the presidency of Lyndon Johnson.

Cultural Legacy

The cultural policies of the Roosevelt years also left precedents that succeeding generations developed further. Among these, government patronage of the arts and the sciences was prominent. Although Congress abolished WPA cultural programs in 1943, it revived them more than twenty years later when it established the National Endowment for the Humanities and the National Endowment for the Arts. The lawmakers acted more promptly in regard to science: they established the National Science Foundation in 1950 to carry on many of the activities of the Office of Scientific Research and Development created during World War II. Unlike the years before 1929, government now became a major supporter of cultural and scientific activities in the United States. In addition, wartime experiences in mass publishing left an impact on the next generation. Many of the young men and women who were involved in such wartime activities as publishing and mass distribution of paperback books for the armed forces carried their experiences into private industry in succeeding decades. The vast expansion of paperback books after 1945 was spawned to a considerable extent by experiences during the Second World War.

Diplomatic Legacy

Many events and policies of the crucial era helped to shape the framework of American foreign policy into the 1980s. Just as the Great Depression contributed to the rise of totalitarian regimes in Germany, Italy, and Japan, World War II diminished their role as major world powers in the next generation. The war also led indirectly to the collapse of the colonial empires of Great Britain, France, the Netherlands, Belgium, and Portugal and the consequent independence of third world nations in Africa, Asia, and the Middle East. The Allied victory in World War II left the world with two superpowers, the United States and the Soviet Union. The struggle between them for dominance in the international balance of powers between 1945 and the 1980s, known as the Cold War, dominated world affairs during those years. It also led to some military confrontations, the most serious occurring in Korea and Vietnam. Only in the late 1980s, with the reconciliation of the superpowers, did the Cold War abate.

The crucial era did much to set the tone of United States foreign policy for the next forty years. Many of the men and women who conducted American diplomacy during these years developed their world views, their assumptions, between 1929 and 1945. Secretaries of State Dean Acheson, George C. Marshall, John Foster Dulles, and Dean Rusk had all developed their approaches during the crucial era. Many were haunted by the specter of British and French appeasement of Nazi Germany in the 1930s that had been epitomized by the Munich Crisis of 1938, when France and England virtually handed Czechoslovakia to Hitler. That incident did much to shape their attitude toward the Soviet Union after 1945, as they hoped to avoid a repetition of such appeasement and the possible consequences of another world war. And, as noted earlier, President George Bush used the analogy of Munich to defend his dispatch of troops to Saudi Arabia in 1990 to deter the expansion of Iraq in the Middle East.

It would be difficult to fix on another span of sixteen years in the twentieth century that left such a comprehensive legacy to succeeding generations as the crucial era. In almost every area of life it left its imprint on the next generation and provided the context in which Americans faced major problems in the second half of the twentieth century—economic insecurity and war. The men and women who shaped events between 1929 and 1945 left a legacy that was to be long remembered and long felt.

Bibliography

General Works: 1929–1941

Perhaps the best-written account of the New Deal is the series by Arthur Schlesinger, Jr., *The Age of Roosevelt* (3 vols., Boston, 1957–1960), a highly sympathetic but unfinished work that does not extend beyond 1936. Volume titles are *The Crisis of the Old Order, The Coming of the New Deal,* and *The Politics of Upheaval.* A shorter, general, one-volume work on the New Deal by William E. Leuchtenburg is *Franklin D. Roosevelt and the New Deal, 1932–1940* (New York, 1963), which restricts itself largely to national and international politics. Students desiring a broad but brief survey will benefit from Dexter Perkins, *The New Age of Franklin D. Roosevelt, 1932–1945* (Chicago, 1957). Edgar E. Robinson, a great admirer of Herbert Hoover, presents an indictment of Roosevelt in *The Roosevelt Leadership, 1933–1945* (Philadelphia, 1955). A stimulating foreign view of the era is by Mario Einaudi, *The Roosevelt Revolution* (New York, 1959). One of the most graphic descriptions of Depression conditions as they affected working people is found in Irving Bernstein, *The Lean Years* (Boston, 1960). This may be supplemented by an excellent collection of contemporary sources about life during the economic crisis in David Shannon (ed.), *The Great Depression* (Englewood Cliffs, 1960). The psychological suffering wrought by the Depression is clearly explained in a fine popular work by Caroline Bird, *The Invisible Scar* (New York, 1966).

More recent general surveys of the period include Peter Fearon, *War, Prosperity, and Depression: The U.S. Economy, 1917–1945* (Lawrence, 1987), an excellent, clearly written account stressing economic developments, and Michael Bernstein, *The Great Depression: Delayed Recovery and Economic Change in America, 1929–1939* (New York, 1988), which concentrates more fully on the Depression decade. A broader, popularly written overview is by Robert S. McElvaine, *The Great Depression: America, 1929–1941* (New York, 1989). Recent years have witnessed increasing interest in Herbert Hoover, and various studies emphasize his flexibility, including Ellis W. Hawley, *The Great War and the Search for a Modern*

189

Order (New York, 1979), and a journalistic description by Gene Smith, *The Shattered Dream: Herbert Hoover and the Great Depression* (New York, 1984). Changing ideas about big government are covered in William J. Barber, *From New Era to New Deal: Herbert Hoover, the Economists, and American Economic Policy* (New York, 1985). A multivolume biography of Hoover by George H. Nash is not yet completed, but meanwhile a very competent one-volume work by Martin Fausold is available, *The Presidency of Herbert Hoover* (Lawrence, 1985). Firsthand reports concerning Americans in the Depression include Richard Lowitt (ed.), *One-Third of a Nation: Lorena Hickock Reports on the Great Depression* (Urbana, 1986), and Robert S. McElvaine (ed.), *Down and Out in the Great Depression: Letters from the "Forgotten Man"* (Chapel Hill, 1983).

Franklin D. Roosevelt

There exists a large body of biographical literature about Roosevelt. One of the best one-volume biographies is *Roosevelt: The Lion and the Fox* (New York, 1956) by James M. Burns. Frank Freidel wrote a multivolume life of Roosevelt—*Franklin D. Roosevelt: The Apprenticeship* (Boston, 1952), *Franklin D. Roosevelt: The Ordeal* (Boston, 1955), *Franklin D. Roosevelt: The Triumph* (Boston, 1955), and *Franklin D. Roosevelt: The Interregnum* [1932–1933] (Boston, 1976). Rexford G. Tugwell, in *The Democratic Roosevelt* (Garden City, 1957), presents a shrewd appraisal as a former close associate and member of the Brains Trust. A charming, warmhearted remembrance of the president by Secretary of Labor Frances Perkins is titled *The Roosevelt I Knew* (New York, 1946). For a short anthology of original source writings by and about Roosevelt, see Gerald D. Nash (ed.), *Franklin Delano Roosevelt* (Englewood Cliffs, 1967). A volume focusing on his personal dimension is by Nathan Miller, *FDR: An Intimate History* (Garden City, 1983). A fuller, more detailed portrait emerges in companion works by Kenneth Davis, *FDR: The New York Years, 1928–1933* (New York, 1985), and *FDR: The New Deal Years, 1933–1937* (New York, 1986). Hugh G. Gallagher, in *FDR's Splendid Deception* (New York, 1985), deals primarily with the president's physical disability and how he overcame it. Geoffrey C. Ward, *A First Class Temperament: The Emergence of Franklin Roosevelt* (New York, 1989), focuses on personality. The most comprehensive new one-volume biography is by Frank Freidel, *Rendezvous with Destiny* (Boston, 1990). On Roosevelt's relationship with his wife, Joseph Lash, *Eleanor and Franklin* (Garden City, 1971), is indispensable. On her circle, see Joseph Lash, *Love Eleanor: Eleanor Roosevelt and Her Friends* (Garden City, 1982). A competent biography of Mrs. Roosevelt is by William T. Youngs, *ER: A Personal and Public Life* (Boston, 1985).

The Hundred Days

The Hundred Days is the subject of a reminiscence by Brains Truster Rexford G. Tugwell in *The Brains Trust* (New York, 1968), and the chief Brains Truster, Raymond Moley, presents his view of this exciting period in *After Seven Years* (New York, 1939). The president's principal speech writer, Samuel Rosenman, reminisces in *Working with Roosevelt* (New York, 1952). Hugh R. Johnson, administrator of the NRA, discusses the establishment of that agency in *The Blue Eagle, from Egg to Earth* (Garden City, 1935), and Edwin G. Nourse et al. in *Three Years of the Agricultural Adjustment Act* (Washington, 1937) describe the growth of New Deal farm programs. Van L. Perkins in *Crisis in Agriculture: The Agricultural Adjustment Administration and the New Deal* (Berkeley, 1969) provides a later and more comprehensive appraisal. Relief efforts are illuminated by Searle Charles in *Minister of Relief: Harry Hopkins and the Depression* (Syracuse, 1963) and in Paul Douglas, *Social Security in the United States* (New York, 1936). Vivid description of the Brains Trust at work are in Elliott Rosen, *Hoover, Roosevelt, and the Brains Trust: From Depression to New Deal* (New York, 1977). See also Samuel B. Hand, *Counsel and Advise: A Political Biography of Samuel L. Rosenman* (New York, 1979). An excellent comprehensive view of the Hundred Days is to be found in James E. Sargent, *Roosevelt and the Hundred Days: Struggle for the Early New Deal* (New York, 1981).

The Experimental New Deal

The experimental phase of the New Deal is covered in general works noted earlier and in various more specialized studies. The NRA is analyzed by Everett S. Lyon et al. in *The National Recovery Administration* (Washington, 1935) and by one of its chief officials, Donald R. Richberg, in *The Rainbow* (New York, 1936). Fiscal policies are discussed clearly by Herbert Stein, *The Fiscal Revolution in America* (Chicago, 1969). A stimulating discussion of experimentation in farm policies is by Richard S. Kirkendall, *Social Scientists and Farm Politics in the Age of Roosevelt* (Columbia, 1966). An excellent survey of labor and labor legislation is by Irving Bernstein, *Turbulent Years: A History of the American Worker, 1933–1941* (Boston, 1970). Experiments with relief can be followed in Donald Howard's book *The WPA and Federal Relief Policy* (New York, 1943) and in Lewis L. Lorwin's *Youth Work Programs* (Washington, 1941). One of the finest comprehensive accounts is by Albert U. Romasco, *The Politics of Recovery: Roosevelt's New Deal* (New York, 1983). On the CWA, see Bonnie F. Schwartz, *The Civil Works Administration, 1933–34: The Business of Emergency Employment in the New Deal* (Princeton, 1984). Good biographies of major architects of the

New Deal include Graham White and John Maze, *Harold Ickes and the New Deal: His Private Life and Public Career* (Cambridge, 1985), and George McJimsey, *Harry Hopkins: Ally of the Poor and Defender of Democracy* (Cambridge, 1987).

Protest against the New Deal

Political reaction against the New Deal is described by Irving Howe and Lewis Coser in *The American Communist Party* (New York, 1957) and by David Shannon in *The Decline of American Communism* (New York, 1959). Donald McCoy, author of *Angry Voices* (Lawrence, 1958), deals with reform-minded third-party groups. A brilliant depiction of Huey Long is T. Harry Williams, *Huey S. Long* (New York, 1969). Abraham Holtzman, *The Townsend Movement: A Political Study* (Syracuse, 1963), is useful, as is Charles J. Tully, *Father Coughlin and the New Deal* (Syracuse, 1965). Charles C. Blackorby, *Prairie Rebel: The Public Life of William Lemke* (Lincoln, 1963), outlines a dissident's view of Roosevelt's policies. The most comprehensive recent work on opponents of the New Deal is Alan Brinkley, *Voices of Protest: Huey Long, Father Coughlin, and the Great Depression* (New York, 1982). Among books dealing with specific individuals are Rodney P. Carlisle, *Hearst and the New Deal: The Progressive as Reactionary* (New York, 1979), Donald L. Miller, *The New American Radicalism: Alfred M. Bingham and Non-Marxian Insurgency in the New Deal Era* (Port Washington, 1979), Donald A. Mulder, *The Insurgent Progressives in the U.S. Senate and the New Deal, 1933–1939* (New York, 1979), and Harvey Klehr, *The Heyday of American Communism: The Depression Decade* (New York, 1984).

The Reform New Deal

The reform phase of the New Deal is brilliantly surveyed in *The Age of Roosevelt* (vol. 3) by Arthur Schlesinger, Jr. It can be followed in briefer form in Broadus Mitchell's *Depression Decade* (New York, 1947). On specialized aspects, see David C. Lilienthal, *TVA: Democracy on the March* (New York, 1944), and Roscoe C. Martin (ed.), *TVA: The First Twenty Years* (University, 1956). Roy Lubove, *The Struggle for Social Security* (Cambridge, 1968), is the best single work on the subject. Paul Conkin, *Tomorrow a New World* (Ithaca, 1959), covers community planning by New Deal agencies. Richard S. Polenberg, *Reorganizing Roosevelt's Government, 1936–1939* (Cambridge, 1966), is a competent monograph on that topic. The New Deal's efforts to develop health policies are discussed in David S. Hirshfield, *The Last Reform: The Campaign for Compulsory Health Insurance in the United States from 1932 to 1943* (Cambridge, 1970). An excellent account of one of the most successful New Deal agencies is D. Clayton Brown, *Electricity for*

Rural America: The Fight for the REA (Westport, 1980). Marion Clawson, *New Deal Planning: The National Resources Planning Board* (Baltimore, 1981), makes a plea for reestablishment of this planning agency. In recent years historians have taken a more critical view of the Tennessee Valley Authority. An example is Michael J. McDonald and John Muldowner, *TVA and the Dispossessed: The Resettlement of Population in the Norris Dam Area* (Knoxville, 1982). On social security, see W. Andrew Achenbaum, *Social Security: Visions and Revisions* (Cambridge, 1989), and Gerald D. Nash et al. (eds.), *Social Security: The First Fifty Years* (Albuquerque, 1988), which contains the reflections of leading framers of the social security system. A shorter survey of New Deal farm policies is by Theodore Saloutos, *The American Farmer and the New Deal* (Ames, 1982). One of the best summaries of New Deal labor legislation is by Irving Bernstein, *A Caring Society: The New Deal, the Workers, and the Great Depression* (Boston, 1985). The decline of reform sentiment is traced by David L. Porter, *Congress and the Waning of the New Deal* (Port Washington, 1980). On the South, see relevant chapters in George B. Tindall, *The Emergence of the New South, 1913–1945* (Baton Rouge, 1967), Pete Daniel, *Standing at the Crossroads* (New York, 1986), and Gavin Wright, *Old South, New South: Revolutions in the Southern Economy since the Civil War* (New York, 1986). For a detailed study of a single southern community, see Dolores E. Janiewski, *Sisterhood Denied: Race, Gender, and Class in a New South Community* (Philadelphia, 1983), Roger Biles, *Memphis in the Great Depression* (Knoxville, 1986), or Douglas L. Smith, *The New Deal in the Urban South* (Baton Rouge, 1988). Several works dealing with individual states have been written, including John D. Minton, *The New Deal in Tennessee, 1932–1938* (New York, 1979), Anthony J. Badger, *Prosperity Road: The New Deal, Tobacco, and North Carolina* (Chapel Hill, 1980), and Ronald L. Heineman, *Depression and New Deal in Virginia: The Enduring Dominion* (Charlottesville, 1983). On the West, see Richard Lowitt, *The New Deal and the West* (Bloomington, 1984), Paul Bonnifield, *The Dust Bowl: Men, Dirt, and Depression* (Albuquerque, 1979), and Donald Worster, *The Dust Bowl: The Southern Plains in the 1930s* (New York, 1979). A study of one state is by James F. Wickens, *Colorado in the Great Depression* (New York, 1979). Shorter surveys can be found in Gerald D. Nash, *The American West in the Twentieth Century* (Albuquerque, 1977), and Michael Malone and Richard W. Etulain, *The American West* (Lincoln, 1989).

Women during the Great Depression

The most concise general survey is Susan Ware, *Holding Their Own: American Women in the 1930s* (Boston, 1982). More specialized studies by Ware on the 1930s include *Beyond Suffrage: Women in the New Deal* (Cambridge,

1981), and *Partner and I: Molly Dewson, Feminism, and the New Deal* (New Haven, 1987). Helpful also are Lois Scharf, *To Work and to Wed: Formal Employment, Feminism, and the Great Depression* (Westport, 1980), Winifred Wandersee, *Women's Work and Family Values, 1920–1940* (Cambridge, 1981), and Lois Scharf and Joan Jensen, *Decades of Discontent: The Women's Movement, 1920–1940* (Westport, 1983). Some general studies of women contain relevant chapters on the 1930s, such as William H. Chafe, *The American Woman, 1920–1970* (New York, 1972), and Lois W. Banner, *Women in Modern America: A Brief History* (New York, 1974). Contemporary accounts that deserve mention are Eleanor Roosevelt, *It's Up to the Women* (New York, 1933), and Mary Beard, *America through Women's Eyes* (New York, 1933). A lively collection of oral histories is provided by Jeane Westin, *Making Do: How Women Survived the '30s* (Chicago, 1976). On black women, see Gerda Lerner, *Black Women in White America: A Documentary History* (New York, 1972).

The New Deal and Minorities

Oscar Handlin, *The Americans*, provides a general survey of ethnic Americans. Raymond Wolters, in *Negroes and the Great Depression* (Westport, 1970), covers selected phases of the subject, and Gunnar Myrdal, *An American Dilemma* (New York, 1944), is still informative. Donald L. Parman, in *The Navajos and the New Deal* (New Haven, 1976), is one of the best works to deal with a large Native American tribe's experiences during the New Deal. On Spanish-speaking Americans, selected portions of Matt S. Meier and Feliciano Rivera, *The Chicanos: A History of Mexican-Americans* (New York, 1972), provide an overview, as does Manuel Servin (ed.), *The Mexican-Americans* (Beverly Hills, 1970). Abraham Hoffman, in *Unwanted Mexican-Americans in the Great Depression* (Tucson, 1974), deals with a deportation incident. On black Americans, see Harvard Sitkoff, *A New Deal for Blacks: The Emergence of Civil Rights as a National Issue* (New York, 1978), a comprehensive work. Robert L. Zangrando, *The NAACP Crusade against Lynching* (Philadelphia, 1980), focuses on one major issue. John B. Kirby, *Black Americans in the Roosevelt Era: Liberalism and Race* (Knoxville, 1980), provides a good overview. Dominic Capeci, Jr., *The Harlem Riot of 1943* (Philadelphia, 1977), is a superb account of a major riot that traces its roots in the New Deal era. Nancy L. Weiss, *Farewell to the Party of Lincoln: Black Politics in the Age of FDR* (Princeton, 1983), is excellent on black Americans' political behavior. On Native Americans, see Graham D. Taylor, *The New Deal and American Indian Tribalism: The Administration of the Indian Reorganization Act, 1934–45* (Lincoln, 1980), Lawrence M. Hauptman, *The Iroquois and the New Deal* (Syracuse, 1981), and Lawrence C.

Kelley, *The Assault on Assimilation: John Collier and the Origins of Indian Policy Reform* (Albuquerque, 1983).

The New Deal and Cultural Life

In recent years much has been written on cultural life during the Great Depression. Daniel Aaron, in *Writers on the Left* (New York, 1961), analyzes one segment of the literary scene, and contemporary literary critics Maxwell Geismar, *Writers in Crisis* (New York, 1942), and Edmund Wilson, *The Shores of Light* (New Haven, 1952), provide perceptive evaluations. A detailed account of the WPA Writers Project by a former participant is Jerre Mangione, *The Dream and the Deal* (Boston, 1972). William F. McDonald's *Federal Relief Administration and the Arts* (Columbus, 1969) is a comprehensive survey, and *Music in the United States: A Historical Introduction* by H. Wiley Hitchcock (2d ed., Englewood Cliffs, 1974) offers a succinct and informative summary of the 1930s. Jane D. Matthews, *The Federal Theatre* (Princeton, 1967), is the best work on this experiment. Marlene Park and Gerald E. Markowitz, *Democratic Vistas: Post Offices and Public Art in the New Deal* (Philadelphia, 1984), shows how cultural nationalism was reflected in New Deal art programs. David Tyack et al., *Public Schools in Hard Times: The Great Depression and Recent Years* (Cambridge, 1984), attempts to place more recent developments in the context of the Depression era. A fine selection from the WPA Guidebooks series is provided by Archie Hobson (ed.), *Remembering America: A Sampler of the WPA American Guide Series* (New York, 1985). On the movies of the era, see the entertaining volume by Gerald Weales, *Canned Goods as Caviar: American Film Comedy of the 1930s* (Chicago, 1985).

Diplomacy during the Depression

The diplomacy of the Depression is capably surveyed by Robert Divine in *The Illusion of Neutrality* (Chicago, 1962) and by Donald F. Drummond in *The Passing of American Neutrality, 1937–1941* (Ann Arbor, 1955). The works of Selig Adler, *The Isolationist Impulse* (London, 1957), and Wayne S. Cole, *America First* (Madison, 1953), deal more specifically with isolationist sentiment. A more specialized and detailed account is by William L. Langer and S. Everett Gleason, *The Challenge to Isolation, 1937–1940* (New York, 1952). Charles A. Beard, in *American Foreign Policy in the Making, 1932–1940* (New Haven, 1946), offers a severe indictment of Roosevelt's policies. One of the best surveys of Roosevelt's diplomacy is Robert Dalleck, *Franklin D. Roosevelt and American Foreign Policy, 1932–1945* (New York, 1979).

C. A. MacDonald, *The United States, Britain, and Appeasement, 1936–1939* (New York, 1981), provides a special focus on efforts to avert war. David Reynolds, *The Creation of the Anglo-American Alliance, 1937–1940: A Study in Competitive Cooperation* (Chapel Hill, 1982), discusses strains between Great Britain and the United States. Wayne S. Cole, *Roosevelt and the Isolationists, 1932–1945* (Lincoln, 1983), is a concise summary of that subject. Howard Lablon, *Crossroads of Decision: The State Department and Foreign Policy, 1933–1937* (Lexington, 1983), analyzes the role of professional diplomats in Roosevelt's diplomacy.

The Road to War

A fine overall survey of the European and world situation is Gordon Wright, *The Ordeal of Total War, 1939–1945* (New York, 1968). Many of the problems of mobilizing American resources in peacetime are surveyed by Eliot Janeway in *The Struggle for Survival* (2d ed., New Haven, 1968) and by Bruce Catton in *The War Lords of Washington* (New York, 1949). Cordell Hull, in *The Memoirs of Cordell Hull* (2 vols., New York, 1948), and Henry Stimson and McGeorge Bundy, in *On Active Service in Peace and War* (New York, 1948), provide a vivid sense of immediacy for these years. A rather detailed account of the worsening international situation is in William L. Langer and S. E. Gleason, *The Undeclared War, 1940–1941* (New York, 1953). On the election of 1940, Ellsworth Barnard, *Wendell Willkie* (New York, 1966), is useful in re-creating the atmosphere. Worsening relations between the United States and Japan can be followed in Herbert Feis, *The Road to Pearl Harbor* (New York, 1950), and in the popular, well-written book by Walter Millis, *This Is Pearl!* (New York, 1947). A scholarly analysis is by Paul W. Schroeder, *The Axis Alliance and Japanese-American Relations, 1948* (Urbana, 1958). A recollection of Pearl Harbor day is vividly recounted by Walter Lord in *Day of Infamy* (New York, 1957). Studies that bear on this aspect of Roosevelt's diplomacy include Thomas A. Bailey and Paul B. Ryan, *Hitler v. Roosevelt: The Undeclared Naval War* (New York, 1979), Richard Collier, *The Road to Pearl Harbor, 1941* (New York, 1981), and the definitive work by Gordon Prange, *At Dawn We Slept: The Untold Story of Pearl Harbor* (New York, 1981). Diplomatic aspects are stressed by Jonathan Utley in *Going to War with Japan, 1937–1941* (Knoxville, 1985). An excellent comprehensive overview is provided by Waldo Heinrichs, *Threshold of War: Franklin D. Roosevelt and American Entry into World War II* (New York, 1988). On Latin America, see Irwin F. Gellman, *Good Neighbor Diplomacy: United States Policies in Latin America, 1933–1945* (Baltimore, 1979).

Roosevelt's Military and Diplomatic Policies during World War II

One of the best books to summarize President Roosevelt's role as commander in chief is James M. Burns, *Roosevelt: The Soldier of Freedom, 1940–1945* (New York, 1970). A leading military analyst, Hanson W. Baldwin, critically appraises Roosevelt's major military decisions in *Great Mistakes of the War* (New York, 1950). Kent R. Greenfield (ed.), in *Command Decisions* (Washington, 1959), offers a more favorable evaluation. A detailed factual summary of United States military policies is A. Russell Buchanan, *The United States and World War II* (2 vols., New York, 1964). Brief surveys of Roosevelt's war diplomacy include Robert A. Divine, *Roosevelt and World War II* (Baltimore, 1969), and Gaddis Smith, *American Diplomacy during the Second World War* (New York, 1964). The wartime conferences of the Big Three are admirably covered in Herbert Feis's *Churchill, Roosevelt, Stalin: The War They Waged and the Peace They Sought* (New York, 1957). New Left critiques of Roosevelt's diplomacy include Gabriel Kolko, *The Politics of War* (New York, 1969), and Lloyd C. Gardner, *Architects of Illusion* (New York, 1970). Books that deal with particular issues include John H. Backer, *The Decision to Divide Germany: American Foreign Policy in Transition* (Durham, 1978), Monty N. Penkower, *The Jews Were Expendable: Free World Diplomacy and the Holocaust* (Urbana, 1983), and Keith Sainsbury, *The Turning Point: Roosevelt, Stalin, Churchill, and Chiang Kai-shek, 1943: The Moscow, Cairo, and Teheran Conferences* (Oxford, 1985). A very readable and comprehensive work is Eric Larrabee, *Commander-in-Chief: Franklin D. Roosevelt, His Lieutenants, and Their War* (New York, 1987). The literature on the atomic bomb continues to grow. James W. Kunetka, *City of Fire: Los Alamos and the Atomic Age, 1943–1945* (Albuquerque, 1979), provides an exciting look at that wartime scene, as does Frank Szasz, *The Day the Sun Rose Twice: The Story of the Trinity Site Nuclear Explosion, July 16, 1945* (Albuquerque, 1984). A fine biography of the man who directed the Manhattan Project is William Lawren, *The General and the Bomb: A Biography of General Leslie R. Groves, Director of the Manhattan Project* (New York, 1988). On oil in the war, see Aaron D. Miller, *Search for Security: Saudi Arabian Oil and American Foreign Policy, 1939–1949* (Chapel Hill, 1980), Michael B. Stoff, *Oil, War, and American Security: The Search for a National Policy on Foreign Oil, 1941–1947* (New Haven, 1980), and David S. Painter, *Oil and the American Century: The Political Economy of U.S. Foreign Oil Policy, 1941–1954* (Baltimore, 1986). On U.S.-Japanese relations, Akira Iriye, *Power and Culture: The Japanese-American War, 1941–1945* (Cambridge, 1981), is authoritative. Ronald H. Spector, *Eagle against the Sun: The American War with Japan* (New York, 1985), is a broad survey. Outstanding also on its subject is David S. Wyman, *The Abandonment of the Jews: America and the Holocaust, 1941–1945* (New York, 1984).

Domestic Mobilization in Wartime

Wartime mobilization is discussed in Eliot Janeway, *The Struggle for Survival* (2d ed., New Haven, 1968), Bruce Catton, *The War Lords of Washington* (New York, 1949), and Richard Polenberg, *War and Society* (Philadelphia, 1972). James P. Baxter III, in *Scientists against Time* (New York, 1946), skillfully summarizes wartime scientific activities. Donald M. Nelson, in *Arsenal for Democracy* (New York, 1948), provides an insider's view. The role of the economy is ably sketched by D. L. Gordon and Royden Dangerfield in *The Hidden Weapon: The Story of Economic Warfare* (New York, 1947) and by W. W. Wilcox in *The Farmer in the Second World War* (Ames, 1947). A comprehensive book on politics during the war still has not been written. Roland Young, *Congressional Politics in the Second World War* (New York, 1956), surveys the legislative scene. D. R. B. Ross, *Preparing for Ulysses: Politics and Veterans during World War II* (New York, 1969), discusses demobilization problems. Two general works about mobilization that have appeared in recent years are Alan S. Milward, *War, Economy, and Society, 1939–1945* (Berkeley, 1979), and Harold G. Vatter, *The United States Economy in World War II* (New York, 1985). Studs Terkl, *The "Good War": An Oral History of World War II* (New York, 1984), has a broad sweep but contains relevant sections on mobilization. A lively, readable account is David Brinkley, *Washington Goes to War* (New York, 1988). Philip J. Funigiello, *The Challenge to Urban Liberalism: Federal-City Relations during World War II* (Knoxville, 1978), is particularly helpful on housing problems. For special aspects of mobilization, see Allan Winkler, *The Politics of Propaganda: The Office of War Information* (New Haven, 1978), Richard A. Smith, *OSS: The Secret History of America's First Central Intelligence Agency* (Berkeley, 1981), and Nelson Lichtenstein, *Labor's War at Home: The CIO in World War II* (Cambridge, 1983). On cultural trends, portions of Richard S. Polenberg, *War and Society* (Philadelphia, 1972), and Geoffrey Perrett, *Days of Sadness, Years of Triumph: The American People, 1939–1945* (New York, 1973), are relevant. Colin Shindler, *Hollywood Goes to War: Films and American Society, 1939–1952* (London, 1979), provides broad coverage. Jarrell Jackman and Carla Borden (eds.), *The Muses Flee Hitler: Cultural Transfer and Adaptation, 1930–1945* (Washington, 1983), traces the impact of European refugees on American culture. Wide scope is provided by Paul Boyer, *By the Dawn's Early Light: American Thought and Culture at the Dawn of the Atomic Age* (New York, 1985).

Women and Minority Groups during World War II

A short comprehensive survey of women's experiences in the Second World War is Susan Hartman, *The Home Front and Beyond: American Women in the 1940s* (Boston, 1982). Leila Rupp, in *Mobilizing Women for War: German and American Propaganda, 1939–1945* (Princeton, 1978), treats the image of women in wartime. Special focus on working women is provided by Philip S. Foner in *Women and the American Labor Movement: From World War I to the Present* (New York, 1980). Karen Anderson, *Wartime Women: Sex Roles, Family Relations, and the Status of Women during World War II* (Westport, 1981), and Maureen Honey, *Creating Rosie the Riveter: Class, Gender, and Propaganda during World War II* (Amherst, 1984), both examine women in the workplace. Ruth Milkman, *Gender at Work: The Dynamics of Job Discrimination by Sex during World War II* (Urbana, 1987), holds to its title. Diane Campbell, *Women at War with America: Private Lives in a Patriotic Era* (Cambridge, 1989), has a broader scope. Andrea Walsh, *Women's Film and Female Experience, 1940–1950* (New York, 1989), analyzes the images of women conveyed by the movies. Mary M. Thomas portrays southern women in *Riveting and Rationing in Dixie: Alabama Women and the Second World War* (Tuscaloosa, 1987). On black Americans in World War II, see Richard M. Dalfiume, *Fighting on Two Fronts: Desegregation of the U.S. Armed Forces, 1939–1953* (Columbia, 1969). On the developments leading to the Fair Employment Practices Committee, see Herbert R. Garfinkel, *When Negroes March: The March on Washington Movement in the Organizational Politics for FEPC* (Glencoe, 1959). The military experience of blacks is fully covered in Ulysses G. Lee, *The Employment of Negro Troops* (Washington, 1966), and that of black pilots in Charles E. Francis, *The Tuskegee Airmen: The Story of the Negro in the U.S. Air Force* (Boston, 1955). Dominic Capeci, Jr., analyzes race relations in *Race Relations in Wartime Detroit: The Sojourner Truth Housing Controversy of 1942* (Philadelphia, 1984). Bernard Sternsher (ed.) presents an interesting collection of sources in *The Negro in Depression and War: Prelude to Revolution, 1930–1945* (New York, 1969). No full account of Native Americans in the war has yet appeared, but see U.S. Office of Indian Affairs, *Indians in the War* (Washington, 1946), and Doris Paul, *The Navajo Code Talkers* (Philadelphia, 1973). A relevant chapter on Native Americans appears in Gerald D. Nash, *The American West Transformed: The Impact of the Second World War* (Bloomington, 1985). On Hispanic Americans, see Manuel Servin (ed.), *The Mexican-Americans* (Beverly Hills, 1970), and the relevant chapter in Nash, *The American West Transformed*. Military contributions are discussed in Raul Morin, *Among the Valiant: Mexican-Americans in WWII and Korea* (Los Angeles, 1963). The literature on Japanese-Americans during the war is very large. See Morton Grodzins, *Americans Betrayed* (Chicago, 1949), and two works by Roger

Daniels, *The Politics of Prejudice* (Berkeley, 1962), and *Concentration Camps USA* (New York, 1971).

The South and the West during World War II

No comprehensive history of the South during the Second World War has yet been written. Some treatment of the subject appears in relevant chapters of George B. Tindall, *The Emergence of the New South, 1913–1945* (Baton Rouge, 1967), and Pete Daniel, *Standing at the Crossroads* (New York, 1986). Sidney Baldwin, *Poverty and Politics: The Rise and Decline of the Farm Security Administration* (Chapel Hill, 1968), touches on aspects of agricultural change. James C. Cobb, *Industrialization and Southern Society, 1877–1984* (Lexington, 1984), covers World War II very briefly. Books that include material on cultural trends in the World War II era in the South include Daniel J. Singal, *The War Within: From Victorian to Modernist Thought in the South, 1919–1945* (Chapel Hill, 1982), and Richard H. King, *A Southern Renaissance: The Cultural Awakening of the American South, 1930–1955* (New York, 1980). On black writers, see Barbara Christian, *Black Women Novelists: The Development of a Tradition, 1892–1976* (Westport, 1980). A short account of the West in the Second World War can be found in Michael Malone and Richard W. Etulain, *The American West* (Lincoln, 1989), and Gerald D. Nash, *The American West in the Twentieth Century* (Albuquerque, 1977). For a fuller analysis, see two other works by Nash, *The American West Transformed: The Impact of the Second World War* (Bloomington, 1985) and *World War II and the West: Reshaping the Economy* (Lincoln, 1990). Contemporary analyses include Wendell Berge, *Economic Freedom for the West* (Lincoln, 1945), and Avram Mezerick, *The Revolt of the South and West* (New York, 1946).

Legacy of the Crucial Era

The impact of the years between 1929 and 1945 can be gauged in books such as those of Robert Wiebe, *The Segmented Society: An Introduction to the Meaning of America* (New York, 1975), and Richard S. Polenberg, *One Nation Divisible: Class, Race, and Ethnicity in the United States since 1938* (New York, 1980). An excellent account stressing biographical detail is William E. Leuchtenburg, *In the Shadow of FDR: From Harry Truman to Ronald Reagan* (Ithaca, 1983), and also incisive is Alonzo Hamby, *Liberalism and Its Challengers: Roosevelt to Reagan* (New York, 1985). Fine assessments of the impact of the New Deal on the United States after 1945 include Harvard Sitkoff (ed.), *Fifty Years Later: The New Deal Evaluated* (Philadelphia, 1985), and Steve Fraser and Gary Gerstle (eds.), *The Rise and Fall of the New Deal Order, 1930–1980* (Princeton, 1989).

Index